ANCIENT FACES

ANCIENT FACES

Mummy Portraits from Roman Egypt

Edited by Susan Walker

The Metropolitan Museum of Art,
New York

Routledge, New York

Editor's note

All catalogue entries were written by Susan Walker except those initialled
as follows:

M.-F. A.	Marie-France Aubert	C. J.	Catherine Johns
R. C.	Roberta Cortopassi	T. M.	Thomas Mathews
J.-L. F.	Jean-Luc Fournet	K. P.	Klaus Parlasca
H.-G. F.	Hans-Georg Frenz	P. R.	Paul Roberts
U. H.	Ulrike Horak	U. S.	Ulrich Schädler

The sequence of entries was prepared by Susan Walker. Where the author's
view of the date of the portrait differs from that of the editor, a note has been
supplied at the end of the entry.

This publication is issued in conjunction with the exhibition 'Ancient Faces: Mummy
Portraits from Roman Egypt', held at The Metropolitan Museum of Art, New York, from
February 15 through May 7, 2000.

The exhibition is made possible in part by The Andrew W. Mellon Foundation.

The exhibition was organised by The Metropolitan Museum of Art, in collaboration with
The British Museum.

The essay by Kurt Gschwantler, 'Graeco-Roman Portraiture', and entries 114 and 116,
by Dr Ulrike Horak, were first published in the exhibition catalogue *Bilder aus dem
Wüstensand: Mumienportraits aus dem Ägyptischen Museum, Kairo*, published by the
Kunsthistorisches Museum, Vienna, in conjunction with Skira, Milan, in 1988, and copyrighted by Kunsthistorisches Museum and by Skira Editore. Printed here by permission.

Entries 4, 33 and 34, by Hans-Georg Frenz; 7, 19, 30–32, 39 and 51, by Ulrich Schädler;
and 56 and 87, by Klaus Parlasca, were first published in the exhibition catalogue
Augenblicke: Mumienporträts und ägyptische Grabkunst aus römischer Zeit, published by
the Schirn Kunsthalle, Frankfurt, in conjunction with Klinkhardt and Biermann, Munich,
in 1999, and copyrighted by Klinkhardt & Biermann and by Schirn Kunsthalle. Printed
here by permission.

Translations from the German are by Russell Stockman.

Entries 49, 74, 89, 90 and 99, by Marie-France Aubert; 50, 54, 62, 63, 86 and 92, by
Roberta Cortopassi; and 65a and 115, by Jean-Luc Fournet, were translated from the
French by Jane Marie Todd.

Published in 2000 by
The Metropolitan Museum of Art, New York, and
Routledge, 29 West 35th Street, New York, NY 10001

Library of Congress Catalog Card Number: 99-76249

ISBN   0-415-92744-7 (hardback)
         0-415-92745-5 (paperback)
         0-87099-930-3 (Museum paperback)

Designed and typeset in Sabon by James Shurmer

Printed in Spain

Frontispiece: Portrait of a man in encaustic on limewood. From Hawara, *c.* AD 125–50
(no. 19).

CONTENTS

ACKNOWLEDGEMENTS

Dorothea Arnold and Marsha Hill of the Department of Egyptian Art at The Metropolitan Museum would like to express their gratitude to the staff of the British Museum who made the New York exhibition possible: Vivian Davies, Morris Bierbrier and Susan Walker, the last of whom oversaw this new edition of the catalogue.

We would like to thank the many institutions who have agreed to participate and the helpful colleagues there: Terry Wilfong, Thelma Thomas, Janet Richards and Robin Meador-Woodruff at the Kelsey Museum of Archaeology, Ann Arbor, Michigan; Laura Burns of Goucher College, Towson, Maryland, and the staff of The Walters Art Gallery, Baltimore, Maryland; Joan Knudson of the Phoebe Apperson Hearst Museum of Anthropology, University of California at Berkeley; Dietrich Wildung and Hannelore Kischkewitz, Ägyptisches Museum und Papyrussammlung, Berlin; Wolf-Dieter Heilmeyer and Gertrud Platz of the Antikensammlung, Berlin; Richard Fazzini and Edna Russmann, of the Brooklyn Museum of Art, Brooklyn; Eleni Vassilika and the Syndics of the Fitzwilliam Museum, Cambridge; Mary Cahill of the National Museum of Ireland, Dublin; Rosalyn Clancey of the Royal Scottish Museum, National Museums of Scotland, Edinburgh; Erika Feucht of the Ägyptologisches Institut der Universität, Heidelberg; Steven Snape of the School of Archaeology, Classics and Oriental Studies, University of Liverpool; Erica Davies of the Freud Museum, London; Barbara Adams, Sally MacDonald and Stephen Quirke of the Petrie Museum of Archaeology; Marion True of the J. Paul Getty Museum, Malibu, California; Raimund Wünsche of the Staatliche Antikensammlungen und Glyptothek, Munich; Roger Moorey of the Ashmolean Museum, Oxford; Christiane Ziegler and Marie-France Aubert of the Département des Antiquités Égyptiennes, and Alain Pasquier of the Département des Antiquités Grecques, Étrusques et Romaines, Musée du Louvre, Paris; Florence Friedman of the Museum of Art, Rhode Island School of Design, Providence, Rhode Island; William Turpin and Ed Fuller of Swarthmore College, Swarthmore, Pennsylvania; Alison Easson of the Royal Ontario Museum, Toronto; and Hermann Harrauer of the Österreichische Nationalbibliothek, Papyrussammlung, Vienna.

We are grateful to the authors who wrote the additional material signed with their initials and to Hellmut Seemann who helped to arrange the use of the German entries.

At the Metropolitan Museum we want to thank first the director, Philippe de Montebello, for his crucial support and Mahrukh Tarapor, associate director for exhibitions, for her decisive assistance. John P. O'Neill, editor in chief, guided the catalogue project from New York, and Hubert von Sonnenburg, Sherman Fairchild Chairman of the Department of Paintings Conservation, and Ann Heywood and Emilia Cortes of the Departments of Objects and Textile Conservation lent their expertise. Barbara Bridgers, manager of the Photograph Studio, also helped substantially. Participants in the ongoing study of the Museum's mummies are David Mininberg, M.D., of New York Hospital and a volunteer in the Department of Egyptian Art; Robert Freiberger M.D., and Rick Perez, both also of New York Hospital. Stephen Mancusi and Peggy Caldwell Ott reconstructed the face of the Museum's complete portrait mummy (cat. no. 9).

Susan Walker would like to thank Dorothea Arnold and Marsha Hill for their kind invitation to catalogue paintings and masks from American collections, for their hospitality in New York and for their support throughout the project. For assistance during the visit, thanks to Emilia Cortes and Miriam Blicka of The Metropolitan Museum of Art; William Turpin and Edward Fuller of Swarthmore College; Richard Fazzini and Edna Russman of the Brooklyn Museum of Art; Cindy Roman of the Wadsworth Atheneum, Hartford; Beth Knox of the Royal Ontario Museum, Toronto. At the British Museum, London, thanks to Dyfri Williams, Keeper of Greek and Roman Antiquities; Vivian Davies, Keeper of Egyptian Antiquities; Morris Bierbrier and John Taylor, Department of Egyptian Antiquities; Paul Roberts and Clare Pickersgill, Department of Greek and Roman Antiquities; Philip Nicholls, Photographic Service; James Shurmer, Colin Grant and Teresa Francis, British Museum Press. Thanks to Christina Rigg of Oxford University for access to an unpublished manuscript on the Deir el-Bahri mummies. Personal thanks to Andrew Solomon and Elizabeth Bartmann (New York), and John and Nicholas Wilkes (London).

DIRECTOR'S FOREWORD

The painted mummy portraits of Roman Egypt almost uncannily bring before us individuals from about two thousand years ago. The powerful promise of the ancient Egyptian afterlife, the pervasiveness and coherence of Roman culture, and the strong naturalism of the Graeco-Roman painting tradition combined to produce these arresting portraits of the gentility of the towns and cities of Egypt beyond the great metropolis of Alexandria.

The original 'Ancient Faces' exhibition at the British Museum in 1997 was the first comprehensive display of these delicate painted panels. Organised at the prescient initiative of Vivian Davies, Keeper of Egyptian Antiquities, and by Morris Bierbrier and Susan Walker of the Departments of Egyptian and of Greek and Roman Antiquities there, it was a groundbreaking undertaking which examined the whole spectrum of funerary arts of the period; situated the panels in relationship to other works showing degrees of assimilation of Roman influences; and brought to bear the most recent scholarship on the dating, technique, and understanding of the panel paintings. Feeling strongly that this remarkable exhibition should come to The Metropolitan Museum of Art in New York, Dorothea Arnold approached Vivian Davies, who responded in his usual forthcoming and cooperative way. This set in motion a highly productive interaction between the respective departments in London and New York. In the meantime, a rich series of exhibitions in Paris, Vienna and Frankfurt introduced other portraits to the public and brought careful consideration to the many yet unsettled questions regarding the panels.

In the present exhibition at The Metropolitan Museum of Art, the first major showing of these panels in North America, Dorothea Arnold and Marsha Hill of the Department of Egyptian Art have added to a core group of portraits from the exhibition in the British Museum more than forty paintings and related objects from German, French, Canadian, and American collections, including a number of non-funerary paintings, while highlighting at the same time the remarkable group of paintings, coffin masks and coffins owned by the Metropolitan Museum. Although the exhibition devotes considerable attention to the complex culture of Roman Egypt experienced by the personalities in the panel paintings, the catalogue concentrates closely on the paintings, their artistry and their social context and meaning.

On behalf of the Museum, I extend my sincere thanks to The Andrew W. Mellon Foundation for its generous support of the exhibition. The Metropolitan Museum of Art deeply appreciates the readiness of the British Museum to lend the objects that form the core of the exhibition, and extends its heartfelt thanks to the other institutions who are lending important objects from their collections. We have been most fortunate to have had the benefit of the inspired scholarship of Susan Walker, who has acted as general editor of the catalogue, written many new entries and an important overview of the ongoing chronological discussions, and given a coherent vision to the whole.

Philippe de Montebello
Director
The Metropolitan Museum of Art

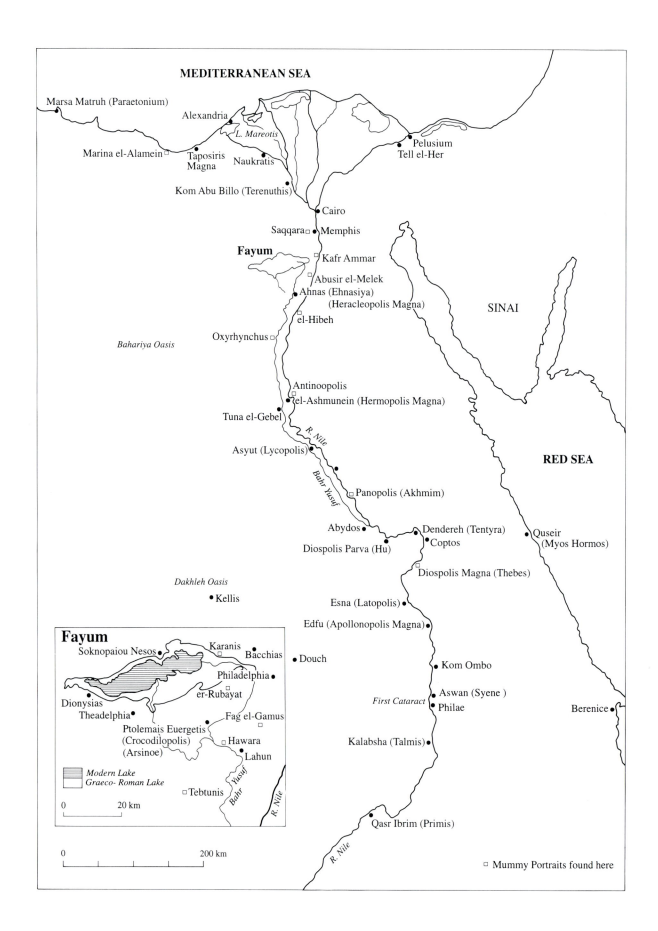

MEDITERRANEAN SEA

Marsa Matruh (Paraetonium)

Alexandria

L. Mareotis

Marina el-Alamein

Taposiris Magna

Naukratis

Pelusium
Tell el-Her

Kom Abu Billo (Terenuthis)

Cairo

Saqqara   Memphis

Fayum

Kafr Ammar

Abusir el-Melek

Ahnas (Ehnasiya)
(Heracleopolis Magna)

el-Hibeh

Bahariya Oasis

Oxyrhynchus

SINAI

Antinoopolis
el-Ashmunein (Hermopolis Magna)

Tuna el-Gebel

R. Nile

Asyut (Lycopolis)

Bahr Yusuf

RED SEA

Panopolis (Akhmim)

Abydos

Dendereh (Tentyra)

Quseir
(Myos Hormos)

Diospolis Parva (Hu)

Coptos

Diospolis Magna (Thebes)

Dakhleh Oasis

Kellis

Esna (Latopolis)

Edfu (Apollonopolis Magna)

Fayum

Soknopaiou Nesos

Karanis

Bacchias

Douch

Kom Ombo

Philadelphia

First Cataract

Aswan (Syene)

er-Rubayat

Philae

Dionysias

Berenice

Theadelphia

Fag el-Gamus

Ptolemais Euergetis
(Crocodilopolis)
(Arsinoe)

Hawara

Kalabsha (Talmis)

Lahun

Tebtunis

Bahr

Yusuf

R. Nile

Modern Lake

Graeco- Roman Lake

0   20 km

0   200 km

Qasr Ibrim (Primis)

R. Nile

□ Mummy Portraits found here

BEFORE THE PORTRAITS: BURIAL PRACTICES IN PHARAONIC EGYPT

John Taylor

The mummy portraits of Roman Egypt were the product of a fusion of two traditions, that of pharaonic Egypt and that of the Classical world. Their style and technique derive from the latter, but their inclusion as part of the trappings of the embalmed body belongs firmly in the context of Egyptian funerary practices. The provision of an idealised image of the deceased, physically attached to the body or in close proximity to it, already had a two thousand year history when the first encaustic panels were painted, and the custom arose in response to a deeply rooted solicitude for the well-being of the dead.

The belief in a life after death was one of the most conspicuous features of the ancient Egyptian civilisation. Much of what is known of their lives and attitudes has survived because of the elaborate preparations they made for the transition from the earthly existence to an eternal life in the hereafter. As an *akh*, or transfigured spirit, the deceased person could aspire to dwell in the earth-bound kingdom of Osiris, the god of the dead *par excellence*, who was himself believed to have suffered death before being resurrected to become ruler of the Underworld. Or he/she might hope to travel through the sky in the barque of the sun-god Ra, the originator of all life who, symbolically repeating the creation of the universe each dawn, offered to mankind the promise of endless rebirths.

It was a fundamental tenet of the Egyptians' beliefs that, in order to become an *akh*, the individual had to survive death in both physical and spiritual forms. The corpse, preserved by mummification, served as an anchor for the spiritual aspects, the *ka* ('life-force') and the *ba* ('spirit of mobility'). But the *ka* also required sustenance if it was to continue to exist. This need could be satisfied by the presentation of food-offerings at the tomb, but as the supply of offerings could not be expected to continue indefinitely, recourse was had to magic in order to guarantee food, drink and other necessaries in perpetuity. These could be provided through magical spells inscribed within the tomb, or through the principle of substitution, whereby two- or three-dimensional images of com-

modities could serve in place of the real thing. By the same principle, any threat to the deceased's eternal survival caused by the accidental destruction of the corpse could be offset by providing a substitute body in the form of a statue or anthropoid coffin. The image of the deceased which these substitutes perpetuated was an idealised one, representing an immortal being endowed with the qualities of divinity; it was not intended to recall the appearance of the deceased in life, and hence an authentic likeness was rarely attempted.

The importance attached to the satisfying of these basic requirements led to the creation, over a period of three millennia, of a complex web of funerary practices and rituals, supported by texts and images, amulets and other objects to guide, assist and protect the deceased on his passage into eternity.

The burials of the Badarian and Naqada I–II cultures (*c.*4500–3300 BC) testify to the existence of a primitive concept of the afterlife some fifteen centuries before the emergence of written language. The simple pit graves of these Predynastic Egyptians contained the unmummified body, placed on its side in a contracted posture and accompanied by pottery and stone vessels containing food and drink, tools, weapons, cosmetic palettes and items of personal adornment. Contact with the hot, dry sand resulted in the natural preservation of the body – skin, bone and hair all surviving in excellent condition. Indeed, the chance discovery of such 'natural mummies' may have been a factor in the early development of beliefs about survival after death.

With the rise of Egypt as a unified state at the end of the fourth millennium BC, burial customs began to reflect the hierarchical structure of Egyptian society more clearly. Kings were buried in huge tombs surmounted by monumental brick superstructures and filled with large quantities of offerings, and the provision made for their subjects grew more elaborate in proportion. In an effort to ensure greater protection, the body was sometimes placed in a simple rectangular coffin of wood, reeds or clay, or in a reused storage vessel. Exclusion of the desiccating sand from contact with the corpse frustrated the processes of natural preservation, but the desire to make increasingly elaborate provision for the dead ensured that coffins and tombs continued to be used. To preserve the body, therefore, experiments in mummification began to be made. Early attempts at wrapping the corpse in linen impregnated with resin were unsuccessful. Only with the introduction of the practice of extracting the internal organs, about 2600 BC, could true embalming be said to have begun. Techniques continued to evolve over the following millennia, reaching a peak of sophistication about 1000 BC. In essence, ancient Egyptian mummification comprised evisceration and the drying of the corpse using natron, a naturally occurring compound of sodium carbonate and sodium bicarbonate (plus sodium chloride and sodium sulphate). The body was subsequently wrapped in sheets and strips of linen. The viscera were preserved separately and the organs regarded as most essential stored in the tomb in chests or 'canopic' jars.

During the Old Kingdom (c.2613–2160 BC) the royal tomb evolved into a massive funerary complex constructed around a stone-built pyramid. Members of the ruling elite were buried under stone mastaba-tombs, which comprised a subterranean burial chamber and decorated offering chapel, the focus of which was the false door (a magical portal through which the spirit of the deceased was supposed to pass from the burial chamber to the offering chapel). Advances in embalming, including removal of the internal organs, led to the preparation of the body in a fully extended position. Even at this relatively early period the aim was not merely to preserve the corpse but to lend it the appearance of a living being; hence the features were modelled in plaster or linen, and the body was sometimes dressed in linen garments of the kind worn in life. In the course of the Old Kingdom the short box-coffins used for contracted bodies were superseded by rectangular wooden coffins and stone sarcophagi designed to contain the body in an extended position. Inscriptions in the tomb and on the coffin included magical formulae to provide the deceased with basic necessities, and jars and bowls for the performance of funerary rituals were also provided, often in the form of model vessels, substitutes for the genuine article. Statues of the tomb owner and his relatives, in stone and wood, became increasingly common; and just as these were to act as substitute bodies for the spirits of those depicted, the preparation of food and drink for the afterlife was taken care of by including statuettes of servants, shown engaged in producing these and other necessaries. Towards the end of the Old Kingdom the first substantial collections of religious texts began to be inscribed on the walls of royal pyramids in the Memphite necropolis. These 'Pyramid Texts', originally reserved for the use of the king, stand at the beginning of the evolution of Egyptian funerary literature.

The breakdown of central authority in Egypt during the First Intermediate Period (c.2160–2025 BC) was marked by a general decline in provisions for the dead and by the rise of provincial workshops which fostered local traditions in the manufacture of funerary equipment. Tombs of officials comprised either a rock-cut chapel with a burial shaft (a type which had appeared in the later Old Kingdom), or a small mud-brick superstructure containing a stela and sited over a shaft leading to a rock-cut burial chamber. An important innovation in the treament of the body was the inclusion of a face-mask of painted cartonnage, placed over the mummy's head. These masks, presenting a highly idealised image of the deceased, represented a formative stage in the evolution of anthropoid coffins, early examples of which were already appearing at the end of the Eleventh Dynasty (c.2000 BC). During the Twelfth Dynasty (c.1985–1795 BC) an anthropoid case often served as the innermost envelope for the body and was enclosed within one or two rectangular coffins. The latter were more extensively decorated than their Old Kingdom precursors and included images of funerary offerings and lengthy extracts from the so-called 'Coffin Texts', a collection of funerary spells deriving in part from the Pyramid Texts but now available without restriction to non-royal persons. Among the developments which took place in embalming, the most notable innovation was the removal of the brain; the organ itself was discarded, but the principal contents of the body cavity (liver, lungs, stomach and intestines) continued to be embalmed and stored in four canopic jars, with lids in the form of human heads. High-status burials included rich jewellery, concealed within the mummy's wrappings or deposited separately in the tomb. Painted wooden tomb statues of the owner continued to be provided, and a range of wooden models representing servants included porters, boats, granaries and scenes of the production of food, drink and other commodities. Sticks and staves, usually of wood and sometimes ritually broken, were also provided.

After the middle of the Twelfth Dynasty further changes occurred. These probably began in the cemeteries associated with the royal residence of Itj-tawy (Lisht) and gradually spread to the provinces. Notable features are a decline in the interior decoration of rectangular coffins and a more restricted use of the Coffin Texts. At the same period wooden models of servants fell out of use, while magical objects used in everyday life (apotropaic wands, rods and figurines) were added to the funerary equipment to provide protection for the dead. These objects, which have allusions to the myth of the sun-god's triumph over his foes, perhaps also served in lieu of the now rarer texts which reflected the same ideas. This period also witnessed the introduction of female figurines, model food offerings, and the mummy-shaped funerary statuettes which evolved into *shabtis* (figurines to perform agricultural labour on behalf of the deceased in the afterlife).

The political decentralisation of the Second Intermediate Period (c.1700–1550 BC) is reflected in the simplification of burials throughout Egypt. Mummies of this period exhibit signs of imperfect embalming, but cartonnage masks continued to be provided, and these were now often decorated with winged headdresses and gilded faces. Alongside the traditional rectangular coffins, a new type of wooden anthropoid case was introduced. This so-called *Rishi* (Arabic: 'feathered') coffin was characterised by prominent winged decoration which has affinities with that of the mummy masks. Many of the *Rishi* coffins were hewn out of single trunks of the native sycamore fig tree. *Shabtis* were crudely carved in wood, with ink inscriptions, and placed in the tomb in model coffins; they were also sometimes employed as votives or buried outside the tomb. Canopic jars seem to have fallen out of use for a time, and the wrapped packages containing the internal organs were placed directly into wooden chests divided into compartments. Otherwise, burial equipment was limited to a few objects, but the period is notable for the introduction of the heart-scarab, an amulet designed to assist the deceased's safe passage through the judgement hall of Osiris – a kind of 'checkpoint' at which the unrighteous might be denied access into the afterlife.

The re-establishment of a unified state at the beginning of the Eighteenth Dynasty (c.1550 BC) inaugurated the New Kingdom, the period of Egypt's greatest influence as a major power in the ancient Near East. Renewed prosperity brought new developments in burial practices, with the emergence of rock-cut tombs with highly decorated chapels (those on the West Bank at Thebes being the best preserved), and a developed and expanded funerary ensemble. Eighteenth Dynasty kings were interred in stone sarcophagi containing up to three richly decorated coffins, the innermost of solid gold. Non-royal individuals were buried in anthropoid wooden coffins

of a new kind, which had superseded the rectangular and *Rishi* coffins. The earliest examples of the new type had polychrome decoration on a white background, but by the middle of the reign of Tuthmosis III (c.1479–1425 BC) black-varnished or black-painted coffins with decoration in gold leaf or yellow paint were the norm. Embalming methods continued to evolve, and removal of the brain via the nose became a standard technique. The mummy was regularly provided with a mask of wood or cartonnage. Canopic jars were made from stone or pottery and stored in wooden shrine-shaped chests. A new collection of funerary texts was introduced into the burial prerequisites. These 'formulae for going forth by day' (conventionally termed the 'Book of the Dead' by Egyptologists) derive in part from the Coffin Texts, to which a number of new formulae were added. They are inscribed in cursive hieroglyphic and first appeared on linen shrouds, but from the reigns of Tuthmosis III and Amenhotep II papyrus rolls became the standard medium for the texts. Although the formulae do not appear in a fixed order, they are illustrated with coloured vignettes. With only a few exceptions, these texts were prepared for the burials of men, but the coffins and other trappings made for women at this period were nonetheless made to a high standard. *Shabtis* were often of fine workmanship, and were usually inscribed with the text of Chapter 6 of the Book of the Dead, the magical spell which was to make the figures work on behalf of their owner. There was an increase in the number of *shabtis* per burial, and from the mid-Eighteenth Dynasty these were stored in shrine-shaped boxes, instead of the miniature coffins characteristic of earlier periods. A notable feature of Eighteenth Dynasty burial practices is the frequent inclusion in the grave of household furniture and personal possessions, such as musical instruments and the tools of the deceased's trade.

Following the short-lived religious revolution led by the pharaoh Amenhotep IV (Akhenaten) in the late fourteenth century BC, several innovations in burial customs can be observed. Wooden coffins with polychrome decoration on a yellow background superseded the earlier black-varnished type; a number of inner coffin lids and mummy boards represent the deceased in the costume and attitude of daily life, and the same iconography is found on the stone sarcophagi, which were now more frequently used for non-royal burials. The number of *shabtis* per burial continued to increase, and papyrus rolls containing the Book of the Dead continued to be supplied. The walls of the kings' tombs were inscribed with a series of compositions known collectively as the

Underworld Books (these included the Amduat, the Book of Gates and the Book of Caverns). They were intended solely for royal use, although exceptions to this rule are known.

In the Twenty-First Dynasty (c.1069–945 BC) the techniques of mummification reached the peak of their perfection. Special attention was devoted to restoring the physical integrity of the body and to making it appear, as far as possible, as it had in life. The embalmed viscera were normally replaced within the body cavity, and subcutaneous packing was employed to fill out the shrunken limbs and features; artificial eyes and false hair helped to create a lifelike impression. Yet throughout this period the economy of Egypt was weak, and one manifestation of this was a reduction in expenditure on tombs and their furnishings. The production of decorated tomb chapels ceased, the sepulchres of earlier periods being reused for new burials. Religious images and texts which had once been painted on tomb walls were now abbreviated, revised and concentrated on the inner and outer surfaces of the coffins and on papyri. A typical burial at Thebes comprised two coffins and a mummy board, *shabtis*, and two rolled funerary papyri, one placed with the body, the other inserted into a hollow wooden Osiris figure. One papyrus usually contained the Book of the Dead, the other the Litany of Ra or Amduat, or an amalgam of texts and vignettes from various sources. The *shabtis* were usually made of blue glazed faience, and were provided in sets of 401 (365 'workers', one for every day of the year, with 36 overseers to control them). Since the internal organs were now replaced in the body cavity, canopic jars were not required, although dummy-vessels were still sometimes provided, out of respect for so ancient a tradition.

The practice of reusing older tombs continued in the Twenty-Second Dynasty (c.945–716 BC); at the same time many burials were made within temple precincts, a practice begun by the kings of the previous dynasty, probably to provide added security. A general simplification of the burial outfit characterises this period. New types of coffins, perhaps first introduced in the Delta, were adopted throughout Egypt. Typical high-status burials at Thebes comprised two to three outer wooden coffins, sparsely decorated on black or unpainted backgrounds, with a polychrome cartonnage envelope, made in a single piece, to contain the mummy. Pairs of papyrus rolls (one usually carrying the Book of the Dead, the other vignettes from the Amduat) were still provided in the ninth century BC, but after this date there was a hiatus in the production of funerary papyri. *Shabtis* were crudely

mass-produced, and no longer bore the *shabti* spell. The only significant addition to the ensemble in this period was the regular provision of a painted wooden funerary stela, usually depicting the deceased adoring the sun-god Ra-Horakhty.

Another major phase of change in burial practices coincided with the Twenty-Fifth Dynasty (c.747–664 BC), and the innovations of that period persisted into the sixth century BC, if not later. While older tombs, and temple precincts, continued to be used for burials, high-ranking officials of the Twenty-Fifth and Twenty-Sixth Dynasties were interred in large and newly constructed sepulchres, those in the Memphite area comprising deep shafts leading to rock-cut burial chambers, while at Thebes the subterranean apartments were crowned by massive mud-brick superstructures. Sets of coffins usually consisted of an outer case of rectangular shape, imitating the appearance of a shrine, and an innermost one representing the mummified deceased standing on a pedestal and leaning against a back pillar. Stone anthropoid sarcophagi were produced in large numbers, particularly fine examples having been found at Giza and Saqqara. The mummy was often covered by a net of tubular faience blue beads, which sometimes incorporated a gold face-mask and figures of deities. The period witnessed the reappearance of the Book of the Dead in a new version, with the individual spells arranged in a fixed sequence. Although there exist few examples on papyri from this period, many extracts were inscribed on coffins and on the walls of tombs. *Shabtis*, too, were redesigned, now closely imitating the form of the inner coffins, with a back pillar and a plinth beneath the feet. They were mould-made from blue-green faience, and usually carried the *shabti* spell. A partial return to the practice of burying the viscera separately resulted in the reappearance of functional canopic jars from the reign of Taharqa (690–664 BC). Amulets placed within the mummy wrappings increased in number and variety; those representing funerary deities became particularly common from the Twenty-Sixth Dynasty. A wooden statuette of the composite funerary deity Ptah-Sokar-Osiris was added to the standard burial ensemble.

The evolution of funerary practices during the first Persian period (525–404 BC) is difficult to ascertain, since few burials have been securely dated to that period. However, the evidence of burial groups dated to the fourth century BC suggests that the practices of the Twenty-Sixth Dynasty continued and developed without a major break.

The fourth century BC and the succeeding Ptolemaic period (305–30 BC) represent the last major phase of traditional ancient Egyptian burial practices. The preservation techniques employed by the embalmers differed little from those used during the preceding centuries. Amulets were provided in profusion, and, as before, great care was devoted to the external appearance of the body. Cartonnage masks were re-introduced, and these were accompanied by pectorals, aprons and footcases of the same material attached to the outer wrappings, and sometimes associated with bandaging in intricate patterns. Stone anthropoid sarcophagi were extensively used. These, and the contemporary wooden coffins, were similar in many respects to those of the Twenty-Sixth Dynasty, but the different bodily proportions (large heads, swollen torsos) and the more restricted range of texts and images employed serve to distinguish them. *Shabtis* and canopic jars continued to be made in the same basic forms as before, but seem to have been less widely used and were often of inferior quality. The Book of the Dead remained an essential component of the well-appointed burial, the texts being inscribed on papyrus sheets and rolls, which were often of substantial length. The same texts were inscribed on linen shrouds and (in the Memphite area) on mummy bandages. Other late religious texts, derived in some cases from temple rituals, were added to the complement of funerary literature.

Mummification continued to be practised during the Roman period (after 30 BC), but the techniques employed were inferior to those of earlier periods, and in many instances the bodies appear to have been in an advanced state of decay before embalming took place. The application of large quantities of resin often took the place of careful embalming methods, and it was common for greater care to be devoted to the external appearance of the wrapped mummy than to the preservation of the corpse itself. Some mummies were encased in painted shrouds, others in decorated stucco cases, while on others elaborate linen wrappings, arranged in complex rhombic patterns, created an impression of richness. A variety of headpieces was available: cartonnage masks (often heavily gilded), realistic plaster heads and encaustic or tempera portraits on wooden panels. In some burials the mummy was enclosed in a rectangular wooden coffin of traditional pharaonic type. Others were painted with scenes in which Hellenistic influences predominated. In many instances the bodies were buried without coffins, and the remaining elements of the traditional pharaonic burial outfit – canopic jars and *shabti* figures – now also fell out of use. Substantial manuscripts containing Book of the Dead texts declined in numbers during the late Ptolemaic period, and by the Roman era these sources had almost ceased to be used. They were replaced by shorter texts, notably the two Books of Breathing, but the funerary text tradition as a whole was by now in decline. Copies of the second Book of Breathing, included in the burials of the Soter family at Thebes (early second century AD) represent the latest known funerary manuscripts from ancient Egypt.

GRAECO-ROMAN PORTRAITURE

Kurt Gschwantler

With but a few exceptions, Egyptian mummy portraits are the only surviving examples of antique portrait painting, and they are accordingly of great value. Virtually all Graeco-Roman panel painting has been lost because it was done on wood, a highly impermanent material. It is only thanks to Egypt's unique climate that mummy portraits have been preserved.

The almost complete loss of antique panel painting is all the more regrettable inasmuch as the ancient writers suggest that Greek painting was even more celebrated than sculpture, with panel painting clearly taking precedence over wall painting. According to Pliny the Elder, only the panel painter could attain true glory (*Natural History* 35, 118). We art historians are placed in a paradoxical position: the ancient writers provide us with an astonishingly complete overview of the development of Greek painting and the lives and works of the major artists, yet not a single panel mentioned survives in the original.

Wall paintings and mosaics in Rome and Campania were often based on Greek models; however, it is rarely possible to glean more than some hint from them about the subject matter and composition of the originals, especially since the surviving depictions draw on an eclectic array of available types and were by no means copied directly from the originals but rather from copies of copies, with any number of intervening stages. In addition, Roman wall painting was subject to its own development and successive styles. While there have been many attempts to link specific wall paintings with certain Greek painters on the basis of picture titles handed down in the literature, it has only been possible to deduce from two or more pictures of identical or similar subject matter an underlying original. For example, in 1874 the Antiquities Collection of Vienna's Kunsthistorisches Museum acquired a mosaic of an erotic scene (fig. 1) that had been unearthed in Centocelle, near Rome, in 1865. Ten years later, in the grounds of the Villa Farnesina in Rome, the remains of a Roman villa with rich fresco paintings (now in the Museo Nazionale, Rome) were discovered, including a depiction of a folding triptych, the centre panel of which corre-

sponds to the mosaic. Although the two pictures differ in detail – the Dionysus statuette (in the upper left corner) and the curtain over the lovers' couch in the mosaic are missing from the fresco, while a small tripod table and a bowl in the fresco take the place of Silenus supporting a vase in the mosaic – they could well represent variations of the same Hellenistic original, the fresco (sadly less well preserved) probably closer to it.

Greek painters were traditionally employed in connection with the cult of the dead and with the production of votive images and decor in temples and shrines. In addition they received over the course of the fifth and fourth centuries BC a growing number of commissions for works of a political nature, leading to an expansion of the repertoire of pictorial subjects previously dominated by the world of gods and heroes. Already by the middle of the fifth century BC the wall paintings in the Stoa Poikile

Fig. 1 Mosaic of an erotic scene, from Centocelle, first century AD (Kunsthistorisches Museum, Antikensammlung, Vienna, Inv. II 9).

(Painted Colonnade) next to the Agora – the work of the leading painters of the time such as Polygnotus, Micon and Panaenus – were confronting the Athenians with past and present glories: historical pictures related their victories at Marathon (against the Persians in 490) and Oenoe (against the Spartans in 460), and mythological ones presented the Iliupersis (destruction of Troy) and an Amazonomachia (battle of Amazons).

But even in the supposedly historical picture of the battle of Marathon the actual background to the fight was closely linked to myth, as is clear from the description by Pausanias, who was able to see these pictures in Athens as late as the second century AD:

> The last part of the painting shows the men who fought at Marathon: the Boiotians from Plataia and men from all over Attica are coming to grips with the barbarians; things are about equal. But in the heart of the battle the barbarians are in flight, pushing each other into the marsh, and the painting ends with the Phoenician ships, and with Greeks slaughtering barbarians as they jump into them. The hero Marathon, from whom the level ground got its name, is standing there, with Theseus rising out of the earth, and Athene and Herakles. The people of Marathon reckon to have been the first to believe Herakles was a god. In the picture of the fighting, you can most clearly make out Kallimachos, who was chosen to be chief Athenian general, and General Miltiades, and the divine hero Echetlos... (*Guide to Greece* I, 15.4)[1]

Presumably the figures in the picture were arranged with the help of the basic principles prescribed for the art of the time by Polygnotus of Thasos, with individuals and groups of warriors stacked one above the other.

The development of portraiture

The gods and heroes, and even the historical figures Kallimachos and Miltiades, must surely have been given the generic, idealised human form found in the sculptures of Pheidias or Polyclitus – Pausanias would only have been able to identify the individual figures with certainty and determine how they related to each other in context with the help of identifying labels, or at least these would have made his identifications much easier.

The art of the fourth century BC gradually abandoned the notion of an ideal human type as theoretically fixed in the 'canon', or system of proportions, developed by Polyclitus, and as implied in the story behind the painting of Helen by Zeuxis: it is said that when the artist was commissioned to paint the picture

of Helen for the temple of Hera Lacinia, the citizens of Croton permitted him to select five maidens, so that he might combine in his painting the most beautiful features of each. The person mainly responsible for the move away from the ideal in Greek art was Lysippus of Sicyon, one of the leading sculptors of the second half of the fourth century BC, who is supposed to have claimed that he 'did not depict men as they are but as they appear'. That phrase refers to Lysippus's revision of the canon of Polyclitus but also to the fleeting nature of appearances (Greek: *kairós*). Lysippus even represented this *kairós* as a kind of personal manifesto in a sculpture.

In terms of the development of portraiture, this involved a tendency to express the subject's unique character, and to this end Greek art up into the late Hellenistic period depicted the entire figure and not just the head or bust. Here it is also appropriate to recall another of Pliny's assertions, to the effect that it was Lysippus's brother, Lysistratus, who first made plaster casts of the faces of living people, poured wax over them and then 'improved' or retouched them. Increased interest in the uniqueness of the individual also led to the so-called invented or reconstructed portraits of celebrated personalities, often long since dead, such as statesmen, philosophers or poets. Widely distributed and copied, these portraits were displayed not only in public spaces but also in Roman houses as three-dimensional sculpture, wall paintings (fig. 2) or mosaics intended to attest to their owner's cultivation.

Fig. 2
Wall painting showing Socrates, from 'Hanghaus 2', Ephesus, first century AD (Ephesus Museum, Selçuk).

The rise of portraiture was accompanied by a growing interest in biographical details, which necessarily led to the creation of legends due to the lack of appropriate sources. Of the numerous anecdotes about Greek artists of the fifth and fourth centuries that have been handed down to us, many may well go back to Duris of Samos (*c.* 340–270 BC), a pupil of Theophrastus, whom Pliny names as a source and who wrote a treatise *On Painting*. Such portraits and biographies were combined towards the end of the Roman Republic in the *Imagines*, published by the public official and scholar M. Terentius Varro. It was the first illustrated Latin book, an encyclopedic collection of 700 painted portraits of distinguished Greeks and Romans, each one accompanied by an epigram and a brief biography.

According to Demosthenes, the strategist Conon in Athens was the first (after the tyrannicides Harmodius and Aristogiton) to have been honoured with a statue in the Agora, commemorating his naval victory over the Spartans in 394 BC. The earliest surviving decrees regarding the commissioning of honorary painted portraits are from the beginning of the second century BC. Most informative in this respect are the inventory lists from the shrine of Apollo at Delos from the time it was administered by Athens after 166 BC. These document the objects preserved in the various sanctuaries. Almost all the buildings in the sacred precinct contained pictures in addition to other votive gifts. Indeed, one of these structures was known as 'the house with the pictures' and was presumably a kind of picture gallery. As a rule, such votive paintings were surely not first-rank works of art, yet the inventories

also include one mention of a picture by Parrhasius, the contemporary and rival of Zeuxis in the fifth century BC. The pictures (Greek: *pínakes*) are distinguished by content, painting technique, type of frame and location. For example, a *pínax eikonikós* was doubtless a portrait. There were framed pictures and others with hinged covers, and they were either hung on the wall or placed on pedestals. The only technique specifically mentioned was encaustic (wax painting; see the essay by E. Doxiadis, pp. 30–31). Paintings fitted with protective folding covers (Greek: *pínakes tethuroménoi*) occur frequently in the wall paintings of Rome and Campania (fig. 3; see also fig. 9); shown as standing on moulded bases, they have the appearance of actual paintings, at times a whole collection of them. There are also pictures standing on pedestal-like columns, sometimes as decorative elements in garden landscapes.

Portraits of Alexander the Great

Documentary records of painted portraits generally concern votive gifts, including numerous donations following victories in gymnastic or artistic contests. From the time of Alexander the Great and his successors it is possible to discern a steady increase in the number of commissions made by ruling houses or by the ruler himself for the purposes of self-aggrandisement and propaganda. Most numerous are mentions of pictures of Alexander the Great, some of them commissioned by himself, others only after his death by his successors to legitimise their rule. After the battle of Chaeronea in 338 BC Philip II had already commissioned a victory monument, the so-called Philippeion, in Olympia, a circular structure containing statues of his family, including one of his son and successor, Alexander. It is said that Alexander only permitted himself to be portrayed in bronze by Lysippus and in painting by Apelles.

As examples of a type of painted princely portrait, it is worth enumerating the paintings of Alexander recorded in literature, with their rich variety of motifs showing the king either alone or in a group, and in historical, mythical or allegorical contexts. Four pictures are reported from the hand of Apelles alone. At Ephesus there were *Alexander Holding a Lightning Bolt* (in the temple of Artemis), in which Alexander was clearly conceived as Zeus, and *Alexander on Horseback*. Two other depictions – one showing a victorious Alexander with Victory and the Dioscuri, and the other portraying him with Mars in chains on his triumphal car as the king who had ended the terror of war – were brought to Rome by

Fig. 3 Wall painting showing a picture (of a bridal procession?) with folding doors, in the Casa del Crittoportico, Pompeii, mid-first century AD.

Emperor Augustus, who wished to be compared with Alexander and donated the pictures to the forum he had built. Lucian's detailed description of *The Marriage of Alexander and Roxana* by Aëtion has inspired any number of artists since the Renaissance, Rubens among them, to create reproductions.

We also know of paintings of Alexander by two Egyptian painters who probably worked on commission from the Ptolemies: *Alexander as a Boy and Alexander with Philip and Athena* by Antiphilus – both of which were in Rome in Pliny's time – and *The Battle of Issus* by Helena of Alexandria, which the Emperor Vespasian donated to his Temple of Peace in Rome. Finally, Pliny writes of a *Battle of Alexander against Darius* painted by Philoxenus of Eretria for King Cassander, a picture he describes as 'second to none'. The originals of all these works have been lost, including the last one by Philoxenus, although it is thought that the well-known Alexander mosaic from the Casa del Fauno in Pompeii (Museo Nazionale, Naples) is a faithful copy of it. Whereas the above-mentioned *Battle of Marathon* in the Painted Colonnade in Athens was made up of a sequence of separate scenes, in the mosaic everything is subsumed within a single composition, the focus of which is Alexander's confrontation with the Persian king as he turns to escape. The definite pathos in Alexander's face is appropriate to a courtly art that largely dispensed with identifying features in favour of the portrait of a superhuman and heroic commander.

Painting in Ptolemaic Alexandria

In connection with the mummy portraits from Egypt, it is of particular interest to determine what role painting, as a part of Greek culture, played in the kingdom of the Ptolemies. In 331 BC, a year after his conquest of Egypt, Alexander the Great founded a new capital and named it Alexandria, after himself. After Alexander's death in 323 BC, the rule of the Ptolemies began with Ptolemy I and continued until Alexandria was conquered by Octavian, the later Emperor Augustus. Under the Ptolemies, Alexandria swiftly became a brilliant metropolis, and the body of Alexander was entombed there with great splendour. Two institutions generously supported by the Ptolemies made Alexandria the intellectual centre of the Hellenistic world as well; only Pergamum in Asia Minor, the residence of the Attalids, could compete with it. These were the Museum, a research facility especially for scholars in the natural sciences and literature, and, closely associated with it, the Library, the most important such institution in the ancient world, which also supported translators and commentators.

The best illustration of the incredible magnificence with which the Ptolemies displayed their wealth and power is provided by Athenaeus in his description of the Dionysian pageant of Ptolemy II (283–246 BC) and the elaborate tent erected on that occasion. In that pageant a fantastic array of gold and silver objects, statues, vessels, jewellery, ivory and precious gems was paraded before the astonished crowd. The huge, palatial tent was adorned with sculptures, golden tripods and eagles, and textiles into which the king's portrait and mythological scenes had been woven. It is also mentioned that there were pictures by painters from Sicyon hung in the spaces between the columns.

This accords with a passage in Plutarch, in which he relates that the Sicyonian statesman and general Aratos sent pictures and drawings to Ptolemy III (246–221 BC), including paintings by Melanthus and Pamphilus, famous Sicyonian painters of the fourth century. Pamphilus was also the founder of the first 'painting academy'. *Hyacinthus*, a work by Nicias of Athens, was also in Alexandria, but after Octavian captured the city it was taken to Rome and later donated by the Emperor Tiberius to the Temple of Augustus. It is tempting to assume that the Ptolemies in Alexandria, like the Attalids in Pergamum, owned a full-scale collection of paintings (Greek: *pinakothéke*), though this cannot be proved.

Wall paintings discovered towards the close of the last century in the villa of P. Fannius Synistor near Boscoreale in Campania possibly provide a glimpse into the world of the Ptolemaic kings. The dining room was painted with imitation architecture incorporating large pictures and with folding paintings on ledges, suggesting the precious picture gallery of a princely court in Hellenistic times. According to an intriguing interpretation by M. Pfrommer, all the pictures are subject to a unifying overall concept intended to glorify the Ptolemaic royal house, and may have been based on a prototype from the second half of the third century BC. In the main picture (fig. 4) Ptolemy III appears enthroned as a naked hero leaning on his sceptre. Next to him sits his step-mother, the deified Arsinoë II, in a pose used to portray deceased women.

The Egyptian court with its self-aggrandising splendour exemplifed not only by the pageant and ceremonial tent mentioned above but also by the *Thalamegos*, the no less magnificent royal barge of Ptolemy III (also described by Athenaeus), must also

Fig. 4
Wall painting with
enthroned couple,
from the villa of
P. Fannius Synistor
near Boscoreale,
*c.*40 BC
(The Metropolitan
Museum of Art,
New York
03.14.6).

have maintained a great number of artists and crafts-men's workshops. However, we read very little about artists who were attached to the court of the Ptolemies or who worked for it. This paucity of sources for the Hellenistic art of the third and second centuries BC is probably a reflection of the more classically oriented tastes of the writers from whom Pliny, for example, drew his information. Pliny ends his history of artists in the early third century BC and asserts that since the 121st Olympiad (296–293 BC) the arts had stagnated and only again attained distinction around the middle of the second century BC.

As for Apelles, whose art represented the absolute apex of Greek painting to critics pledged to classicism, the sources tell of two encounters with Ptolemy I in Alexandria. According to Lucian (*Slander* 2–5), Apelles was slandered before the king by the painter Antiphilus in an affair of some political seriousness. The intrigue was uncovered, however, and Apelles was richly rewarded and Antiphilus presented to him

as a slave. As a result of that unfortunate experience, Apelles is said to have painted the picture *Calumny*. Lucian describes it and its many allegorical figures so precisely that a great number of artists since the Renaissance have ventured to paint this subject as well. The earliest is the *Calunnia di Apelle* by Sandro Botticelli (in the Uffizi, Florence).

In the second story, too, Apelles first falls out of grace with Ptolemy. Responding to a false invitation, he turned up as a guest at a royal banquet. The king was enraged, but Apelles promptly revealed the identity of the man who had tricked him in a few deft strokes with a piece of coal. Since the first of these anecdotes is flawed by anachronisms, the most we can derive from them are the two points that Apelles was possibly engaged by Ptolemy I and that he was confronted by rivalry and intrigue, something that seems perfectly plausible at Ptolemy's court, where both 'foreign' and native artists were employed.

The only important painter from Egypt mentioned

in the written sources is Antiphilus (Pliny, *Natural History* 35, 114.138), whom we have already encountered as the painter of portraits of Alexander the Great and a rival of Apelles. He was an Egyptian by birth and the pupil of a certain Ctesidemus. Pliny does not rank him among the very finest painters, certainly, yet Antiphilus was clearly sufficiently well known from a number of his pictures in Rome that the knowledgeable Varro mentions him in one passage as representing the whole art of painting just as Lysippus represented sculpture. Among his other portraits was a *Ptolemy Hunting*. He also produced pictures of the gods and mythological scenes, including a very famous depiction of Pan 'on the lookout' – hence his nickname *Aposkopeuon* – shading his eyes with his hand. Indeed in antiquity a grotesque figure called *Gryllos* gave his name to caricatured genre figures, which appear to have been especially typical of Alexandrine art.

Aside from the painter Helena of Alexandria already mentioned, there is a reference in an epigram of the poetess Nossis of Egypt (*c.* 300 BC) to the self-portrait, dedicated to Aphrodite, of an otherwise unknown courtesan named Callo. Two letters preserved on papyrus from a painter by the name of Theophilus take us to a realm at some remove from 'high' art, providing a glimpse of a miserable professional life more typical of craftsmen than artists. The letters were written to Zenon, the secretary to a district commissioner in Fayum, and date from the third century BC. The first of them refers to wall paintings in the house of some official for which he is submitting a bill. In the second letter he also mentions panel paintings: 'Since your works are finished and there is nothing more to do, and I am sitting here without even the bare necessities, you would do well if you were to assign to me some of the panels you require after all, so that I might have employment and sustenance...'

Painting in contemporary Italy

In the paintings of Rome and Campania there are only a very few examples of portraits of contemporaries. More common are the portraits of famous Greek statesmen, philosophers or poets mentioned above, like that of Socrates from Ephesus (fig. 2) or the well-known seated one of the comedy writer Menander, which gave its name to the Casa del Menandro in Pompeii. One of the few examples of a contemporary portrait is that of a married couple from Pompeii (fig. 5), which imitates a panel painting in its format and framing. The portrait of the man, Terentius Neo –

we know his name from a graffito – is particularly notable for its realism. A papyrus roll, a writing tablet and a stylus identify the couple as cultivated citizens.

In republican Rome there must have been a tradition of painted portraits associated with the ancestor cult. In Book 35 of his *Natural History* Pliny begins the section on ancient painting with the sad assertion that such pictures are a thing of the past:

Portrait painting (*imaginum pictura*), which best assures the preservation of a person's likeness for posterity, has completely died out. There are now hanging bronze shields with silver faces on them... To their subjects it is more important to be valued on the basis of the [expensive] material than to be recognised. Moreover, people stuff their galleries with old pictures and take pleasure in portraits of strangers... Our forefathers, however, placed in their halls only those objects that should be seen. They had no pictures by foreign artists or images in bronze or marble. Portraits of moulded wax were kept in special cupboards for use at family burials, so that when someone died he was accompanied by the whole host of ancestors (*Natural History* 35, 2.4–6).

Pliny's report on the use of wax masks at the funeral ceremony (*pompa funebris*) is impressively confirmed by the Greek historian Polybius, who

Fig. 5 Wall painting with portrait of a married couple, from the House of Terentius Neo in Pompeii, AD 50–75 (Museo Nazionale, Naples 9058).

have looked like we cannot know. They may partly have been painted predecessors of the metal shield busts (*clipeatae imagines*) that Pliny scorns and that are also repeatedly shown in Pompeian wall paintings (fig. 6). Shields decorated with draped female busts are fixed at some height from the ground to two horizontal strips of wood suspended between slender columns.

Two such shield busts, probably painted ones, can be seen on the inner wall of a sarcophagus from Kerch, on which there is a rare depiction of a painter in his studio (fig. 7). In relation to mummy portraits, the picture is intriguing in several ways. The painter is clearly working on a picture in encaustic, for he is heating his painting utensil or possibly even the wax pigment over a basin of coals. In front of him on a column is a picture with hinged doors, on which he has laid out a square grid. Three darker spots arranged in a triangle could possibly be thought of as marking the arrangement of a family portrait (see fig. 10). Just to the right is an easel with an as yet unpainted panel in a so-called eight-end frame of the type we know from the Fayum (fig. 8). The same sort of frame can be seen on a picture hanging between two shield busts on the wall. On all three we can see draped busts; the frames of the shields are decorated.

Fig. 6 Wall painting with shield busts (*clipeatae imagines*), in the Casa del Bell'Impluvio, Pompeii, mid-first century AD.

Fig. 7 Part of the inside of a stone sarcophagus from Kerch showing a painter in his studio, *c.* AD 100 (Hermitage, St Petersburg).

around the middle of the second century BC was particularly struck by this Roman ritual inasmuch as it was so very different from Greek practices.

This image consists of a mask, which is fashioned with extraordinary fidelity both in its modelling and its complexion to represent the features of the dead man... And when any distinguished member of the family dies, the masks are taken to the funeral, and are there worn by men who are considered to bear the closest resemblance to the original, both in height and in their general appearance and bearing (*History* 6, 53).[2]

The importance of these death masks in the development of realism in republican portraiture has been overplayed in the past, although as one of a number of contributing factors they can hardly be dismissed. What the 'painted portraits' mentioned by Pliny might

Fig. 8 Framed portrait of a woman from Hawara, AD 50–100 (British Museum, London, GR 1889.10-18.1).

Fig. 9 Portrait with folding doors showing a man, and the gods Isis and Serapis, AD 180–200 (J. Paul Getty Museum, Malibu, 74 AP. 20–22).

Mummy portraits from Roman Egypt

The mummy portraits of Roman Egypt came into being as the result of the blending of two traditions. In style and technique they are a product of Graeco-Roman portrait painting, though in function they are integral to the preparation of mummies in the last phase of the ancient Egyptian cult of the dead. One cannot but wonder just how the convergence of Egyptian culture with the painted portraits of the Romans came about. When Pliny asserts that portrait painting relating to the ancestor cult had died out by his time – the *Natural History* was published only after his death in AD 79 – this does not necessarily apply to the whole empire. Aside from the fact that the production of mummy portraits probably began as early as the reign of Tiberius (AD 14–37), Roman citizens working abroad as administrators in the new province of Egypt would surely have clung to older Roman traditions. Ancestor portraits were of particular significance, socially and politically, for members of the aristocracy.

Even in Egypt, very few examples of panel paintings from the many other areas of public or private life have survived, though they must have been quite common. The only framed panel painting came to light during Flinders Petrie's excavations at Hawara (fig. 8). This painting of a female bust, probably executed in tempera and held in an eight-end frame, was found together with a mummy and probably served as a stand-in for the missing mummy portrait. Judging from its frame, its smaller size and the bit of cord attached to the frame, it must have originally been a wall painting.

One picture with folding doors (fig. 9), the origins of which are sadly unknown, differs from mummy portraits in its execution but doubtless still had to do with the cult of the dead. It is a panel portrait of a man to which side panels with busts of the gods Isis and Sarapis have been attached to form a triptych; the wings were hinged to the frame so that they could be closed.

In addition to painted portraits in the private sphere and votive gifts in temples and shrines, there must have been countless painted portraits of emperors and their families, especially since they would have been considerably cheaper to produce than busts or statues. Two inscriptions from the first century confirm their existence. The first refers to festivities in honour of the imperial family in Gythium, Laconia, where painted portraits (*eikones graptaí*) of the deified (*divus*) Augustus, his wife Livia and the reigning emperor Tiberius were set up on a stage. The second comes from Ephesus and records the decision of the priests of Demeter to mark the occasion of the birth of twin sons to Drusus Caesar (Drusus the Younger) in the year AD 19 by commissioning paintings of the Ephesian Artemis, of Livia as Demeter Sebaste and of the twins as the new Dioscuri.

Interestingly enough, the only surviving painted portrait of an emperor comes from Egypt (fig. 10). The picture, painted in tempera on wood, includes bust portraits of Septimus Severus, his wife Iulia Domna, and his two sons Geta and Caracalla. Such depictions of rulers together with their families and complete with sceptre and imperial regalia were intended to suggest dynastic continuity. This picture also documents the effectiveness of the *damnatio*

memoriae, or obliteration of all remembrance, imposed after Caracalla murdered his brother Geta in AD 212: even on this panel painting the head of Geta has been effaced. The circular picture, or tondo, which probably derived as a type from the shield bust, may well have been produced on the occasion of the imperial family's visit to Egypt in AD 199.

1 Pausanias, *Guide to Greece,* trans. Peter Levi (Harmondsworth, 1971), vol. 1, 45–6.

2 Polybius, *The Rise of the Roman Empire*, trans. Ian Scott-Kilvert (Harmondsworth, 1979), 346–7.

Fig. 10 Tondo with portraits of the Emperor Septimius Severus and his family, *c.* AD 200 (Antikensammlung, Staatliche Museen zu Berlin 31329).

MUMMY PORTRAITS AND
ROMAN PORTRAITURE

Susan Walker

The portrait as a record of an individual's personal appearance in his or her lifetime has long been regarded as one of the most successful and enduring genres of Roman art. Even today, many people would have no difficulty in recognising, say, Julius Caesar from his surviving portraits, so strong is the sense of personal identity conveyed in surviving images of him on coins, gems and in sculptured heads.

Some Roman portraits were set up in public areas, like modern commemorative statues of distinguished individuals. Many more were placed in tombs; as in many modern societies, surviving relatives remembered their loved ones with an image recalling their appearance in life. In the Roman Republic, funerary portraits were restricted to the nobility and to the families of serving magistrates. The portrait masks made then had an exemplary role; they were intended to instil in younger members of the family group the virtues practised by their ancestors. Under the Empire this very specific function of portraiture gradually fell into disuse, and portraiture became instead one of many means of expressing loyalty to the reigning emperor and his family, private citizens aping even the imperial physiognomy (e.g. no. 11).

It is the latter type of Roman portrait that found its way to Egypt, appearing in the middle of the first century AD and remaining in use for some two hundred years. In Egypt the portraits were made for a specifically local purpose, that of covering the head of the mummified individual represented in the portrait. To this end, the portraits were painted on wooden panels that were inserted over the mummy wrappings (e.g. nos 9, 60) or on linen shrouds that covered the mummy (e.g. nos 1, 56). Portraits were also painted on plaster heads that were attached to a variety of materials used to enclose and protect the mummy: wooden coffin lids (e.g. no. 73), linen bags (no. 98) or even on cartonnage or mud cases. Whatever the material, the purpose of the portrait remained consistent: to serve as a record of the deceased as he or she had appeared in life.

By careful assessment of the hairstyles, clothes and jewellery worn by the subjects of the mummy portraits, it is possible to date them, in many cases within a decade or so, by reference to similar objects of known date from elsewhere in the Roman Empire. This is in itself an interesting aspect of Roman culture, which was in a sense an ancestor of the 'jeans and coca-cola' phenomenon universally recognised today. Even in remote parts of the Roman Empire, attempts were made to follow imperial court fashions, and certain features of everyday life (not merely clothes but also, say, tableware and even Latin handwriting) appear in astonishingly consistent form across the Empire at a given time. The close relationship of the mummy portraits to metropolitan Roman fashion may be explained by the strong likelihood that the subjects of the portraits were themselves engaged in local administration on behalf of the imperial authorities. They thus had the motivation and, through personal and official contacts, the means to dress like Romans living in Rome. Similar types of portrait, strongly reflecting Roman influence but specifically designed for local use and exactly contemporary with mummy portraits, are found at Palmyra in Syria and Cyrenaica in eastern Libya.

However, careful study of the portraits reveals that the physical appearance of the subjects offers a considerably more varied picture than their dress. It does indeed appear that the artists of the mummy portraits (of whom we know nothing) recorded the personal features of their subjects. Thus a pair of portraits from the same tomb at er-Rubayat (no. 46 and National Galleries of Scotland, Edinburgh 1902.70) were first linked together by observation of shared physiognomical features (eyes, cleft chins, deep clefts above and below the lips, which are themselves strikingly similar). Now that the paintings are known from archival evidence to be from the same tomb, further inferences can be made: the suggestion, first made some sixty years ago, that the portraits are by the same painter, may be confirmed; as the paintings very probably represent members of the same family (from the age difference, perhaps mother and son), it may be surmised that the same artist was engaged to paint a number of family portraits; the paintings do represent personal features in detail; the boy's portrait, hitherto regarded as difficult to date for lack of any chronologically significant features, may now be dated in relation to the woman's portrait, which includes jewellery, hairstyle and clothing fashionable in the late second or early third century AD.

Other 'couples' may be associated in the same manner, though there is no supporting documentary evidence to trace them to the same tomb (no. 35 and Vienna, Kunsthistorisches Museum x300; BM EA 65346 and Eton College ECM 1473). Examples of paintings showing distinctive personal characteristics include a panel portrait from Hawara of a woman with very strong, almost masculine features (no. 3, cover picture); a fat man from Kafr Ammar (no. 59), and a young man with facial hemiatrophy, the subject of a fine portrait from Hawara (no. 6). Many more portraits show a keen sense of individuality: skin tone, facial hair and bone structure are meticulously recorded and, within the corpus, considerably varied.

It is often observed that the subjects of the portraits seem very young, and concluded that the paintings must have been commissioned during the lifetime of the subject. However, such a view makes it difficult to interpret portraits painted on shrouds or other components of the coffin, and portraits of children, most of whom surely died with little warning. Though exceptions are known, C.A.T. scans of all the complete mummies represented here reveal a correspondence of age and, in suitable cases, sex between mummy and image (e.g. no. 85). Some portraits of middle-aged or elderly people have survived (e.g. nos 10, 64, 67), but it must be concluded that many of the portraits reflect the low life expectancy recorded in census returns from Roman Egypt.

Related to the notion that the portraits were painted in life is the idea that they were hung in houses and only later were attached to the mummies. Certainly the panel portraits were cut down from a rectangle (no. 61) to an arched (e.g. no. 3), clipped (e.g. no. 44) or shouldered (e.g. no. 49) shape, the final product corresponding to local traditions at, respectively, Hawara, er-Rubayat and Antinoopolis. However, mummy portraits are necessarily close to life size in scale, and the only surviving framed portrait (BM Painting 85, significantly found propped against a mummy without a portrait) is much too small to have served as a mummy portrait. There is no evidence to show how and when the latter were commissioned, but it is not out of the question that they were painted around the time of death to be carried in the procession (ekphora) of the deceased through the town or village, whence the body and the portrait were taken to the embalmers for mummification and cutting of the panel to fit the wrappings. Such a procedure,

which is inferred from the papyrological evidence for the sequence of events at funerals of the well-to-do in Roman Egypt, would explain the existence of some double-sided portraits, which could have been displayed in the procession, the appearance of three portraits of the same young man (not exhibited) tucked into one of the mummies excavated at Hawara, and the evidence for cutting of the panels. It is likely that, after embalming, the mummies were entombed, the Egyptian habit of 'dining with the dead' noted by Greek and Latin authors taking place not at home but in a pavilion associated with the tomb, of which a fine example has recently been excavated at Marina el-Alamein.

The *ekphora* is a Greek rite, and in various respects the portraits reflect an interest in Greek culture. In the Fayum it is likely that the portraits represent members of a group of descendants of the Greek mercenaries who had fought for Alexander and the early Ptolemies and were granted land after the Fayum had been drained for agricultural use in the early years of Ptolemaic rule. The colonists settled and married local women, adopting Egyptian religious belief. By the time of the Roman conquest, the population of the Fayum was very mixed. To Roman eyes the descendants of the colonists were Egyptians, but in their own view the colonists were Greeks, and they represented themselves as such to the Roman authorities, who charged them with the task of administering the towns and villages of the Fayum, offering in exchange privileged status and a reduction in the rate of poll-tax.

Until the reign of Septimius Severus (AD 193–211) the smaller communities of Roman Egypt had no town councils. They were represented at higher levels of authority by the alumni of the gymnasium, the traditional centre of Greek education, to which entry was carefully screened. Several of the portraits show youths, their ages meticulously suggested by varying degrees of facial hair, and the portraits often embellished with gold leaf (e.g. no. 31). It is likely that these images represent youths who had received a traditional Greek education. Many are shown unclothed (e.g. no. 20), complementing surviving literary accounts of the contemporary fashion for a well-developed tanned body. Another visual indicator of interest in Greek culture is the appearance of bearded men (e.g. no. 6) in the years before the Emperor Hadrian, who through his personal commitment to Greek culture, made beards a universal fashion (e.g. nos 56, 70).

The mummy of Hermione (now at Girton College, Cambridge) offers a particularly interesting example of the interest in Greek culture shown by the subjects of mummy portraits. Unusually, her name and profession are written on the shroud: *Hermione grammatike*. The latter word is usually translated as 'teacher of [Greek] grammar'. However, a recent study has shown that *grammatikoi* (overwhelmingly men) were honoured by the Greek-speaking communities of the eastern Roman Empire as upholders of Greek cultural traditions within the framework of Roman rule. The rare examples of female *grammatikai* (both from North Africa) are thought to represent an advanced degree of acceptance of Roman authority, within which traditional culture was allowed to flourish. It is perhaps in this context that the fine portrait of the young Hermione, whose skeleton suggests that she did no manual work in her lifetime, should be interpreted.

As the communities of Roman Egypt were redeveloped in the course of the second century AD, reflections of local pride may be seen in the portraits, some of which exhibit a sense of local identity. In the first century AD men and women wore tunics and mantles, the former decorated with the dark stripes (*clavi*) indicative of social rank in Rome, but in Egypt perhaps reflecting a more general sense of affiliation to Roman customs. During the second century AD a second tunic appeared, worn beneath the first and often distinguished by a decorative neckline which appears to vary from site to site. Thus some of the women of Antinoopolis wear an undertunic decorated at the neck with purple triangles (e.g. nos 50, 52). The subjects of the portraits from Antinoopolis present an austere appearance, their hair tightly confined (e.g. nos 50, 52–4). This is perhaps a reflection of the contemporary fashion among Greek communities to stress their classical past. Although – or, more likely,

because – Antinoopolis was a new foundation of Greeks, created by the Emperor Hadrian in memory of his love for the Bithynian youth Antinous, who had mysteriously drowned in the Nile in AD 130, interest there in classical Greek culture seems especially strong.

Towards the middle of the third century AD there was a radical change in fashion in favour of the dalmatic, a wide tunic with very broad *clavi* and wide sleeves (nos 98–9). The subjects of some shrouds from Antinoopolis wear the dalmatic, which otherwise is hardly represented in the corpus of mummy portraits. Interestingly, the papyrological references to the descendants of Greek military colonists tail off at the same time, reflecting a breakdown in civic and perhaps also social organisation in the Fayum at a time of weakness of central authority. It appears that the wealthier inhabitants of the Fayum settlements moved to the urban centres of the Nile valley, where the dead, clothed as eastern Mediterranean subjects of the Roman Empire, continued to be gently escorted by the jackal-headed Anubis into the presence of the mummified Osiris. A remarkable coexistence of a Greek cultural heritage, a Roman domination of the political and social order, and a faith in the only pagan religious system to offer a coherent vision of the afterlife thus survived in some centres into the fourth century AD. Throughout the three centuries of mummy portraiture there is no evidence of any break in continuity or of any conflict between the disparate elements of this delicately balanced way of life. For, provided the worship of their emperor was accepted and carried out in the approved manner, the Roman ruling authorities tolerated local systems of religious belief, even those as bizarre to Roman eyes as the Egyptian way of dealing with their dead.

THE FAYUM AND ITS PEOPLE

R.S. Bagnall

The mummy portraits are often called 'Fayum portraits' because so many of them were found in the cemeteries of the Fayum district of Egypt. Portraits have turned up, however, in many other parts of Egypt, ranging from Upper Egypt to the Mediterranean coast west of Alexandria. If we ask who the people represented in the portraits are, we are thus asking a question that is about all of Roman Egypt, not just about the Fayum. But it is for the Fayum that we have the most striking collocation of portraits and documents, for it holds almost as prominent a place in the sources of papyrus texts from Roman Egypt as it does among those of the portraits. Here better than anywhere else we should be in a position to know something about these people whose faces, clothing and adornment meet us so vividly.

Even so, the task of retrieving their identity and character is anything but simple. For one thing, few portraits bear any name, and even those that do rarely tell us what we would need to know in order to identify the individuals with confidence: father's and mother's names, place of residence, perhaps date of death. So we must proceed at a less specific level, asking what the nature of the elite of the Fayum was during these centuries: for the elite is what we are talking about. Only a tiny fraction of those who came up with the money to pay for mummification (which was not cheap) also found the wherewithal to pay the extraordinarily skilled artists responsible for these portraits.

With the Fayum, however, we have another critical difficulty. It was in many ways a most unusual area of Egypt, and we cannot take it for granted that what we find there was true throughout the land. This is the problem of typicality: was the elite of the Fayum similar to the top strata of other parts of the country? For that matter, was the population as a whole at all typical of Egypt? Or are we dealing with something so distinctive that it must be considered an isolated case? Historians have often been at pains to stress the Fayum's individuality, its uniqueness. To see why this is so, and what it might mean for our purpose, we must step back to the half-century after the death of Alexander the Great (died 323 BC), when the Ptolemies were consolidating their Egyptian kingdom and making the Fayum into what it was by the time the Romans arrived.

Very little is actually known about the Fayum during the few hundred years before the early third century BC. It has some monuments showing that parts of it were inhabited more than 1500 years earlier, but we have to work backward from what we can identify of the activity of the early Ptolemaic kings to see what they found there. One virtual certainty is that the land looked very different. The Fayum is a low-lying area, watered by the Nile through a long branch canal, the Bahr Yussuf, which runs parallel and to the west of the main river channel for a long way before reaching the entrance to the Fayum basin. There the water divides into a network of canals that bring the water around the edge of the basin and into its centre. The fields of the Fayum are in turn drained by channels that bring what remains of the water into the Birket el Qarun, called Lake Moeris, or just 'the lake', in antiquity.

The size of this lake depends essentially on how much water is let into the Fayum from the Bahr Yussuf, and the amount of land available for cultivation depends in turn on the size of the lake, as well as on competent maintenance of the irrigation and drainage network. To oversimplify: more water let in means a bigger lake and less usable land; less water means a smaller lake and more potentially usable land. The Ptolemies figured this out and started both to shrink the lake and to create the canals, drains and dikes that would make the land cultivable. Over time, the Fayum acquired a greatly enlarged zone of cultivation and became one of the richest agricultural areas of Egypt, with particularly high concentrations of gardens, orchards and vineyards.

It was not simply love of improvements that led the Ptolemies to do this, not even just a desire for more revenue. Rather, they had a need for new land, for they had adopted a common Macedonian practice of supporting their army by giving the soldiers plots of new land from which they could derive an income. As kings of Egypt, the Ptolemies owned a lot of land, but most of it had existing tenants farming it, and simply removing them was not a very attractive policy for many reasons. So new land was enormously useful to the kings. And into the Fayum they put large numbers of new settlers, mainly their Greek soldiers. But not all of the settlers were Greeks or soldiers. After all, the military settlers were not very interested in digging ditches, building dikes and bringing land under cultivation themselves. They wanted someone else to do this and pay them rents, which would support them and their families no matter where they were at the moment – and sometimes they were certainly away on military service.

These other people who did the hard labour were Egyptians, and there are clues in the village names, the personal names and the gods of the Fayum that people were brought from all over Egypt to settle the rich new land and make it work. The importation of these people is even mentioned explicitly in some papyri of the middle of the third century. Some came from the Delta, some from Upper Egypt, while others came from the nearby Oxyrhynchite and Memphite nomes.

From these twin streams of immigrants came a Fayum with a remarkably diverse population. About 30 per cent were Greeks – we will ask in a moment just what that meant – and the rest Egyptians, coming in this village from Oxyrhynchus, in that from the middle of the Delta, in another from the Thebaid, in still another from the region of Memphis. More than in other parts of Egypt, there was considerable heterogeneity in the gods worshipped. As Egyptian personal names are mainly derived from those of the gods of a particular community, many names are distinctive to one or a few places. Sometimes we find names known only in one or two Fayum villages and in some remote place in another part of Egypt. The Fayum might then be seen as a kind of microcosm of Egypt, with more Greeks than elsewhere but also a more varied Egyptian population than was typical.

We must now ask what the word 'Greek' meant in this description of how the Fayum came to have its population. In the Ptolemaic system all people were divided into two groups, Hellenes (Greeks) and Egyptians. Hellenic – or 'not Egyptian' – status was based on official national origin, and virtually all foreigners qualified as Hellenes: Thracians, Paeonians, Judaeans, Idumaeans – all sorts of people that a classical Athenian would have been aghast to think of as Greeks. For most purposes, the term meant 'immigrant' or 'foreign settler'. The third-century census records show us a population in which ethnic designations apply not so much to individuals as to entire households. The wife of a Hellene is therefore a Hellene, no matter what her ancestry. The results

were from our point of view quite remarkable: one could become a Hellene. About half of the Fayum's Greeks were military men and their families, about half civilians.

Ptolemaic ethnicity thus looks a bit slippery. That should not actually be surprising if we know anything about ethnicity in modern societies, for ethnic terms and categories are always based in historical circumstances and forces, and people struggle to control them. Ethnicity does not exist in isolation from the relationship of one group to another; there is no consciousness of ethnicity except where one must talk about one group as against another. There may be, as in Ptolemaic Egypt, official definitions of ethnicity, and these are what we find in official or legal documents; but we cannot assume that they are identical to the way terms were used in private speech. Certainly ethnicity is not simply equivalent to race (itself an elusive and perhaps illegitimate concept), to geographical origin, to language or to culture.

The complex, contested, relational and mutable character of ethnicity is undoubtedly at the root of our difficulty in speaking of the ethnicity of particular individuals or families. When Dionysios, alias Plenis, entered the army around 105 BC, he acquired the status of Macedonian instead of that of 'Persian'. But at the same time that he bears the ethnic of the conquerors, he moves freely in the world of the Egyptian temples, is himself holder of a priestly office and is designated in some texts as a royal cultivator, the very definition of the purely Egyptian peasant. He could write with a high degree of competence in both demotic Egyptian and Greek. There is absolutely no doubt that he was recorded in the royal accounts as holding the status of Hellene; that is, he occupies a position in the dominant class of Egypt, the royal system. Yet his ethnicity is not exhausted by the official designation. The editors of his archive concluded that Dionysios came from a predominantly Egyptian background. What he represents is a pattern in which individuals operate in multiple social roles, each with their own official ethnicity: being a 'Macedonian' soldier is Hellenic, being a priest or a royal cultivator is Egyptian.

We do not know what Dionysios, alias Plenis, thought of all this. But he and others managed to operate in two spheres. His bicultural class may not have been vast in numbers, but neither was it trivial. We must not suppose that later Ptolemaic Egypt was a society divided tidily into Greeks and Egyptians. The Graeco-Macedonian military settlers, civilians of Greek descent, official Greeks of Egyptian or mixed descent, and Egyptians untouched by the presence of foreigners all coexisted in the countryside. Official ethnicity had moved from representing the national origin of the head of the household to being a heritable status, and from that to being an acquirable status.

Faced with a situation of this complexity, the Romans took an entirely different approach, one rooted in their categories of legal status. As in the Ptolemaic period, we find a distinction between Greeks and Egyptians. But those words mean something different: Hellenes turn out to be a subcategory of Egyptians, not their opposite! In the Roman class structure of Egypt there were several strata. At the top were the holders of Roman citizenship; below them were the citizens of the three, later four, Greek cities of Egypt: non-Romans, but citizens. Of these, Alexandria occupied a somewhat higher niche than Ptolemais, Naukratis or Antinoopolis, but the citizens of all four were recognisably Greeks by any definition. The Romans did not call these people Hellenes, however; they identified them collectively as 'citizens', *astoi* in Greek. The third stratum was composed of Egyptians, peregrine non-citizens in Roman terms, and it included all of the inhabitants of the country outside of the two citizen groups already mentioned.

This 'flagrant divorce between social reality and juridical categories', as one scholar has called it, called for further subcategorisation. And so within the Egyptians the Romans distinguished a privileged group of residents of the *metropoleis*, or chief towns of the nomes, and these were variously called *metropolitai* or *Hellenes*. Their chief privilege was to pay poll-tax at a lower rate than other 'Egyptians', but they were not, unlike citizens, exempted altogether. They also emerged as the governing class of the *metropoleis*. But they were still 'Egyptians'.

This kind of 'ethnicity' is obviously just as much a creation of the Roman legal and administrative system as the Ptolemaic official categories were of their system. As with Ptolemaic society, it raises for us the question whether the inhabitants of Egypt saw matters, either initially or eventually, as the Romans did. That is, when the Romans drew the line between ethnic groups in a different place from that used by the Ptolemies, altering legal ethnicity, was perceived ethnicity changed along with it? Here the Jews serve as a valuable test case. The so-called Acts of the Pagan Martyrs preserve vignettes of Alexandrians speaking before the emperor. In one of them Isidoros says, 'I accuse them [the Jews] of wishing to stir up the entire world . . . We must consider the entire mass. They are not of the same temperament as the Alexandrians, but live rather after the fashion of the Egyptians. Are they

not on a level with those who pay the poll-tax.' Isidoros thus glides effortlessly from legal ethnicity, reflected here in subjection to the poll-tax, to way of life, or perceived ethnicity. Tendentious he is, of course; the Alexandrian citizens were the closest thing to winners in the Roman redesign of Egypt, and Isidoros had every interest in exaggerating the distinctions. But at least his words suggest that the Roman innovations produced a new zone in which ethnicity was contested.

Do we then have any means of asking how these newly created 'Egyptians' saw themselves? Did they all 'live after the fashion of the Egyptians' and see themselves as such, or did some of them see themselves as Greeks? This is the nub of the problem. There is little or no direct evidence for questions of self-perception in this population. Sometimes it is possible to discern the ways in which a member of the village elite identified his interests with those of the ruling power, like local elites all over the Roman Empire. It would not be unreasonable to imagine that such people thought of themselves as both Greeks and Romans, perhaps even as Egyptians, Greeks and Romans simultaneously. We cannot say if the notion of these as disjunctive categories even came into the thinking of such people.

It would be natural to suggest that language was still a basic discriminant of culture, and even of ethnicity. But we face here the basic problem that Greek very quickly became almost the only written language of Roman Egypt. Those bastions of Egyptian identity, the temples, operated mainly in Greek, at least so far as written documentation is concerned, although they preserved much literature in demotic for many decades. The relationship of spoken to written language is extremely complex in this society, and someone capable of operating in Greek might nonetheless have thought of it as an alien language – the language of foreigners.

Our best tool turns out to be names, not so much because they are inherently attached to an ethnic group but because they tell us something of what sense of social and religious location parents had in naming their children. The urban elite of the Fayum was the body that referred to itelf most formally as 'the 6475 Hellenes in the Arsinoite nome' – probably the descendants of the Ptolemaic military settlers, for in some documents the term for military settlers is part of the description of the status. When we look at their men's names, we find that only a little over 20 per cent are Greek names commonly found outside Egypt and with no special Egyptian connection. Another 24 per cent are dynastic names or linked to the initial settlement of the Fayum. A handful (5 per cent) are of Roman origin. But the largest block, some 44 per cent, are based on the names of gods, and almost all of these are either clearly or possibly Greek renderings of Egyptian theophoric names or else Greek formations on the names of Egyptian gods. The overall character of this 'Greek' onomastic repertory is unmistakably rooted in Egyptian religion.

When we compare this group to the residents of several villages in the Fayum, we find mainly a drop, in varying degree, in the Greekness of the names. That is, the names are still largely based on the Egyptian gods, but more of them are, linguistically speaking, Egyptian formations, not Greek formations. Some villages have many more Greek names than others, but none comes close to the distinctive blend of this elite group. In both the city and the villages, however, we find that women's names are more often Egyptian, and less often Greek, than men's are. No one, probably, will argue that in an 'ethnic' sense generations of intermarriages kept producing Greek boys and Egyptian girls; we must instead see that the gender differences reflect the more public roles played by men and the sense that those roles – being trained in the gymnasium, for example – were Greek.

By now it is obvious that the ethnicity of the elite inhabitants of the Roman Fayum cannot be seen in simple binary terms, Greek *or* Egyptian. Some of these people may indeed have seen matters in such terms, but the way they named their children suggests something much more complex. When we move from the elite to the villages, the degree of overall connection to Egypt changes very slightly, but the Greekness of that connection declines. It seems reasonable to conclude that most of the Greek-speaking inhabitants of the region, and especially of its elite, saw themselves as *both* Greek and Egyptian. This duality, even plurality, of identity was commonplace in the Roman East, where it was in no way necessary to abandon local pride and identification in order to participate in the metropolitan culture of the Greek regions of the Roman Empire. And what form could better exemplify this complex ethnicity than the combination of Graeco-Roman clothing, hairstyles, and jewellery with the quintessentially Egyptian funerary practice of mummification?

TECHNIQUE

Euphrosyne C. Doxiadis

The Fayum corpus of painted portraits is of paramount significance in the history of art because it embodies the great Greek painting tradition. Almost all the work in that tradition has been lost to time and the elements, the Mediterranean not sharing the exceptional preservative conditions of the Egyptian desert. The paintings of the Fayum, sheltered in this way, are a dazzling testament to the sophistication of the Alexandrian school from which they are derived and show us the heights that had been reached in the rendering of nature. It is not until some fifteen centuries later, in the faces painted by Titian or Rembrandt's depiction of his own features as he saw them reflected in the mirror, that the same artistry that characterises many of the anonymous painters of the Fayum is witnessed again.

In addition to the Greek painting tradition, which, ancient sources tell us, reached its peak at the time of Apelles in the fourth century BC, there came Egyptian influences, particularly in relation to the beliefs and techniques surrounding the preservation of the human form for the attainment of immortality. Of these two strands, the sophistication of the first and the intensity of the second combined to produce moments of breathtaking beauty and unsettling presence in the paintings that survive.

Within the Fayum corpus two different painting media – tempera and encaustic – have been used either on wood (from a variety of trees) or straight onto the linen mummy shroud. 'Tempera' describes the method whereby pigments are mixed with a water-soluble binding agent, most frequently an animal glue; 'encaustic' in modern times has come to signify all painting methods in which pigments have been mixed with beeswax, whether melted in its natural brittle condition or emulsified by chemical mixture with bicarbonate of soda. The following is a more detailed discussion of these two types.

The portraits in tempera were painted either on white gesso or on dark khaki or grey grounds. In the first case the white ground glows through the paler colours, giving luminosity to the faces. The portraits on dark grounds, which may have originated in attempts to imitate the colour and tone of the wooden panel or of the khaki colour of natural linen, acquire greater depth as the lights and darks of the portrait respectively stand out and recede to greater effect.

Whether on light or dark grounds, the tempera used in life-size portraits of adults was applied delicately throughout since it dries quickly and does not offer itself to blending with other tones. Fine, almost hair-width brushes were used to apply extremely fine lines, which depict a form through hatching and cross-hatching in a manner closely resembling the technique of engravers of the fifteenth century onwards. The results, which can be clearly observed in the portraits, are delicately calligraphic, as if inscribed with a fine-nibbed pen. Much rests on this very precise rendering, and there is a type of portrait that relies on near-perfect drawing for depicting the features; a millimetre off can skew a likeness leaving a flawed portrait for posterity.

In the smaller portraits of children, a different technique was adopted. A uniform flesh tone, comprising two or three different tones roughly blended together, was applied flatly in a manner that works only because of the smaller size of the faces.

The technique of ancient encaustic, in which most of the Fayum portraits were painted, remains something of a mystery. From the eighteenth century onwards a number of artists and scholars have tried to uncover its secrets, an effort that accelerated with the finds of larger numbers of such portraits at the end of the nineteenth and beginning of the twentieth century and continues to occupy researchers from various disciplines to this day. Instructions for the procedure perished with the loss at an early date of ancient treatises on painting, the most famous among them being the 'volumes' of Apelles that Pliny the Elder describes in his *Natural History*. There does, however, survive in Pliny's monumental work a recipe for Punic wax that can be easily followed and applied today and that produces an excellent painting medium. Following in the long line of researchers I have experimented extensively with the recipe and its product, a malleable emulsified wax that can be used cold and produces results that fit well with the evidence of the Fayum portraits.

From the growing literature on scientific tests carried out on the paintings and the visual evidence of the portraits themselves, it is clear that several types of encaustic have been used, the painter achieving different effects according to a number of variables: the use of hot or cold wax, the painting surface of wood or linen stiffened with animal glue or gesso, the colour of the underpainting or the wood grain visible beneath the features, and the choice of brush or hard tools, the latter used heated or cold.

Hot beeswax would be mixed with a hardening agent such as resin (Chios mastic, for instance) before it was used for painting, while it appears that cold Punic wax was mixed with egg (B. Ramer's scientific analysis of the portrait of a young man, no. 48, revealed the presence of egg in the encaustic impasto) and sometimes a small amount of linseed oil. The choice of tools was determined by the effect desired but also in part by the type of wax used; for instance, those portraits painted with brushes throughout were almost always produced in the more malleable medium of emulsified cold wax as can be seen in an 'athlete' (no. 24) and the mummy of Artemidorus (no. 32). Some of the portraits are painted with brushes in the first instance, before the application of a hard tool to blend in the tones and add texture and depth by adding 'wound' marks to the thick wax impasto. In most cases this technique is confined to the flesh areas, such as in a portrait of a woman (no. 50) but it may also be used more generally, as in a portrait of a man (no. 23).

In conclusion, one cannot overemphasise the diversity of techniques used in the Fayum corpus. The subtlety and roughness, the finesse and asperity, seen in the portraits attest to the idiosyncrasy of each individual painter. Although they are unsigned works, the 'handwriting' of each painter is visible in the brush-strokes and tool-marks scored in the thick wax impasto of the ancient faces, and in the application of paint in the most masterful encaustic portraits shows an uncanny similarity to oil-painting. It is therefore not surprising that the portraits have been compared to the works of the Impressionists, who shared their ancient colleagues' inspired use of medium. The rich textures and colours and the great variety of individual styles reveal the presence of unique individuals in the painters as much as the subjects.

THE DISCOVERY OF THE MUMMY PORTRAITS

Morris Bierbrier

In December 1615 the Italian traveller Pietro della Valle (1586–1652), who was in Egypt *en route* to Persia and India, visited the site of Saqqara near Cairo. There 'excavations' were occasionally carried out by the local inhabitants in their search for mummies to satisfy the rare tourist and, more importantly, the brisk trade in *mumiya* or mummy dust for medicinal purposes. Della Valle was shown two mummies with fine painted portraits which he promptly acquired. After numerous adventures the traveller and his collections reached Italy safely, and the mummies were published in his account of his travels which appeared in 1650–3 and was translated into several languages. However, the engravings of the portraits did not illustrate their artistic quality and they made no great impact on the connoisseurs of art but were regarded as mere curiosities. They disappeared from view for a time but were acquired for the Dresden collection in 1728.

It was not until extensive excavations were undertaken by the British and French consuls at the beginning of the nineteenth century that further portraits came to light. The first and second collections of the British consul Henry Salt (1780–1826) passed to the British Museum and the Louvre in 1823 and 1826. Most of the objects were found by his agents Belzoni (1778–1821) and d'Athanasi (1798–1854) and included a small group of mummy portraits, one still on a mummy (no. 115). Unfortunately, the provenances of these portraits are not clearly indicated, but they probably originated from either Saqqara or Thebes where most of Salt's efforts were concentrated. The Theban provenance was considered dubious until recently when fragments of mummy portraits were indeed discovered there. Salt, by training an artist, was quick to realise the significance of his finds. He wrote in October 1815: 'One case contains two Greek mummies – one of which is of great value, as it has upon it a portrait painted on wood in the incaustic style of the antients...The specimen I send home may tend to throw a light upon this subject & to illustrate thereby the early history of the art.' A trickle of portraits and portrait shrouds from Saqqara and probably Thebes, entered European collections throughout the course of the nineteenth century but failed to attract much attention.

The situation was dramatically changed in the late 1880s by extensive discoveries made in the Fayum. In 1887 the local inhabitants unearthed one or more major cemeteries near er-Rubayat which contained many mummies with wooden portraits. An astute Austrian businessman named Theodor Graf (1840–1903) quickly bought up all the portrait finds. These he exhibited in various European cities and in New York before selling many of them and scattering them throughout the world. These portraits are usually designated as the first Graf Collection. After his death his heirs sold the remaining portraits in the 1920s, these now being known as the second Graf Collection. Unfortunately, the Graf portraits lacked a firm archaeological context, especially as the mummies to which they had been attached were either not preserved or more likely discarded by the discoverers. Unlike previously discovered portraits, they were almost entirely painted in tempera and not the wax encaustic technique.

At about the same time in 1887–9 Flinders Petrie (1853–1942) discovered a major Roman cemetery at Hawara, also in the Fayum, in which were buried many mummies with fine encaustic portraits. Petrie carefully recorded the archaeological context of his finds although not in as much detail as modern researchers would have liked. His letters are more evocative: 'Then a report of another mummy, and by the time they have lunched a procession of three gilt mummies is seen coming across the mounds glittering in the sun.' He also preserved intact several mummies with their portraits and salvaged many portraits which were in poor condition but can now be reconstructed with modern conservation techniques. Most of the portraits in the collections in Great Britain derive from Petrie's discoveries at Hawara. He himself returned to the site in 1911 and was rewarded with further finds. Further portraits were discovered by German expeditions to Hawara in the 1890s. This sudden flood of portraits stimulated great interest in artistic circles and it is suggestive that Petrie gave many of his best finds to the National Gallery.

However, artistic interest soon waned especially as critics tended to view them as an isolated phenomenon without due consideration of their Egyptian and Roman context.

Because of the great numbers which had been found in the Fayum, the portraits have erroneously been termed Fayum portraits, but in fact subsequent archaeological work has demonstrated that they were used as part of funerary equipment throughout the country. In the Fayum the papyrologists Bernard Grenfell (1869–1926) and Arthur Hunt (1871–1934) found portrait burials at Tebtunis in 1899–1900; at er-Rubayat in 1901, thereby confirming the location of some, if not all, of the Graf discoveries; and at Fag el-Gamus in 1902. South of the Fayum two mummies with portraits were found at el-Hibeh in 1903. From 1897 the French archaeologist Albert Gayet (1856–1916) made important discoveries of portrait mummies and shrouds in Middle Egypt at the site of Antinoopolis, founded by the Emperor Hadrian in honour of his dead favourite Antinous who drowned in the Nile in AD 130. Further portraits were uncovered at Akhmim by the German Carl Schmidt (1868–1938) at the end of the nineteenth century and in subsequent work at the site. All these major discoveries were made by 1914 and interest in the portraits lessened as no further evidence was uncovered.

The study of mummy portraits was inhibited by the fact that they were considered a classical development by Egyptologists, who were more interested in the dynastic period, but were considered an Egyptological aspect by classicists, who tended to ignore them. Art historians also saw them as of only archaeological concern. Certain specialists continued to study them, most notably Klaus Parlasca who compiled the first catalogue of all known portraits and thus made them available to other scholars. Fortunately, scholarship has now progressed so that Egyptologists and classicists no longer view their subjects in isolation, and the growth of interdisciplinary studies has led to the revival of interest in Roman Egypt, the culture of which period is now appreciated for its own sake rather than being dismissed as of no importance by Egyptologist and classicist alike. New studies have illuminated aspects of this hybrid culture including the mummy portraits. Coincidentally new portrait discoveries have been made at Thebes, possibly at el-Hibeh, and more recently in 1991 at Marina el-Alamein on the edge of the Delta, thus proving that the use of portraits in burials was by no means confined to the Fayum or Middle Egypt but was spread throughout the country.

A NOTE ON THE DATING OF MUMMY PORTRAITS

Susan Walker

The first edition of *Ancient Faces*, published in 1997, contained no discussion of the controversial matter of the dating of mummy portraits from Roman Egypt. The topic has been a matter of lively debate since the first discoveries of large groups of mummy portraits in the Fayum cemeteries in the late nineteenth century, and remains controversial after the series of exhibitions following the British Museum's version of *Ancient Faces*. There follows here a brief résumé of attempts to date the portraits, with a concise explanation of the methods used by the present author. The résumé draws on the much fuller account given by Borg (1996, 19–26).

The Viennese antiquarian and dealer Theodor Graf first proposed a Ptolemaic date and a royal context for his collection of mostly tempera paintings stripped from the tombs of er-Rubayat in the north-east Fayum in the 1880s; in this he was supported by the Egyptologist Georg Ebers, both men impressed by the high quality of many of the paintings (Ebers 1889, 1893). However, the contemporary excavation and rapid publication of the cemeteries of Hawara in the south-east Fayum by the British Egyptologist W. Flinders Petrie also revealed paintings of superb quality which were rightly recognised as Roman. Petrie later revised his reconstruction of the evolution of mummy portraiture, which in its original form postulated a linear development from undecorated mummies, through gilded masks with Egyptian and then Greek decoration, to painted panels. The discovery of the Egyptian-style mask of Titus Flavius Demetrios (Walker and Bierbrier 1997, 84–5, no. 74), his name derived from the Flavian emperors (AD 69–96), thus pushed the beginning of the panel portraits later, into the second century AD.

Two scholars, R. Graul and C. C. Edgar, reviewed the new corpus, and made important observations on the dating which are still valid today. Graul (1888, 1889) noted that portraits of inferior quality might coexist with finer work, and Edgar (1905) effectively demolished the cases for a Ptolemaic date and for Petrie's evolution, carefully comparing the hairstyles of the portraits with those of Roman stone sculptures, and using the evidence offered by Roman papyri and inscriptions. Both Edgar and Petrie dated the end of the production of painted portraits to the middle years of the third century AD. However, A. Reinach began in 1914 a catalogue of the surviving works, sadly not completed. He argued that the production of shrouds from Antinoopolis continued beyond the painted portraits into the tetrarchic period (see further below). In 1922 P. Buberl published a catalogue of Graf's collection in which the Roman dating was fully accepted, and qualitative differences were understood to have existed throughout the production of the portraits, which Buberl, like Edgar, dated from the first to the third centuries AD. Significantly, Buberl constructed a stylistic development of the paintings from expressionism through naturalism to a formal flat style.

Heinrich Drerup's dissertation on the dating of mummy portraits (1933) was published as a concise overview, with thirty-four paintings illustrating a chronological structure which fitted contemporary notions of decline in the mid-third century AD and revival in the fourth. Many of the tempera portraits, much cruder in appearance than those painted in encaustic, were deemed to be of late antique date, their production stretching through the fourth century AD. The comparison with sculptured portraits, though scrupulously applied in the catalogue entries, suffered from the poor contemporary understanding of later Roman portraiture in stone. In its place a greater reliance was placed upon the stylistic features of the portraits, which assumed the role of a dating criterion in their own right. The dominance of stylistic analysis may be seen in the wider mid-twentieth century context of archaeological and art-historical scholarship in which an increasing technological sophistication coincided with a reluctance to contextualise artefacts within ancient social structures, both developments fuelled by modern global political conflicts.

The tendency to impose a dating system based upon perceptions of style informed work published in the 1960s and 1970s and thereby has resonance even today. Thus, following the publication in 1966 of a highly successful monograph, of lasting value for its detailed consideration within an archaeological context of a vast range of portraits in all surviving media, Klaus Parlasca began work on a corpus of portraits on wood and linen shrouds. Three volumes have appeared (1969, 1977, 1980), comprehensive in coverage, bibliography and illustration, a monumental achievement difficult to challenge. Compilation of the corpus also heralded a period of increasing specialisation within the genre. Günther Grimm's monograph (1974), which also followed Drerup's dating, was concerned with mummy masks and shrouds. Even monographs written in the 1990s (Doxiadis 1995, Borg 1996) have been restricted to two-dimensional paintings.

The publication of Parlasca's third volume in 1980, largely of tempera portraits, met with some criticism for an apparently arbitrary judgement of quality (Jucker 1984). A doctoral thesis on the chronology and social context of the encaustic and tempera portraits was prepared by Barbara Borg, who returned to earlier principles of dating by means of a strict comparison with the hairstyles of portraits made in other media (especially stone), combining her comparisons with a sensitivity to stylistic and technical developments, and a careful consideration of the known social context of the paintings. Borg's detailed analysis, supported by an improved understanding of later imperial portraits in stone, has reinstated tempera painting as contemporary with encaustic. Borg's views informed the widely accessible and brilliantly illustrated monograph by Euphrosyne Doxiadis, which appeared in 1995 in Greek, French and English.

Since the British exhibition of 1997, most of which was also shown in Rome with an Italian translation of the catalogue, exhibitions of mummy portraits using much of the material but not the catalogue have appeared in Greece (Doxiadis 1998), France (Aubert and Cortopassi 1998) and Germany (Parlasca and Seeman 1999). An exhibition of portraits mostly held by Cairo Museum was mounted in Vienna with an accompanying catalogue (Seipel 1998). Dating of the paintings exhibited has fallen into two camps, one allowing dominance of the perception of stylistic change over comparison with portraits in other media (Aubert and Cortopassi 1998, Parlasca and Seeman 1999), the other giving greater weight to the comparison of the hairstyles and physiognomies of the subjects of both encaustic and tempera paintings to Roman portraits in other media (Walker and Bierbrier 1997, Doxiadis 1998, Laubenberger in Seipel 1998, *passim*).

For the British Museum's exhibition, researched in a climate of lively controversy between the two camps, it was decided to take an independent view based on close observation of the paintings themselves. For all the paintings borrowed from British collections, the study included preparation of detailed annotated sketches of the more complex pieces, and for all these portraits the catalogue entry was drafted on a portable computer with the portrait to hand. While it cannot be claimed that the method is foolproof, it is certainly more reliable than photography alone, obliging the researcher to spend a long time looking at each portrait, and to understand what is seen, for a drawing cannot be undertaken without comprehension of the details of its subject. Drawing also proved a valuable aid to memory, allowing wider, speedier and more reliable recall of details for comparison. Significantly, the criteria for dating by external comparison were expanded beyond the hairstyles and physiognomies inspired by the fashions of the imperial court to include details of dress and jewellery. These last elements, seen to be consistent in portraits well dated by hairstyle, were related to finds of jewellery and clothing in and outside of Egypt, and to representations of dress in painting, mosaic, gold glass and sculpture from elsewhere in the Roman empire. These methods and criteria have also been used for the supplementary entries written for this edition of the catalogue by the present author.

It was also decided to group the portraits by site, a decision that proved critical to the understanding of their date. For it soon became apparent that painters worked in ateliers associated with particular villages, and the choice of medium was more reflective of geography and relative economic prosperity than of date. It was also clear that the subjects of the portraits, whether painted in tempera, encaustic or (as often happened) in a mixture of the two, wore similar clothes, jewellery and hairstyles, however carefully their individual appearance had been captured by the artist. This observation applied also to three-dimensional portrait masks, which followed the same pattern of development as panel paintings and shroud portraits. Only the gilded masks from Hawara seemed to have a different life-span, apparently beginning in the Ptolemaic period and falling out of use in the early second century AD.

It was clear when the exhibition was opened that more work needed to be done on the later antique masks from Deir el-Bahri and on the shroud portraits from Antinoopolis. Opportunities for understanding this group of portraits were much enhanced by the opening in early 1998 of a permanent gallery of funerary art from Ptolemaic and Roman Egypt in the

Musée du Louvre. The display included an important selection of recently conserved shroud portraits from Saqqara and Antinoopolis. Detailed study of these revealed a close correspondence with wall paintings and especially gold-glass portraits from the cemeteries of Rome, mostly of fourth-century date. A progression from plain to more decorative fashions may be traced through the later third century and well into the fourth. The results of this research have been published as a short paper in the catalogue of the Frankfurt exhibition (Walker in Parlasca and Seeman 1999, 74–8), where, however, the catalogue entries, prepared by H. G. Frenz, reflect a different view.

To summarise the position taken here, mummy portraits in encaustic on wood and in tempera on linen were first made about AD 30–40, some two generations after the imposition of Roman rule in Egypt. The rise of portraits offering a Romanised appearance of the subject coincides with papyrological evidence for increased contacts of the leaders of the Fayum settlements with the Roman imperial authorities, contacts which were aimed at maintaining a relatively privileged position for those who described themselves as the descendants of the Greek veteran soldiers settled in the Fayum by the early Ptolemies (Walker in Bierbrier 1997, 1–6). Panel paintings in tempera may have been devised slightly later, but were certainly produced by about AD 70. Paintings on wood in either medium, and sometimes in mixed media, continued to be made with no sign of any interruption until the early third century AD. To the present author's knowledge there are only two of certain later date, an unprovenanced portrait of a woman now in Mariemont (Parlasca and Seeman 1999, 238, no. 146, dated to about AD 300) and a portrait of a young woman apparently from Antinoopolis and now in the Museo Egizio, Turin (Parlasca II, no. 476, there described as male and dated to the Hadrianic period, but from the jewellery surely a girl, and from the dress also about AD 300).

Painted plaster masks appear to show a similar pattern of development: those not sporting Egyptian wigs may be compared to panel and shroud portraits with an often striking correspondence of hairstyle, dress and jewellery. In their form they show an evolution from a flat portrayal of the individual on the bier, prevalent in the first century AD, through a raised head in the second century, to an almost vertical head and shoulders in the third. Gilded masks, in contrast, indicate a continuous development from the Ptolemaic to early Roman period, showing strongly Romanised features very similar to painted portraits in the mid-first century AD. They do not appear to have been made later than the early years of the second century AD, and are unusual in that several masks incorporate within the portrait an inscription giving in Greek the name of the deceased, his or her patronymic and age at death. These masks may have been commissioned by wealthier families.

Painted shroud portraits were certainly made before the middle of the first century AD. Somewhat eclipsed by the growth in popularity of panel painting in the later first century, they enjoyed great popularity through the second and third centuries. It is in this medium that the transition to late antique fashions may be most clearly documented. A number of shrouds from Antinoopolis clearly show individuals dressed in the dalmatic, a sleeved tunic with broad and often elaborately decorated *clavi* (stripes) which became standard dress for elite women in the second half of the third century AD. Men and boys also adopted a sleeved tunic, but with narrow sleeves. Both garments were often decorated with woven rectangles of a contrasting colour (*tabellae*) or roundels (*orbiculi*). The painted plaster and linen masks from Deir el-Bahri also show men and women dressed in sleeved tunics of this sort.

As noted above, dalmatics hardly appear on painted panel portraits or indeed on painted plaster masks, and that is reason enough to agree with Barbara Borg and her early twentieth-century predecessors that the painted panels were not much produced after the middle years of the third century. More recently Borg has been assembling evidence for the decline of the Fayum settlements in the third century AD (Borg 1998, 96–101). It appears from the evidence offered by the shroud portraits that the elite populations of the region moved from the Fayum to urban centres in the Nile valley, certainly Antinoopolis and perhaps also Memphis and Thebes. In relative security they maintained their traditions of pagan burial long after the official adoption of Christianity as the religion of the Roman emperor, if not of all of his subjects.

CATALOGUE

PORTRAITS AND MUMMIES FROM HAWARA

The portraits in this section were excavated in the cemeteries at Hawara (south-east Fayum) by W. M. (later Professor Sir William) Flinders Petrie, in three campaigns conducted in 1887–8, 1888–9 and 1910–11. The mummies, of which only 1–2 per cent had portrait panels, were found packed into pits lined with stone or brick in a manner suggesting that the portraits had formerly been entombed or at least displayed elsewhere. Almost all the portraits found at Hawara are painted on very thin panels of lime, a Mediterranean wood not native to Egypt. The panels were cut to an arched shape to fit the mummies. Most of the paintings are executed in the encaustic technique, and the subjects of the portraits display an enthusiastic adoption of Roman fashion in hairstyles, jewellery and clothing. It is likely that Hawara was the cemetery of the nome capital Ptolemais Euergetis (also known as Arsinoe), which might explain the urbanised character of the portraits. However, papyrological evidence shows that burial near the pyramid complex, known to the Greeks as the labyrinth, built by Amenemhat III (1842–1797 BC), was considered a privilege, and the cemetery may also have included burials of persons domiciled elsewhere.

Many of the painted panels were detached from their mummies, the latter being too poorly preserved to transport from the site. Some finds were deposited in the Cairo Museum. The objects exported by Petrie were dispersed among his financial backers in the United Kingdom, where they are now held in national, local and university collections, most notably the Petrie Museum in University College London, where Petrie held the first chair of Egyptology endowed by Amelia Edwards. During his excavations Petrie kept notebooks and journals, which have been used here to reconstruct groups of burials.

1 Portrait of a woman in tempera and encaustic with added gold leaf on a linen shroud

AD 50–70

H 51.7 cm, W 37 cm

Excavated by Petrie at Hawara in 1888 (Petrie YY) with a canvas portrait (Petrie yy) as yet unidentified

Presented by the National Gallery in 1994

London, British Museum EA 74709 (formerly National Gallery 1266)

Though the figure is painted in tempera, the hair appears waxy and was apparently painted in encaustic. The fragmentary linen shroud has been remounted, and much of the paint is abraded. The jewellery was added in gold leaf. The surface is coated with varnish.

The woman wears a green tunic with black *clavi*. Unusually she has no mantle. Her right arm is raised across her body and holds a pinkish-red lucky knot; her left arm rests beneath.

In her hair the woman wears a red band, an ornament characteristic of Neronian portraits. The central parting is gilded. In her pierced ears the woman wears ball earrings typical of the later first century AD, and round her neck is a necklace of gold beads linked by cylindrical elements, with a central shell pendant. On both forearms are gold snake bracelets. On the third finger of her right hand is a gold ring, now mostly lost.

The hair is lightly waved with banks of curls at the sides of the head, and long locks at the side of the neck, that on the proper left side worn in a knot of the sort more often seen at the nape of the neck, here

1

2 Portrait of a woman in encaustic on limewood

AD 55–70

H 35.8 cm, W 20.2 cm

Excavated by Petrie at Hawara in 1911 (Petrie 58)

Presented by the National Gallery in 1994

London, British Museum EA 74716 (formerly National Gallery 2914)

A large crack splits the panel from top to bottom through the proper right eye, and a shorter crack runs through the left eye. The paint surface is damaged in several places. Traces of the mummy wrappings appear at the upper corners. The background was painted in bluish grey with long brush-strokes.

The figure appears very large in relation to the background and is shown in three-quarter view. She wears a claret-coloured tunic with a very dark crimson *clavus* edged with gold, visible on the proper right side. A mantle of mauvish tone is draped around the shoulders.

The woman wears gold ball earrings (painted with white highlights) typical of the later first century AD. She wears around her neck a gold chain with pendant crescent with ball-shaped terminals: this too is painted with creamy-white highlights. It is not out of the question that she originally had an ornamental chain across the hair, separating the bun on the crown from the locks in front – a feature of other Neronian portraits. Of this, nothing survives but a greyish ground. The front hair is arranged around the brow in two banks of snail-shaped curls, expanded to four above the ears. Locks fall behind the ears to either side of the neck; the necklace has been painted over the lock on the proper right side.

The eyes (especially the proper left eye) are large and rounded, with arched eyebrows. The nose is rather shorter than the norm; the lips are full and painted rose pink. The creamy flesh is tinted pink on the cheeks and chin, and a creamy-white

bound in gold. The eyes are large and round, with eyebrows and eyelashes drawn with individual strokes resembling stitches, very characteristic of painting in tempera. The slightly opened lips are painted red, and there are cream highlights on the nose.

In general composition the portrait is reminiscent of contemporary work in gilded cartonnage (e.g. no. 27).

BIBLIOGRAPHY

Petrie, *Hawara*, 17, 42, pl. 11; Petrie, *Portfolio*, pl. 5; Petrie, *Portraits*, 3, 11; Shore pl. 17; Parlasca III, 44, no. 584 (bibl.), pl. 140, 3; Doxiadis 1995, no. 47, 47; A. Bowman, *Egypt after the Pharaohs* (London 1996), 139, pl. 81; Doxiadis 1998, 137 no. 7 with pl. p. 27; Aubert and Cortopassi 1998, 66–7, no. 23

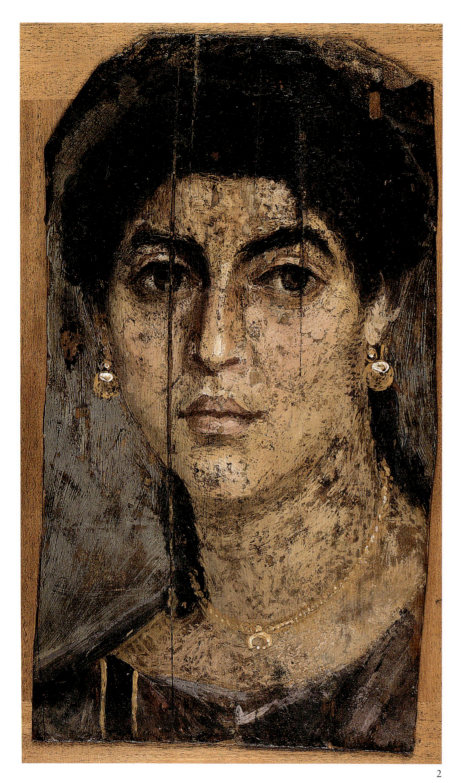

2

highlight runs down the nose and above and below the lips.

BIBLIOGRAPHY

Petrie, *Portraits*, 7, 14; Petrie, *Portfolio*, pl. 7; Shore pl. 2; Parlasca I, 29, no. 13 (bibl.), pl. 4; Doxiadis 1995, 200, no. 48; Borg 1996, 31, 91, 106, 126, 169; Doxiadis 1998, 136 no. 6 with pl. p. 22; Aubert and Cortopassi 1998, 140–1 no. 86; Parlasca and Seeman 1999, 102 no. 2.

3 Portrait of a woman in encaustic on limewood

AD 55–70

H 41.6 cm, W 21.5 cm

Excavated by Petrie at Hawara in 1888 (Petrie vv)

Presented by the National Gallery in 1994

British Museum EA 74713 (formerly National Gallery 1270)

Longitudinal cracks run through part of the panel at intervals. Part of the painted surface is lost to the left of the figure. The background is grey beneath the head and neck, and greenish below the drapery (the green appears at the base of the panel).

Shown turned in three-quarter view, the subject wears a mauve tunic and a mantle drawn in a deeper shade, with dark red folds. The black *clavus* over the proper right shoulder is edged with gold and has no stitching. The mantle is worn over the proper left shoulder, its edge rolled back, and may be seen as a line on the proper right shoulder as it falls down the woman's back.

The jewellery consists of gold ball earrings and a gold necklace with pendant crescent with circular terminals.

The black hair is centrally parted (the parting is obscured by a crack in the panel). A row of snail curls frames the brow, and banks of them are shown at the sides of the head. The hair is plaited into a low bun at the back of the crown.

The dark eyes are very round; the arched eyebrows meet over the bridge of the long nose. The pink lips are slightly open. The cheekbones and chin are long and oval; they are tinted pink, with ochre used to model the contours. The strength of the eyes, neck and shoulders render this a powerful portrait, suggesting an athletic quality more appropriate to a male subject.

The hairstyle, jewellery and drapery indicate a date in the reign of Nero.

BIBLIOGRAPHY

Petrie, *Portfolio*, pl. 10; Shore pl.11; Parlasca 1, 47–8, no. 80 (bibl.), pl. 19, 3; Doxiadis 1995, 201, no. 54; Borg 1996, 166; Doxiadis 1998, 137 no. 8 with pl. p. 28; Parlasca and Seeman 1999, 118–9 no. 19.

4 Portrait of a young woman in encaustic on wood

About AD 70

H 37 cm, W 20 cm

Excavated by Petrie at Hawara in 1888 (Petrie OO)

Berlin, Staatliche Museen, Ägyptisches Museum und Papyrussammlung 10974

This portrait shows a young woman turned slightly to the right. The woman has a round face with a low forehead, heavy arched eyebrows, and wide-set eyes, whose gaze, following the turn of the head, passes by the viewer. Her mouth is large, with slightly drooping corners and a full, somewhat pendulous lower lip. Her hair frames her forehead in several rows of ringlets that become fuller at the sides and almost completely cover her ears. Behind this section of ringlets the rest of her hair is caught in an ochre-coloured band. The woman wears a reddish brown tunic with broad, black-violet *clavus* bordered in white and a dark violet cloak lies across her left shoulder. In the corners of the neck opening one can see the netlike edges of an additional undergarment that was painted in a yellowish brown and then gilt. The woman's jewellery consists of earrings made up of a small sphere with a large disk suspended from it and a thin, dark ribbon necklace with a crescent

3

4

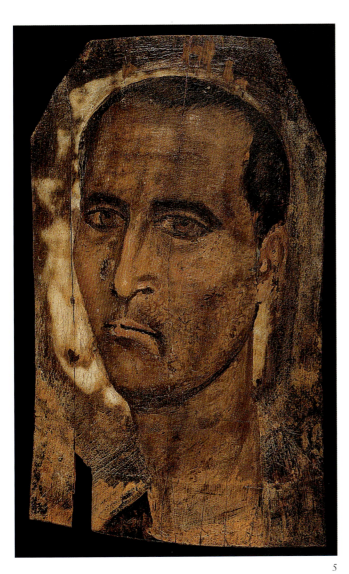

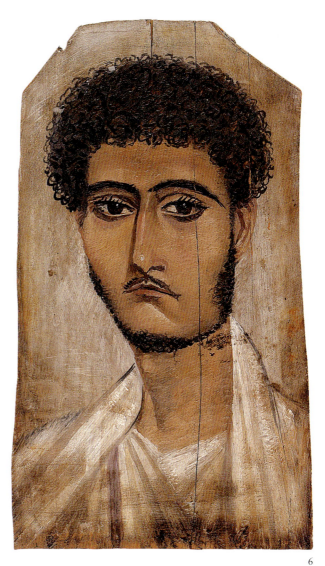

5

6

pendant. The pieces of jewellery were applied in three-dimensional stucco and gilt.

The grain of the panel runs horizontally. The long sides are trimmed, the upper corners rounded. The light falls from above, producing strong highlights on the forehead and nose and distinct shadows below the eyes, nose, lower lip and chin. The coiffure reflects the style around the year AD 70.

H.-G.F.

BIBLIOGRAPHY

Parlasca I, 44 no. 67, pl. 11; Borg 1996, 96f, 166, 169; Parlasca and Seeman 1999, 115 no. 16.

5 Portrait of a man in encaustic on limewood

About AD 70–100

H 32.2 cm, W 22.2 cm, TH 0.2 cm

Excavated by Petrie at Hawara in 1911 (Petrie 52)

University College London, Petrie Museum UC 19608

The panel has suffered two vertical fissures and several small cracks along the lower edge; towards the left side a piece is lost. The wax was perhaps melted and another coat applied. The edges of the panel are strongly marked and hard to read.

The subject is a thin man of mature years. He wears a cream mantle

around his shoulders, now difficult to discern. No tunic is visible at the base of his long neck. His close-cropped black hair recedes at the temples. The large almond-shaped eyes are brown, the nose is very long and pointed, and the red lips down-turned. The skin is tanned, with thick paint on the cheeks. There is a resemblance to the painting of the young man with facial hemiatrophy, of slightly later date, excavated by Petrie in 1888 (no. 6).

BIBLIOGRAPHY

Petrie, *Portraits*, pl. VIIA (52); Parlasca I, 35, no. 32 (bibl.), pl. 8.4; Parlasca and Seeman 1999, 125 no. 28.

6 Portrait of a young man in encaustic on limewood

About AD 70–120

H 38.3 cm, W 22.8 cm

Excavated by Petrie at Hawara in 1888 (Petrie U)

Presented by the National Gallery in 1994

British Museum EA 74707 (formerly National Gallery 1264)

A vertical fissure runs through the panel from top to bottom, with slighter splits on either side. The painting is otherwise well preserved. The background is creamy grey.

The youth wears a creamy-white tunic and mantle; a narrow mauve *clavus* appears on the proper right side of the tunic. The mantle is draped over both shoulders. The brush-strokes suggest thick folds of cloth, though the line of the tunic is visible on the proper right shoulder.

The hair is very curly, with strands escaping from the edge of the coiffure. The beard is very short and trimmed square around the chin and cheekbones; this may be a sign of early (Flavian-Trajanic) date, which would accord with the resemblance in style to no. 5.

The eyebrows are very long, as are the prominent upper lashes over the slanting brown eyes. The red lips are closed and turn down beneath a narrow moustache. The mouth and chin give the painting an unsatisfactory appearance, but, as Parlasca notes, this is more likely to represent a facial disability, in 1999 recognised as a hemiatrophy, rather than any inability on the part of the painter, who is in other respects competent. The flesh is painted in warm honey tones with touches of pink and cream highlights on the nose and chin.

BIBLIOGRAPHY

Petrie, *Hawara*, 46; Shore pl.9; Parlasca I, 79, no. 194 (bibl.), pl. 47, 4; Borg 1996, 79, 105; Doxiadis 1998, 140 no. 19 with pl. p. 63; Aubert and Cortopassi 1998, 106 no. 57 with pl. p. 109; Parlasca and Seeman 1999, 134–5 no. 36.

7 Portrait of a young man in encaustic on wood

About AD 40–80

H 43 cm, W 22.4 cm, TH 0.3–0.4 cm

Excavated by H. Brugsch at Hawara in 1892

Berlin, Staatliche Museen, Ägyptisches Museum und Papyrussammlung 19722

The discoloration below the head and along the edges of this panel, irregularly shaped at the top, show that in the mummy only the head of the portrait was visible. The young man, drawn into the picture from the left, casts what appears to be only a fleeting glance at the viewer in passing. He wears either a mantle drawn high around his long neck or a tunic. The almost triangular shape of the head, the round, deep-set eyes beneath high, projecting brows, the prominent nose and chin, and the suggestion of soft beard above the slightly open mouth give the work its individuality. The distinctive lighting adds to the impression that the portrait is true to life. Apparently falling from above and to the left, light strikes the area around the subject's right eye, places a highlight

7

on his left cheekbone and casts the lower left half of his face in half shadow. His hair consists of very short curls that cling to the head like a dense cap, only slightly retreating above the eyes.

There is an interesting inscription on the back consisting of the letter sequence σεσεμ, apparently what is left of σεσεμειομαι. The same word appears in a more complete inscription on the portrait of Eutyches, the freedman of Kasianos, in New York (no. 65). Its interpretation is debated. Most likely it is to be understood in the sense of 'countersign, confirm'. The proposition that this is a reference to the act of freeing a slave is less plausible: why should a legal act be documented on the back of a portrait? It would seem more reasonable that the inscription has something to do with the painting on the front, and was meant to confirm the portrait's resemblance to the subject.

According to Barbara Borg's stylistic analysis, the portrait was possibly produced by the same hand as the portrait from a mummy in New York (no. 9).

U.S.

BIBLIOGRAPHY
Parlasca I, 38 no. 42 pl. 11,4; Doxiadis 1995, 54 pl. 37, 126, 139, 197 with illus.; Borg 1996, 70, 91, 98, 106, 154, 192 pl. 3; Borg 1998, 38ff illus. 45; Parlasca and Seeman 1999, 71, 115 no. 14.

8 Portrait of a man in encaustic on limewood

About AD 80

H 42.5 cm, W 20.9 cm, TH 0.2 cm

Excavated by Petrie at Hawara in 1888 (Petrie AJ)

Presented by the National Gallery in 1994

British Museum EA 74718 (formerly National Gallery 3139)

The panel is fissured from the upper edge through the proper right ear. It has been cut on the right-hand side. The lower edge is unpainted.

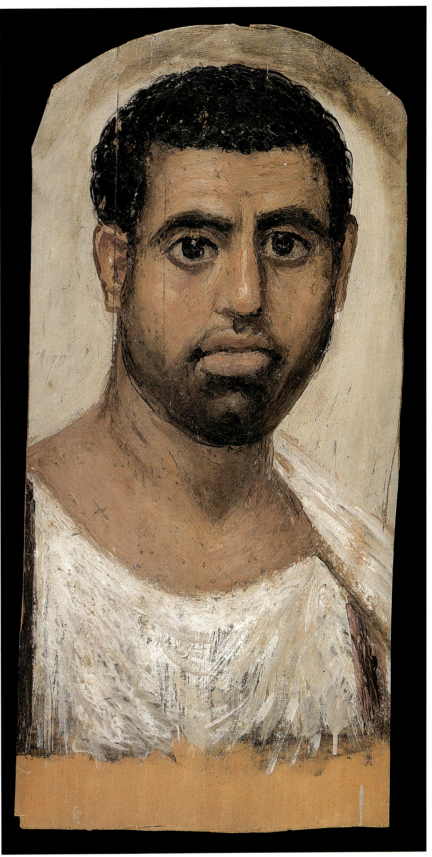

8

The greyish background is obscured above the head by marks of wrappings. The wax was melted after excavation and a thin layer of paraffin wax applied.

The garments are rendered impressionistically; the paint is unusually thick, and in places appears to have been applied with fingers. The subject wears a white tunic with violet *clavi* appearing on both sides. The white mantle is worn over the proper left shoulder and disappears behind the neck. The garments are drawn in pink, also used to shade the face and neck.

The dark curly hair is cut close to the head. The eyebrows are lightly arched and the large eyes are unevenly set. The full, reddish-pink lips are turned down. Shading around the chin and cheeks suggests a swarthy appearance. The contour is carelessly drawn in brown.

The rendering of the hair and the shape of the face recall portraits of the Emperor Titus (AD 79–81).

BIBLIOGRAPHY

Petrie, *Hawara*, 46, pl. 10, 13; Parlasca I, 39, no. 49 (bibl.), pl. 13, 1; Doxiadis 1995, 196, no. 34; Borg 1996, 72, 85, 97; Doxiadis 1998, 139 no. 11 with pl. p. 39; Aubert and Cortopassi 1998, 102–3 no. 54; Parlasca and Seeman 1999, 115–16 no. 15.

9 Mummy with an inserted panel portrait of a youth, in encaustic on limewood

About AD 80–100

Mummy L 1.69 m, W (shoulders) 45 cm; footcase H 39 cm; portrait as exposed H 38.1 cm, W 18 cm

Excavated by Petrie at Hawara in 1911 in an enclosed tomb of mudbrick walls laid on stone footings, with a mummy wearing a gilded mask, two further mummies with portraits (now Edinburgh 1911.210.3 and Seabury Western Theological Seminary, Chicago) and a mummy in plain wrappings

New York, The Metropolitan Museum of Art, Gift of the Egyptian Research Account and the British School of Archaeology, 1912 11.139

9

An area of paint is lost from the portrait panel immediately to the right of the youth's neck and jaw. The mummy wrappings are damaged, especially on the right shoulder, but in other respects the mummy is well preserved.

The subject of the portrait is a youth, his doleful appearance accentuated by a down-turned mouth and large, deep-set, shadowed eyes. He wears a white mantle now visible only against the left side of his neck. The curly black hair is cut square around the brow, and worn high above the crown of the head. On his head is a gilded wreath of narrow leaves and berries, with a central oval motif. The eyebrows are almost straight, the round brown eyes are painted with highlights, the skin tone is sallow, the lips thick, and painted pink; above them is a slight downy moustache. The face is thin, with prominent cheekbones and a projecting small chin.

X-rays and C.A.T. scans have revealed a mummy of sex appropriate to the portrait, but apparently considerably older (30–35 years ± 5 years) at the time of death. The discrepancy is unusual in portraits of young people. Possibly the subject of this portrait was related to that of the other male portrait now in Edinburgh, and the portraits were muddled by the embalmers. In 1998 a drawn reconstruction of the face was commissioned from the forensic artist Stephen Mancusi, who prepared the drawing from the scans without knowledge of the painted portrait. It was evident from the scans that the youth's left eye was asymmetric with the other, a medical condition not reflected in the portrait.

The portrait has been dated to the Flavian period by Parlasca, and it does compare well with no. 8, a portrait of a mature man from Hawara, dated to about AD 80. The portrait mummy now in Edinburgh was also dated to the late first or very early second century AD in the London version of *Ancient Faces* (Walker and Bierbrier 1997, 47 no. 22), and both portraits are

dated to the Flavian period by Borg
(1996, 72 n. 363). Borg notes the
resemblance in style and technique
with a portrait found at Hawara by
H. Brugsch in 1892 and now in
Berlin (no. 7), perhaps the work of
the same artist (Borg 1996, 98 and
pls 2–3; 1998, 38–9, figs 45–6).
Unlike those on the Edinburgh
mummy, the elaborate wrappings,
intended to recall the net worn by
Osiris, have no gilded plaster discs
to ornament the lozenges and the
horizontal bands around the chest,
and the feet are completely enclosed
by the wrappings, with no gilded
footplate.

BIBLIOGRAPHY
Petrie, *Man* 11 (1911), 146, fig. A, pl. K;
Petrie, *Records of the Past* 10 (1911),
306ff, fig. 3; Petrie, *Portfolio*, pl. 22;
Parlasca, *Mumienporträts*, 50 n. 234,
51 n. 247 no. 2, 252–3; Parlasca I, 40
no. 50 (bibl.); Corcoran 9 no. 17, 20,
Group I; Borg 1996, 70, 72, 98, 106,
122, 129, 184, pl. 2; Borg 1998, 38–9,
pl. 46.

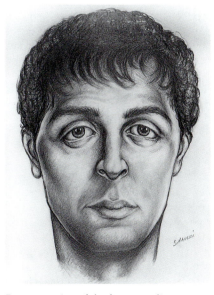

Reconstruction of the face according to a
C.A.T. scan of the mummy, by Stephen
Mancusi and Peggy Caldwell Ott

9

10 Portrait of an elderly man named Demetri(o)s, in encaustic on cypress wood

About AD 95–100

H 37.3 cm, W 20.5 cm

Excavated by Petrie at Hawara in 1911

Brooklyn Museum of Art, Charles Edwin Wilbour Fund 11.600-B

The much warped panel has lost small patches of paint, especially at the sides and near the base. There are two long cracks in the wood, on either side of the nose, perhaps occasioned by the removal of the panel from the mummy in 1939. The area of the portrait exposed within the mummy wrappings is clearly visible as a darkened zone of the grey background, surrounded by a yellowish line representing the edge of the wrappings.

The subject is an elderly man dressed in a white tunic of very fine, almost transparent cloth, the *clavus* magenta to violet in tone. Around his neck the man wears a folded mantle. In his hair is a wreath of gold leaves, preserved only on the left side of the panel. The hair is painted as loose silvery white curls on a dark brown ground. Towards the brow the curls become flat strands. The dark brown eyebrows are lightly arched, the nose very long and hooked. The dark brown eyes are painted white along the edge of the lower lid; the sockets are deeply shadowed. The cheeks are red, and the area of the shaved beard is brown with silver highlights. The flattish lips are a deep pink. The nose, brow and neck are lit with white highlights. The cheekbones are high, and the chin small and prominent.

Although the artist evidently intended to represent an elderly man, it is difficult to reconcile the image offered by this portrait with the age at death of the mummified individual. The text, ΔΗΜΗΤΡΙC ΛΠΘ ('Demetri(o)s, lived eighty-nine years'), was inscribed in gilt letters on the red stuccoed covering of the mummy. X-rays confirmed the age and sex of the burial. It is noteworthy that this panel is painted all over its surface, a possible indication of the rare reuse of a portrait painted in life. Alternatively, perhaps, Demetri(o)s was expected to die after an earlier bout of illness but survived to have the portrait then commissioned reused. However, there is another instance of a mismatch between the age (and reconstructed appearance) of the mummified individual and his portrait, also excavated by Petrie at Hawara in 1911 (Copenhagen, Ny Carlsberg Glyptotek 1425). Moreover, some would judge no. 8 to represent a man younger than the forty-five to sixty-year-old suggested by his surviving skull. It could be that artists were sometimes requested to make their older subjects look younger than their years.

The appearance of the portrait compares well with images of the Emperor Nerva (AD 96–8), and the portrait probably dates from the closing years of the first century AD.

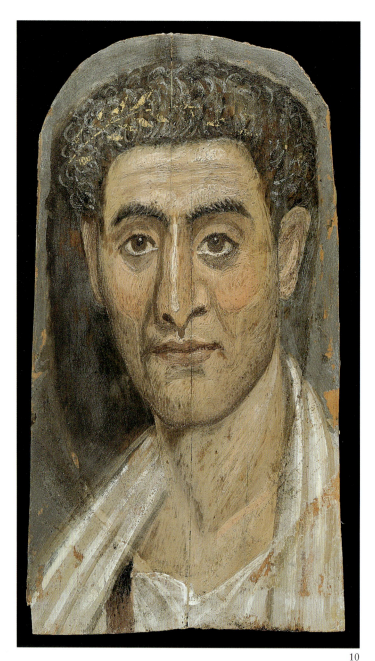

10

BIBLIOGRAPHY

Petrie, *Portraits* 5, 9, 15, pl. 21 centre
(complete mummy); Petrie, *Portfolio*,
pl. 12; Petrie, *Man* 11 (1911), 146,
pl. K, fig. B; Petrie, *Records of the Past*
10 (1911), 303, fig. 2; Parlasca,
Mumienporträts, 20 n. 17, 66, 79 n. 2,
84, 190, pl. 17 no. 4; Parlasca 1, 35
no. 34, pl. 9, 2; Doxiadis 1995, 69
pl. 56, 202; Borg 1996, 12, 16, 73,
105, 107, 129ff, 146ff, 151, 194.

11 Portrait of a man in encaustic on limewood

AD 100–20

H 42.1 cm, W 23 cm, TH 0.24 cm

Excavated by Petrie at Hawara in 1888
(Petrie JJ), found with a badly rotted
portrait of a girl (Petrie jj)

Presented by the National Gallery in
1994

British Museum EA 74708 (formerly
National Gallery 1265)

The panel is cut down at the sides as
well as at the top. A crack extends
from top to bottom through the
centre. The lower part was left
unpainted.

The surface of this expressive
portrait was worked with a spatula,
and the background is more thickly
rendered with brush-strokes than is
usual. The wax was remelted by
Petrie, and a thin coat of paraffin
wax was applied to conserve the
surface. The mummy was wrapped in
coarse linen, which has left diagonal
impressions framing the portrait, so
only the face and upper neck were
visible.

The original depiction of the
subject without clothing was thus
concealed. Of mature years, he may
have been portrayed as an athlete or,
in the aristocratic manner, heroised.
The hair, black and cropped close to
the head, is very similar to Roman
court portraiture of the Trajanic
period, as is the shape and
contouring of the face, which
confronts the viewer directly in the
Roman manner. Short black brush-
strokes on the chin may indicate
stubble. The outline of the face is
drawn in reddish brown, also used to

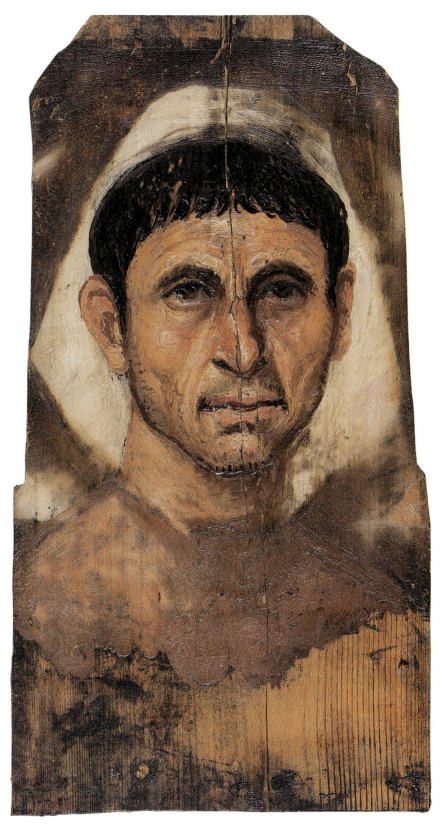

11

part the lips. The face is painted in ochre and burnt sienna tones, with highlights in pink and cream. The brown eyes are deeply recessed and shaded. The Romanised appearance could indicate high social status, but the overall impression (somewhat lessened by inconfident painting of his left ear) is of maturity and physical strength, the latter expressed in the rugged physique and sunburned countenance.

BIBLIOGRAPHY

Petrie, *Hawara*, 42, 43, pl. 10; Petrie, *Portfolio*, pl. 23; Shore pl.5; Parlasca I, 67–8, no. 148 (bibl.), pl. 35, 3; Doxiadis 1995, 205, no. 71; Borg 1996, 12, 74, 107, 159, pl. 58.1; Doxiadis 1998, 134 no. 2 with pl. p. 10; Aubert and Cortopassi 1998, 142–3 no. 87; Parlasca and Seeman 1999, 127–8 no. 30.

12 Portrait of a woman in encaustic on limewood

AD 100–20

H 39.6 cm, W 22.6 cm, TH 0.25 cm

Excavated by Petrie at Hawara in 1888 (Petrie J)

Presented by the National Gallery in 1994

British Museum EA 74712 (formerly National Gallery 1269)

Minor cracks run from the broken upper edge of the panel. Patches of the painted surface are lost over the proper left cheek. The lower edge of the panel is unpainted.

The face, slightly turned to the viewer's left, is drawn in yellow ochre lines on a background of greenish-grey distemper. The flesh tones were built up from the undercoat, which blends into them around the edges of the cheeks and chin to give volume to a plump face.

The tunic and mantle are painted in purple with reddish tones. The *clavus* on the proper right shoulder is almost black, the seam on the shoulder appearing as a gap in the paint.

The bun is secured with a round-headed gold pin; the hoop earrings are strung with an emerald between

12

two pearls. Around her neck the woman wears a gold chain with a pendant emerald in a circular gold setting. A second necklace is threaded with emeralds interspersed with gold.

The black hair rises in tiers of curls above the brow and is coiled into a large plaited bun on the crown of the head. The eyes are very large and brown, with fine plucked eyebrows rendered perhaps with the *cestrum*. The small pink lips are pursed. There are pink highlights on the ivory cheeks and cream on the nose, above the mouth and on the double chin. The drapery and jewellery are carelessly painted in comparison with the head and neck, but in general the painting suggests refined affluence by judicious use of the palette (as Doxiadis observes). Borg (1996, 96–7) has linked this portrait with the image of Isarous (Walker and Bierbrier 1997, 45–6 no. 19), an earlier work by the same artist.

The hairstyle follows the fashion of the court of Domitian (AD 81–96), but the jewellery and the drapery of the mantle over the proper left shoulder only suggest a date in the early years of the second century AD.

BIBLIOGRAPHY

Petrie, *Portfolio*, pl. 18; Shore pl.12; Parlasca I, 51–2, no. 94 (bibl.), pl. 22.2; Doxiadis 1995, 199, no. 42; Borg 1996, 13, 34, 91, 93, 96f, 103, 106, 170f, pl. 57, 1; Doxiadis 1998, 140 no. 14 with pl. p. 48; Aubert and Cortopassi 1998, 102, 104 no. 53; Parlasca and Seeman 1999, 112–3 no. 13.

13 Portrait of a young woman in encaustic on wood

AD 110–20

H 43.7 cm, W 34 cm

Excavated by Petrie at Hawara in 1911 (Petrie 50), found under Petrie 49 (UC 30082)

Edinburgh, National Museums of Scotland, Royal Museum of Scotland 1951.160

There are some vertical fissures in the upper edge of the panel, but the painting is well preserved, with some

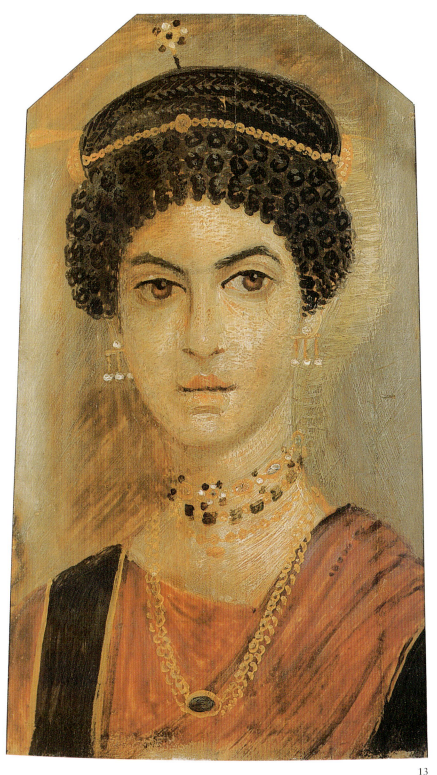

13

surface flaking on the proper right cheek. The lower edge of the panel is unpainted. An orange undercoat gives the painting a warm tone. The background is greyish cream.

The woman wears a bright crimson tunic, with dark purple *clavi* edged with gold, the latter rendered in yellow paint. Over her left shoulder is draped a mantle of similar cloth, arranged in the manner of contemporary portraits in bronze or stone.

The subject wears a remarkable number of jewels and was dubbed by Petrie 'The Jewellery Girl' (MS Notebook 37, p. 49). In the top of her bun is a pin set with pearls and garnets. The bun is gathered with a gold chain with a central medallion and decorated gold boxes at either side; above these a long pin is apparently worn across the back of the head. Adorning the ears is a pair of trident earrings with a central pearl set above the bar and three pendant pearls. Of four necklaces, the uppermost matches the pin in the top of the bun, with large pale stones, perhaps aquamarine, in gold settings between the small pearls and garnets. Beneath is a necklace of squared emeralds separated by gold beads, and below that a chain of gold beads with a gold pendant. Hanging low on the breast is a plaited gold chain with a large oval stone, perhaps an emerald intaglio, in a heavy gold setting.

The woman's black hair is arranged in four tiers of snail-like curls, with a large plaited bun on the crown of the head. Given the refinement of the jewellery, the complexion is unexpectedly sallow, with raised eyebrows giving the subject a quizzical air. The large, brown, almond-shaped eyes are slightly lowered; the nose is shorter than most and slightly retroussé. The lips are painted bright red and the mouth left slightly open.

The lack of corkscrew locks in front of the ears and the flattened bun suggest a date in the late Trajanic period.

14

BIBLIOGRAPHY

Petrie, *Portfolio*, pl. 17; Parlasca I, 53, no. 98 (bibl.), pl. 23, 2; Doxiadis 1995, 206, no. 72; Borg 1996, 34, 107, 129f, 168, 170f, 192.

14 Portrait of a woman in encaustic on wood

About AD 100–20

H 33 cm, W 23.5 cm

Excavated by Petrie at Hawara in 1911 (Petrie 46)

Oxford, Ashmolean Museum 1911.354

Unusually, the panel is split by transverse fissures. The upper part of the painting is damaged by an early attempt at conservation with paraffin wax. The paint is applied thickly throughout, against the grain of the wood.

The woman wears a brown tunic of heavy cloth and a scarlet mantle over her proper left shoulder and around her neck. A dark *clavus* appears on the tunic below the proper right shoulder.

The ears are adorned with hoops of gold threaded with pearls and emeralds. The upper necklace is of gold with squarish links. The lower necklace is of unusual form, consisting of a gold band edged in red with a square pendant. The hair is arranged in small curls around the face, and piled into a bun at the crown. The eyes are large and round, their shape echoed by the brows. The nose is unusually short and the mouth small, leaving a large expanse of chin. The flesh is very pale, and the general effect is of indulged opulence.

The jewellery, hairstyle and clothing suggest a date in the Trajanic period. The hairstyle compares well with an early second century bust from Cyrene (Walker and Bierbrier 1997, no. 270).

BIBLIOGRAPHY
Petrie, *Portraits*, 4, 6, 8, 10, pl. 5A; Parlasca I, 51, no. 92 (bibl.), pl. 21, 7; Parlasca and Seeman 1999, 123 no. 26 (AD 69–79).

15 Portrait of a young person in encaustic on wood

About AD 100–30

H 33 cm, W 16.6 cm

Excavated by Petrie at Hawara in 1911 (Petrie 53) with Manchester 5379 (Petrie 54 = Parlasca I, no. 132, not exhibited)

Manchester Museum 5378

The lower right corner of the panel is lost. Three major vertical fissures run through the length of the panel. The painted surface is damaged, especially around the eyes and on the proper left cheek. Traces of mummy bands are preserved at the lower left corner, where the panel is unpainted. The background is greyish olive.

The portrait is of a young person turned to the left. The clothing is indistinct, and the painting may represent a naked youth. Around the neck is a plaited leather chain, with a pendant lunula.

The dark hair is combed into a fringe on the forehead, and there is no sign of any bun at the crown or nape. There are traces of a band, perhaps the base of a gilded wreath, over the crown of the head, with a tie appearing over the figure's left shoulder. The skin is a creamy ivory and the large dark eyes almond-shaped, with long upper lashes; the nose is long and hooked; the cheek-bones prominent; and the lips painted red.

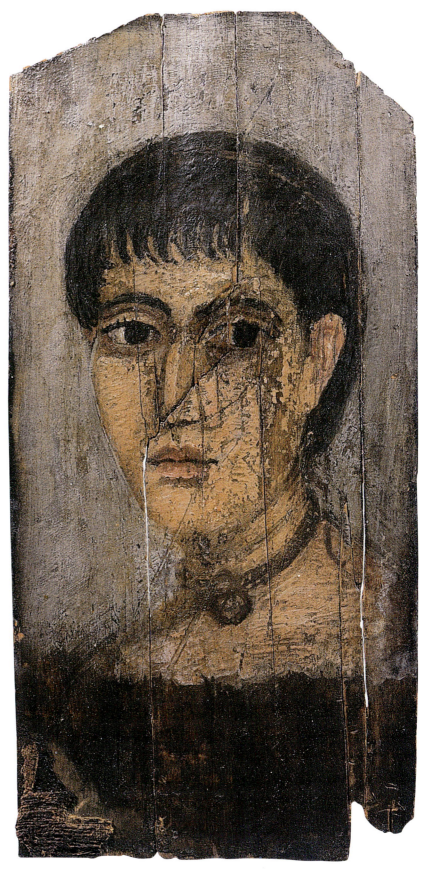

15

The hairstyle indicates a date in the early decades of the second century AD.

BIBLIOGRAPHY

Petrie, *Portraits*, 11, pl. 5; Parlasca I, 131 no. 133 (bibl.), pl. 32, 3.

16 Portrait of a woman in encaustic on limewood

AD 100–20

H 38.2 cm, W 20.5 cm, TH 0.15 cm

Excavated by Petrie at Hawara in 1888 (Petrie AA), found with a male portrait (Petrie Y) now in Cairo (CG 33236)

Presented by the National Gallery in 1994

British Museum EA 74706 (formerly National Gallery 1263)

The upper edge of the panel is broken, and three vertical fissures extend from the broken edge.

This painting demonstrates a very sophisticated use of colour on a grey background; the drapery is painted in three tones of purple, with careful shading and highlighting, also used to form the tones of the face. The original wax was remelted by Petrie; a thin layer of paraffin wax was added to conserve the surface.

The subject wears a cyclamen purple tunic, apparently draped to fall off the proper left shoulder (the line of the drapery is visible beneath a mantle of slightly darker hue). Both garments are of fine cloth; the mantle is worn over both shoulders. The woman wears gold hoop earrings set with three round emeralds, and two necklaces, of which the upper is set with longer emeralds interspersed with two gold elements, and the lower with small amethysts and a large central emerald in a gold setting, from which hang two pearls.

The hair is curly and cut fairly close to the head, with locks falling in front of the ears. The eyes are large, with lightly curved lower lids and arched eyebrows; of refined appearance, the woman's ivory flesh is lightly tinted on the cheeks, with cream highlights on the nose.

The style of the hair (especially the locks in front of the ears) and of the jewellery suggests a date in the early years of the second century AD.

BIBLIOGRAPHY

Petrie, *Hawara*, 15, 44, frontispiece, n. 9; Petrie, *Portfolio*, pl. 16; Shore pl. 14; Parlasca I, 85, no. 218 (bibl.), pl. 54, 2; Doxiadis 1995, 198, no. 41; Borg 1996, 130, 166, 171, pl. 5, 2; Doxiadis 1998, 140 no. 13 with pl. p. 47; Aubert and Cortopassi 1998, 106–7 no. 55; Parlasca and Seeman 1999, 130–1 no. 32.

17 Portrait of a woman wearing an Egyptian hairpiece

About AD 100–10

H 41.7 cm, W 22 cm

Excavated in 1888 by W. Flinders Petrie in a tomb at Hawara (Petrie H) with Parlasca I, 112 (Petrie L)

Formerly in the collection of H. Martyn Kennard; given by W. E. H. Massey to the Royal Ontario Museum

Toronto, Royal Ontario Museum 918.20.1 (G 6127)

16

17

The panel is broken on the right side and has several vertical fissures. It is roughly shaped around the upper edge. There is a nail hole in the centre of the top of the panel, matched by another aligned with it at the base. The lower margin of the panel is unpainted and has traces of the mummy wrappings, which also appear at the top. The line of exposure may be gauged from the paint loss across the neckline of the tunic and at the right side of the painted area. Small areas of paint are lost over the surface of the painting. Petrie reports the removal of cloth from the face, perhaps represented by the blotchy area on the brow above the nose. In recent years minor paint flakes have been reattached. Minute traces of brush hair were noted on the subject's right cheek. Originally Petrie had intended to keep the mummy with its gilded wrappings 'so perfectly preserved' (Petrie, *Journal*, 12–17/2/1888), but in his excavation notebook he recorded that in the event the two mummies found in this tomb were not kept, and only the panel portraits were removed from the site.

The subject wears a purplish crimson tunic, cut low on the neck and shoulders, and a mantle of the same colour, worn high on the neck. The paint on the clothing is very faded. In her hair is a finely executed garland, perhaps of myrtle leaves, in applied gold leaf. She wears gold bar earrings adorned with a central pearl on the bar and with three suspended pearls. On her neck is a string of pearls and oblong emeralds, and beneath this a gold chain with a suspended amulet case.

The woman has a strong face with high cheekbones, a long nose, thick dark red lips and a prominent chin. Her face is shaded in brownish ochre, giving her a very tanned appearance, with lighter pinks and whites above and below the mouth and on her left cheek. The neck is also darkly shaded. The upper lid of the right eye is much longer than the lower, which turns upwards, suggesting eye disease. The fine dark brows are lightly arched.

The painting has been rightly dated to the turn of the first and second centuries AD; that much is clear from the natural hair, drawn in tight braids into a large flat bun at the crown, behind the unusually flamboyant hairpiece of corkscrew locks hanging out from the head well beyond the ears. In contrast to the unusual wig and high skin colour, the subject's jewellery and clothing are quite conventional.

Petrie noted that the two mummies H and L were covered in cloth 'resined on'; mummy L was 'knocked about the feet and not beautiful in its wrappings'. The portrait from mummy L was in the collection of Dr J. Mäder of St Gall, Switzerland, by the 1960s. It is very similar to the portrait now in Toronto, the female subject also portrayed with corkscrew locks, her fashionable Roman bun appearing behind, secured with a long pin. The resemblance of the two subjects is strong, and it is not out of the question that they were members of the same family, perhaps sisters.

BIBLIOGRAPHY
Petrie, *Hawara* 16, pl. 10; Petrie, *Roman Portraits* pl. 8; Parlasca, *Mumienporträts*, 52; Parlasca I, 56, no. 109 (bibl.); H. Zaloscer, *Porträts aus dem Wüstensand* (Vienna-Munich 1961); D. Thompson, *The Artists of the Mummy Portraits* (1976), 11, fig. 24; F. M. Ricci (ed.), *El-Fayyum* (1985) 80, pl. p. 81; R. DePuma, *Roman Portraits* (exh. cat., Iowa City, 1988), 80 no. 33, pl. p. 81; D. Kleiner and S. B. Matheson, *I, Claudia: Women in Ancient Rome* (Yale 1996), 196 no. 143; Borg 1996, 35, 96.

18 Portrait of a young woman in encaustic on limewood

AD 120–40

H 35.3 cm, W 20.2 cm

Excavated by Petrie at Hawara in 1888 (Petrie AG)

Presented by the National Gallery in 1994

British Museum EA 74705 (formerly National Gallery 1262)

The panel is not painted at the upper corners, which have not been cut down. The direction of brush-strokes suggests an arched top. Black strips of resin remain at the sides of the panel. The painted surface is damaged in various places. Lead white was used as a ground, hematite for the pink robe, a copper-based pigment for the necklace and jarosite (iron sulphate) for the flesh tones. The background is a greenish grey.

The woman wears a tunic and mantle of mauve, with touches of cyclamen. Both *clavi* are visible: they are black with gold edges, and a row of stitches in white, representing the shoulder seam, runs towards the corner of the neckline of the tunic on the proper right side. On her left side a white undertunic is visible (the paint extends across the neck, but the remainder is probably an undercoat for flesh tones left incomplete). The mantle is folded back across the proper left shoulder, and appears above the line of the right shoulder.

The jewellery comprises a pair of hoop earrings, strung with three pearls, and two necklaces, much damaged. The upper necklace included emeralds and perhaps garnets and pearls; no emeralds appear in the lower necklace, which is set with larger stones perhaps linked with garnets. The woman's bun is secured with a large gold pin on the proper right side; traces of a second pin may appear on the left side, but the head of the pin is obscured by paint loss and resin.

The hair is drawn up from the face in the neo-classical style typical

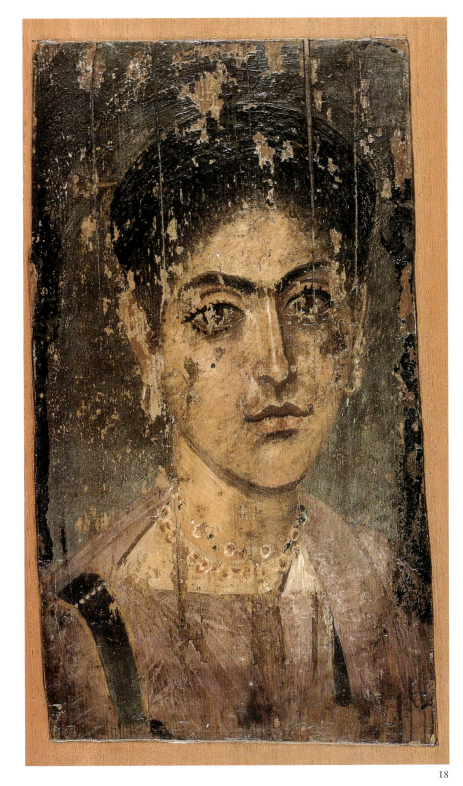

18

of Hadrianic portraiture, and wound around the back crown in a tightly drawn coil of plaits. The eyes are brown, large and almond-shaped. The thick eyebrows nearly meet over the nose, which is long with cream highlights. The lips are red and slightly open. Touches of red on the chin and cheeks enliven the lightly tanned complexion. The subject is shown in three-quarter profile.

BIBLIOGRAPHY

Petrie, *Hawara*, 44; Parlasca II, 30 no. 529; Doxiadis 1995, 208, no. 80; Borg 1996, 44f, 94f, 107, 171, pl. 19.1; Doxiadis 1998, 140 no. 15 with pl. p. 53; Parlasca and Seeman 1999, 134 no. 35.

19 Portrait of a man in encaustic on wood

About AD 125–50

H 37 cm, W 20 cm

Excavated by R. von Kaufmann at Hawara in 1892

Munich, Antikensammlung, Inv. 15013

Acquired in 1962 from descendants of Dr Seidel, the excavator's physician

The young man, placed in the picture at an angle, turns slightly to the left so as to gaze not quite frontally at the viewer. Imagined light illuminates the face quite generally from the upper left, but produces highlights above the right eyebrow, on the nose, mouth and chin, and in the hollow of the throat. In combination with the warm yellow and reddish tones and the shadows around the small, sensitive mouth, these give the portrait a distinctly lifelike three-dimensionality. The slightly drooping lower eyelids enhance the impression that this is a specific individual.

The dense curls framing the forehead in a gentle curve were applied in several layers of thicker and thinner black pigment. The face is ringed by a full curly beard, shaved on the cheeks in the manner familiar from portraits of the Emperor Hadrian of the so-called ΔO type (M. A. Wegner, *Das Römische Herrscherbild* II 4

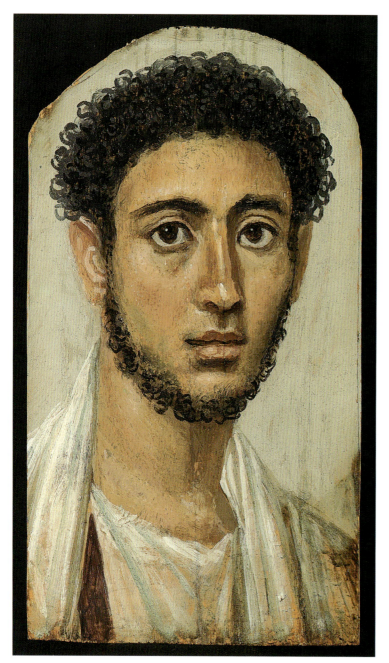

19

BIBLIOGRAPHY

Parlasca I, 78 no. 189 pl. 46.1;
Doxiadis 1995, 7 pl. 6, 100, 126, 135,
195 with illus.; Borg 1996, 75, 92,
103f, 107 pl. 12,1 (see pl. 12,2, Petrie
Museum Inv. UC 30088); Borg 1998,
88, 96f illus. 118; Parlasca and Seeman
1999, pp. 71f., 131 no. 34.

20 Portrait of a young man in encaustic on limewood

About AD 140–60

H 39.6 cm, W 27.8 cm, TH 0.2 cm

Excavated by Petrie at Hawara in 1911
(Petrie 8), found with two other
portrait mummies (Petrie 7, as yet
unidentified, and Petrie 9, Nottingham
11–61)

University College London, Petrie
Museum UC 19610

The unusually large panel is split
from top to bottom in two places.
The bottom and lower left edge of
the panel are unpainted; the margins
of the painted area are unusually
neat. The painting is also distinguished by the pose of the sitter, who
appears in three-quarter left profile,
his face turned to confront the
viewer.

The young man appears naked
against a creamy background, his
skin tanned a ruddy brown (Petrie
nicknamed the portrait 'The Red
Youth'). Strength and a developed
musculature are suggested by thick
brushwork and careful shading.
By contrast, the face is smoothly
painted and well lit.

The black hair is arranged with
three locks falling on the brow and is
only slightly dishevelled around the
edge of the head. The arched eyebrows meet above the bridge of the
nose. The enormous round eyes are
dark brown, the damaged proper left
eye giving a glassy appearance. The
young man has a short straight beard
and moustache. The full lips are
painted red.

The portrait was found with
another of a bearded man dated to
the late Antonine period and now in
Nottingham (11–61). The hairstyle of
the present portrait indicates an

[Berlin 1956], 229; S. Schröder,
*Katalog der antiken Skulpturen des
Museo del Prado in Madrid I: Die
Porträts* [Mainz 1993], 204 no. 54;
Borg 1996, 74 n. 375 [bibl.]).

The young man wears a white
tunic, its wide right-hand *clavus*
partially visible beneath the *pallium*
drawn high around his neck and
shoulders. The rendering of the
clothing is distinctly painterly; it is

executed in thin white, grey-green,
grey-brown and orange-ochre
pigments without contour lines.
Barbara Borg has noted that in this
and in other technical aspects the
Munich portrait closely resembles a
female portrait in the Petrie Museum,
London (UC 30088), which may
therefore have been executed by the
same painter.

U.S.

20

earlier, though still Antonine date. The size and quality of the painting suggest that the subject was a member of a family of some importance.

BIBLIOGRAPHY

Petrie, *Portraits*, 12; Petrie, *Portfolio*, pl. 21; Parlasca 1, 83 no. 211 (bibl.), pl. 52.3; B. Ramer, 'The Technology, Examination and Conservation of the Fayum Portraits in the Petrie Museum', *Studies in Conservation* 24 (1979), 1–13, pl. 6 fig. 5; B. Adams, 'The Petrie Museum of Egyptian Archaeology', *Biblical Archaeologist* (Dec. 1984), 243; S. Walker, *Greek and Roman Portraits* (1995), 106, fig. 77; Doxiadis 1995, 205, no. 70; Borg 1996, 16, 75, 159; Doxiadis 1998, 135 no. 3 with pl. p. 15; Aubert and Cortopassi 1998, 110–11 no. 58; Parlasca and Seeman 1999, 140–1 no. 43.

21 Portrait, perhaps of a priest, in encaustic on limewood

About AD 140–60

H 42.5 cm, W 22.2 cm, TH 0.4 cm

Excavated by Petrie at Hawara in 1911 (Petrie 56)

Presented by the National Gallery in 1994

British Museum EA 74714 (formerly National Gallery 2912)

The panel is cracked through the right side from the upper edge to the subject's proper left ear. A row of four nail holes indicative of reuse, or perhaps of attachment to a frame, runs across the panel 6.3 cm below the upper edge, and a row of three holes 9–9.5 cm above the lower edge. The background is a greenish cream.

The subject, a man of mature years, wears a creamy-white tunic with violet/pink *clavus* on the proper right shoulder. A mantle with brownish folds with cream highlights is worn over the proper left shoulder and around the back of the neck, but does not appear on the other side. The upper edge of the tunic and the central fold below the neck is rather clumsily drawn with a thick cream line. A shoulder seam appears as diagonal hatching across the *clavus,* lined up with the corner of the neck of the tunic.

In his hair the subject wears a narrow fillet, with a central gold star with seven points laid on a purple ground. The rest of the fillet is grey with cream highlights, perhaps representing an original in silver.

Below the fillet the dark brown hair falls in three locks on the brow in an arrangement typical of individuals associated with the cult of Sarapis. The hair is curly and even, the outer strands are tidily arranged. The beard and moustache are straight. The flesh is sunburned, with pink and cream highlights. The close-set, light brown eyes stare at the viewer; the impression of a severe intensity is heightened by the narrow down-turned mouth. The arched eyebrows are rendered with diagonal strokes.

There are difficulties in reconciling this portrait of an individual with luxuriant hair with the convention of representing priests of Egyptian cults with shaven heads. Parlasca (1966) suggested that the star and corkscrew locks on the brow could represent the deceased as the god Sarapis. Against this view is the conventional mortal clothing. Goette (1989) suggests the subject may be a novice of the cult who died before ordination.

A date in the early Antonine period is indicated by the cut of the hair and beard, giving a boxy, solid appearance to the head, and by the naturalistic style of the painting of the head and neck, rendered with much greater care than the drapery.

BIBLIOGRAPHY

Petrie, *Portfolio,* pl. 15; Shore pl.8; Parlasca, *Mumienporträts,* 87–8; Parlasca I, 82, no. 206 (bibl.), pl. 51, 2; H. Goette, 'Kaiserzeitliche Bildnisse von Sarapis-Priestern', *MDAIK* 45 (1989), 173–86; Corcoran 71–2; Doxiadis 1995, 195, no. 31 and p. 234; Borg 1996, 78, 112, 166, 175; Borg 1998, 70–71 pl. 85; Doxiadis 1998, 137–8 no. 10 with pl. p. 34; Parlasca and Seeman 1999, 138–9 no. 41.

21

22 Portrait of a young man in encaustic on limewood, with a gilded stucco frame

AD 150–70

H 42.7 cm, W 22.2 cm, TH 0.4 cm; frame W 2.2 cm

Excavated by Petrie at Hawara in 1888 (Petrie Z)

Presented by the National Gallery in 1994

British Museum EA 74704 (formerly National Gallery 1261)

The panel is fissured in the centre from top to bottom. The surface of the gilt frame is very crazed, but the original vine-scroll decoration is visible in places, as is the reddish bole beneath. The frame surrounds the background in greenish grey, but does not extend over the painted drapery. A band, perhaps of shellac, extends across the bottom of the panel.

The subject wears a white tunic with pink *clavus*, the seam below the shoulder shown as darker pink bands. Over the proper left shoulder is a white mantle, which extends to the back of the neck but it is not shown on the proper right side. The dark brown hair is abundant and curly, with long whiskers in front of the ears, almost joined to a thin beard. Above the full red lips is a moustache. All the facial hair, including the eyebrows, is painted in a lighter brown. The hazel eyes are large and rounded, with prominent upper lashes. The skin is painted in warm pinks and umbers, with thick strokes in a lighter shade. There is a slight resemblance to the Emperor Lucius Verus (AD 161–9), and in general the portrait typifies images of young adult males of the middle years of the second century AD.

BIBLIOGRAPHY

Petrie, *Portfolio*, pl. 28; Shore pl.10; Parlasca 1, 80, no. 198 (bibl.), pl. 48, 4; Doxiadis 1995, 203, no. 61; Borg 1996, 80, 129, 166; Doxiadis 1998, 140 no. 18 with pl. p. 58; Aubert and Cortopassi 1998, 46, 49 no. 11; Parlasca and Seeman 1999, 137 no. 39.

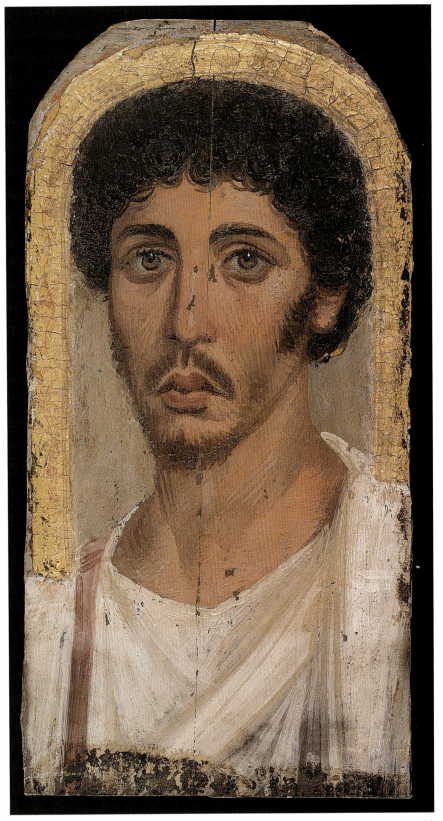

22

23 Portrait of a woman in encaustic on wood

AD 140–60

H 42.5 cm, W 21.2 cm

Excavated by Petrie at Hawara in 1888 (Petrie s)

Presented by Jesse Haworth

Manchester Museum 2266

The panel is well preserved, with traces of linen binding indicating the original extent of the exposed portrait, which was set within an octagonal frame. The background is cream.

The woman wears a purple tunic with a border or undertunic of black decorated with a lattice motif in gold thread. No *clavi* are visible, as her shoulders are draped in a crimson mantle (in the style of contemporary Cyrenaican marble portraits). In her ears are gold hooped earrings threaded with pearls, and around her neck is a necklace of emeralds.

The woman's hair is parted centrally and looped back over the ears to be wound into a bun worn high on the crown. The austere style is matched by the gravity of her countenance, a sensitive portrayal suggesting final illness. The eyebrows are long and straight, and the hooded dark eyes deep-set and sad, with shadows beneath them; under the long straight nose the mouth is turned down, and the complexion is sallow. The face is carefully lit with white highlights.

The hairstyle and the draping of the mantle indicate a date in the early Antonine period.

BIBLIOGRAPHY

Petrie, *Hawara*, 45, A, B; Parlasca I, 64–5, no. 137 (bibl.), pl. 32, 6; Doxiadis 1995, 74, 204, no. 65; Borg 1996, 49, 163, pl. 28; Borg 1998, 95, fig. 117.

24 Portrait of a woman in encaustic on limewood

AD 160–80

H 36 cm, W 18 cm, TH 1 cm

Excavated by Petrie at Hawara in 1888 (Petrie GG), found with a portrait mummy of a girl (Petrie HH, now Cairo CG 3325)

Presented by the National Gallery in 1994

British Museum EA 74710 (formerly National Gallery 1267)

The panel is fissured at the left side and an unfortunate early attempt at conservation has damaged the proper right eye and brow. The surface is lightly coated with paraffin wax. The background is greenish grey.

The subject, of refined appearance, wears a plain white tunic beneath a magenta mantle, the folds indicated in darker paint. The mantle appears to swathe the subject in a manner strongly reminiscent of sculptured stone and terracotta busts of the day, especially those from the North African provinces.

The jewellery comprises two gold

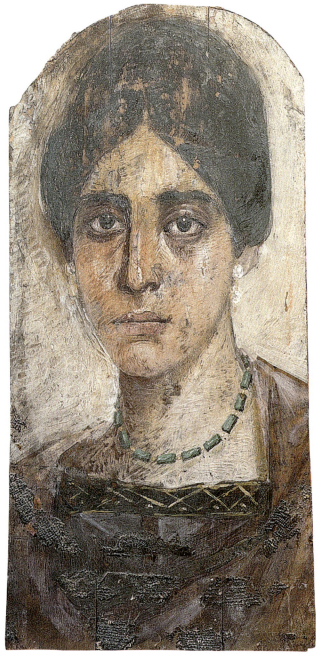

23

circular hoop earrings with pendant pearls and two necklaces, the upper of emerald beads linked with gold, and the lower a twisted gold chain. The hair is waved back from the face with a few snail curls around the central parting. The bun towards the rear is sketchily painted in lighter grey. A few strands escape around the outer edge of the coiffure.

The dark brown eyes have flat lower lids; the strongly arched eyebrows meet above the long nose. The closed lips are orangey pink. Cream highlights are used in the centre of the face, which elsewhere is rendered with a warm cream and pink tone. The shape of the face and high cheekbones recall Cyrenaican portraits.

BIBLIOGRAPHY

Petrie, *Hawara*, 45, frontispiece no. 2; Petrie, *Portfolio*, pl. 25; Shore pl.13; Parlasca II, 36 no. 276 (bibl.), pl. 67; Doxiadis 1995, 199, no. 43; Borg 1996, 164, pl. 30; Doxiadis 1998, 140 no. 17 with pl. p. 57; Parlasca and Seeman 1999, 143 no. 45.

25 Portrait of a woman in encaustic on limewood

About AD 190–220

H 31 cm, W 21.5 cm

Excavated by Petrie at Hawara in 1888 (Petrie QQ)

Presented by the National Gallery in 1994

British Museum EA 74703 (formerly National Gallery 1260)

The panel is broken by vertical cracks and strips of paint are lost around them. The flesh surface (originally ivory) has been worked with a spatula (compare the 'Jewellery Girl', no. 13). Traces of the mummy wrappings appear as diagonal lines at the upper and lower corners of the panel. The background is grey with a touch of cream.

The woman wears a white tunic, the folds clearly rendered with broad brush-strokes, with dark red *clavi*. White stitches representing the

24

25

on the nose, but this part of the face is particularly damaged.

BIBLIOGRAPHY

Petrie, *Hawara*, 45; *Portfolio*, pl. 8 (colour); Parlasca II, 68, no. 400 (bibl.), pl. 99.2; Doxiadis 1995, 208, no. 79; Borg 1996, 66; Doxiadis 1998, 140 no. 21 with pl. p. 69; Aubert and Cortopassi 1998, 110, 113, no. 60; Parlasca and Seeman 1999, 136 no. 37.

26 Portrait of a woman in encaustic on fir, with added gilding

About AD 190–220

H 32.1 cm, W (base) 22.7 cm (top) 20.9 cm, TH 1.5 cm

Excavated by Petrie at Hawara in 1911 (Petrie 23), found below Petrie 22 (as yet unidentified)

Presented by the National Gallery in 1994

British Museum EA 74717 (formerly National Gallery 2915)

The panel is cracked vertically to the right of the centre through to the subject's brow. Much of the surface is lost or altered through melting of the original wax. A thick coat of paraffin wax has been applied.

The panel is not cut down at the upper corners. The background to the portrait, in lead white, appears as a rectangle within black borders. The subject is shown in frontal pose, dressed in a pinkish-red tunic with orange-gold *clavi*. She wears no mantle. Madder mixed with a little Egyptian blue was used for the robe; the *clavi* were painted with Egyptian blue and ochre. The jewellery is added in gold leaf: trident earrings with pendant pearls painted in white; a necklace composed of long gold strips set vertically, and a herring-bone chain with a pendant stone (perhaps a garnet or amethyst) in a gold setting. In the hair is a triple gold wreath of lozenges and triangles, some detached from their original setting, and a central circular element.

The proper left eye is large and

shoulder seam appear below the proper right shoulder. The mantle is worn over the proper left shoulder and appears as a line above the right shoulder; touches of ochre are used to highlight this and the *clavus*.

Round the neck is a gold chain with a pendant crescent, matched by gold hoop earrings. This, and the form of the dress, might suggest a date a century earlier than that offered by the hairstyle. The hair is black and curly, cut close to the head in African style, but markedly frizzy around the outer edge in the manner of later second- and third-century coiffures. It is possible that the subject was dressed (and perhaps even buried) in ancestral clothes and jewellery for the occasion of the portrait.

The eyes are brown and almond-shaped, with markedly arched eye-brows fading at the outer edges. The lips are pink, with a slight smile. Cream highlights are used here and almond-shaped with a squarish brown pupil. The eyebrows are arched. The proper right eye and much of the nose are severely damaged. The thin dark red lips are covered in gold leaf.

A central parting is clearly visible in the hair, which appears to be cut close to the head. Though Parlasca considered the portrait to resemble those from Antinoopolis and therefore dated it to the Hadrianic period, the frontality of the portrait (despite a slight turn of the face), the lack of mantle, the form of the jewellery and the central parting suggest a date in the late Antonine or Severan period.

BIBLIOGRAPHY
Petrie, *Portraits*, 10, pl. 5; Parlasca I, 67 no. 145 (bibl.), pl. 34.6; Borg 1996, 58f; Parlasca and Seeman 1999, 136 no. 38.

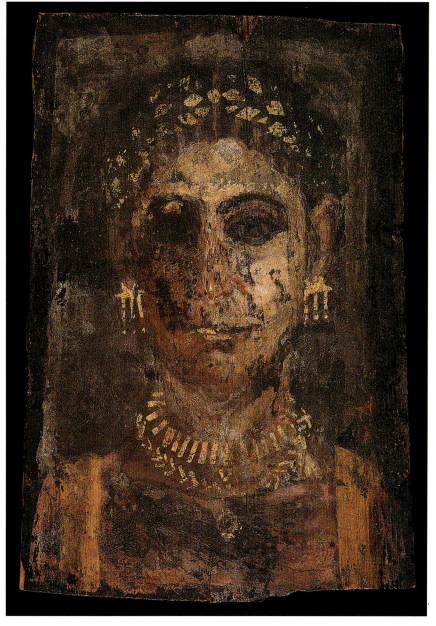

26

GILDED MASKS FROM HAWARA

Like the painted portraits (nos 11–53), the gilded masks were excavated by W. M. Flinders Petrie in the cemeteries at Hawara. The masks were derived from pharaonic traditions of belief, in which the mask served as a substitute for the head of the deceased, endowing the individual with the attributes of deities and thereby assisting his or her passage to the afterlife; in many instances, the gilded face is surrounded by scenes representing protective deities, painted in registers on the lappets and at the sides and back of the head. Gilded masks with individual portrait features date back to the earliest years of the Roman occupation of Egypt. They do not appear to have been made much after the beginning of the second century AD, though one burial group includes objects of later date with a mummy mask apparently dating to the first or early second century AD.

The earliest masks are of men, masks of women with mostly very Romanised portrait features appearing in the mid-first century AD. It is striking that few painted panel or shroud portraits of men appear to date before the reign of Vespasian (AD 69–79), and it may be the case that in the early Empire most men were commemorated with masks. It is also of interest that, in contrast to the portraits, a high proportion of the gilded masks bear inscriptions giving the name of the deceased individual, sometimes with other personal information. One of these, Titus Flavius Demetrius (Walker & Bierbrier 1997, 84–5, no. 74), is the only Roman citizen known from the entire corpus of mummy portraits. Notwithstanding his status, Flavius Demetrius' mask is of traditional Egyptian appearance; without the evidence of his name, one might be inclined to date it earlier than the late first or early second century AD. All these features suggest that gilded masks were made for persons of relatively high social status; a group of inscribed examples, including no. 28, were discovered by Petrie between 23 and 30 March 1888, suggesting that they were excavated in a particular area of the cemetery at Hawara.

27 Portrait of a woman in gilded and painted cartonnage

AD 40–60

H 55.2 cm, W 41 cm, TH 11 cm
Excavated by Petrie at Hawara in 1911; the back is marked with an 'N'
Petrie Museum UC 28084

The proper left eye is lost and the bust is joined from many fragments. Some of the surface is damaged.

Portrayed is a woman dressed in a tunic, a dark wine-red *clavus* edged with red appearing below the proper right shoulder. Her mantle is drawn over her head to form a veil; this is edged in wine-red as if to frame the portrait. In her hair the woman wears a rolled band, once painted, perhaps to represent cloth. She wears large gold ball earrings, with two small discs between the upper and lower balls. Above the tunic is a gold necklace with pendant balls, probably pearls, while over the tunic is a second gold chain with pendant figures of Sarapis, Harpocrates and Isis. The woman's right hand is raised to hold a garland of rose petals; on her right arm is a gold armlet above the elbow, and on the forearm a large double-headed snake bracelet. Similar jewellery is worn on the proper left arm, while on the left hand is a thick-bezelled ring on the forefinger, a triple ring on the third finger and a double ring on the fourth.

The hair is parted in the centre, and lightly waved to either side, with four tiers of curls above the ears, long single corkscrew locks hanging behind them and a row of snail-shaped curls across the brow. The eyebrows are painted in the Egyptian manner as elongated black lines. The surviving proper right eye is set

27

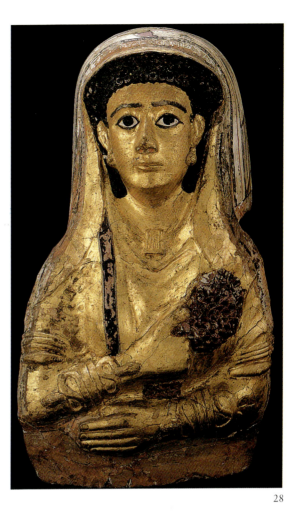

28

in a bronze case, the edges serrated to represent bronze lashes. The dark blue glass iris and pupil is set into the alabaster eye in a separate bronze casing. The nose is straight, the thick lips slightly smiling and the chin small and round and set in folds of flesh, reminiscent of Ptolemaic fashion.

The snail-shaped curls with no break at the parting may indicate a date as early as the AD 40s (the hairstyle is associated with Claudius' second wife Messalina); the jewellery is consistent with a Claudian or Neronian date.

BIBLIOGRAPHY

Petrie, *Portraits*, pl. x, 2; Petrie, *Funeral Furniture and Stone and Metal Vases* (London 1937), 19, 356.

28 Painted and gilded cartonnage mask of a woman named Aphrodite, daughter of Didas, aged twenty

AD 50–70

H 53.5 cm, W 30.8 cm, TH 23.8 cm

Excavated by Petrie at Hawara in 1888 with another gilt-faced mummy, the bandages inscribed 'Souchas, brother of Didas, son of Ampholas'

Given by H. Martyn Kennard to the Victoria and Albert Museum in 1888, and presented by the Trustees to the British Museum in 1979

British Museum EA 69020

Apart from slight damage around the edges, the front of the mask is well preserved. The woman wears a tunic with a *clavus* (now black, but originally purple) visible below the proper right shoulder; a veil is draped over her head and shoulders. She wears ball earrings and a necklace comprising a gold chain with a central plaque showing three divinities, perhaps two Demeters with Harpocrates. On both arms are elaborate snake bracelets, triple armlets and a second armlet with enlarged bezel. No finger rings are visible. In her right hand she holds a wreath of pink flowers. The hair, painted black, is arranged in three tiers of snail-shaped curls with no central parting. Banks of curls surmount the ears; ringlets fall behind them onto the shoulders.

The eyes, eyebrows and lashes are simply painted in black and white. The nostrils are painted orange. The lips are slightly opened.

The inscription is of raised gilt letters applied to the painted ground of the veil, behind the gilded edge.

On the top of the head is a vulture wearing the crown of Upper Egypt (here coloured pink instead of the traditional white), its wings enfolding the head of the deceased. The badly damaged scene at the back originally showed Osiris (only his crown is preserved), whose head was flanked by falcons and mummiform divinities. The gilding on the front lies on a ground of pinkish-orange paint visible at the sides and the lower edge.

Cited by Grimm as the latest and most individualised of the Romanised gilded cartonnage masks from Hawara, the portrait is regarded as Flavian, though the particular combination of jewellery, drapery and hairstyle does not rule out a late Claudian or Neronian date.

BIBLIOGRAPHY

Petrie, *Hawara*, 16f, pl. 4, 3; Petrie, *Ten Years' Digging in Egypt* (London 1893), 97, fig. 73 lower l.; Preisigke, *Sammelbuch* I, 4177; Parlasca, *Mumienporträts*, 111, 167 n. 105; Grimm, *Mumienmasken*, 49, 53, 108, 114, 117, 127 A6 (bibl.), pl. 74, 4 (throughout cited as Victoria and Albert Museum Inv. 1687–1888); Parlasca and Seeman 1999, 110 no. 11 (compare the painting pp. 208–9 no. 116).

PORTRAITS FROM ER-RUBAYAT (PHILADELPHIA)

The portraits associated with the cemetery at er-Rubayat were mostly acquired in the 1880s by the Viennese dealer Theodor Graf, who exhibited them at several venues in Europe and America to great public acclaim, selling them to various institutions and private collectors. Only for the tomb group excavated in 1901 by the papyrologists Grenfell and Hunt (including no. 46) is the provenance of er-Rubayat secure.

It has recently been confirmed that the cemetery was the burial ground for the inhabitants of Philadelphia, a large community in the north-east of the Fayum some 12 km distant from the modern settlement of er-Rubayat, from where the paintings were probably sent out of the Fayum (Roberts in Parlasca and Seeman 1999, 49–50). Most exhibit a consistency of technique, being painted in tempera usually on thick panels of oak, which like the lime used at Hawara is a Mediterranean wood not native to Egypt. (One of the paintings excavated by Grenfell and Hunt is on yew, the other is yet to be analysed.) Most of the panels are clipped at the upper corners. However, this section includes a number of portraits in encaustic attributed to er-Rubayat by association with Theodor Graf or other dealers; they are not typical of the cemetery and may originate elsewhere, perhaps even Hawara where Petrie records excavation of four to five portrait mummies in his absence by the dealer Faraq (Petrie, MS Journal, 24 October 1888–23 May 1889, p. 6).

Many of the tempera portraits have been dated to the third and fourth centuries AD on grounds of the apparent crudity of their style. However, careful observation of the hairstyles, jewellery and clothing worn by the subjects of the portraits reveals that they are approximately contemporary with the grander encaustic panels from Hawara; the apparent crudity derives from the tempera technique and does not feature, for example, in the encaustic paintings nos 30–32 and 37–8, all works of considerable distinction.

Unlike their contemporaries at Hawara, many of the subjects of second-century AD paintings from er-Rubayat wear undertunics decorated at the neck, a feature of dress that may be linked to the desire to express a local identity.

29 Portrait of a woman in tempera and encaustic on limewood

About AD 70–100

H 41.5 cm, W (max.) 22 cm

Said to be from er-Rubayat

Formerly in the Graf Collection, and from 1893 in that of Dr Ludwig Mond; given to the National Gallery with no. 85 in 1924

London, National Gallery 3931

The trapezoidal panel has slight vertical fissures, and paint is lost in several areas, especially to the right of the portrait. Originally the right and lower margins were left unpainted, but areas of the mantle have been filled with crimson paint. Marks of bands appear around the lower, left and upper edges of the panel, where they are stained blue. The upper corners are only slightly cut.

The subject wears a crimson tunic with a wide black *clavus* edged with gold and a darker crimson mantle over the shoulders. She wears gold ball earrings, of which the proper left is original, outlined in ochre and painted in yellow and white, while the other is restored in outline. Around the neck is a thick plaited gold chain and, below, a necklace of oblong emeralds interspersed with gold elements.

As with other mixed-media portraits (e.g. no. 1), the dark hair is very thickly painted and the curls not well differentiated except around the brow. The arched eyebrows and almond-shaped eyes are distinctively worked with cross-hatching. The woman has high cheekbones, a small square chin and a long nose. The thick lips, bow-shaped and painted pink, are slightly down-turned, with the slanted eyes giving the subject a menacing air. The skin is painted in warm tones of cream and pink, with orange shading at the neck beside the tunic. The flesh and hair is painted in encaustic, while the drapery is more crudely rendered in tempera.

A Flavian date is suggested by the style of the earrings and the hair, and by the richly coloured tunic and mantle (compare no. 3). The double necklaces are more characteristic of slightly later portraits, though not unknown in the later first-century repertoire (e.g. Cairo 33241 = Doxiadis 53). The mixed technique is also found in other first-century paintings (e.g. no. 1).

BIBLIOGRAPHY

Parlasca I, 53 no. 99 (bibl.), pl. 92; Borg 1996, 13, 15, 33, 170, pl. 9; Aubert and Cortopassi 1998, 102, 105, no. 54; Parlasca and Seeman 1999, 146–7 no. 47.

30 Portrait of an old man in encaustic on wood

AD 75–150

H 34.5, W 19 cm

Said to be from er-Rubayat

Acquired in 1928 from the Graf Collection

Berlin, Staatliche Museen, Antikensammlung 31161/15

The panel, cut at the top in the form of a trapezoid, presents one of the few mummy portraits of old men. Bathed in a soft, diffuse light with the proper right eye as the focus, the well-proportioned face, turned slightly to the left, emerges from the darkness somewhat blurred. A broad but diffuse ray of light illuminates only the forehead, the cheekbones, and the nose. As a result, the cheeks, like the shadowed eyes, appear somewhat sunken. The small bright eyes, the left somewhat lower than the right, are ringed with pink and gaze slightly to the side. Semicircular brows, traced with the *cestrum*, arch above them, and the suggestion of

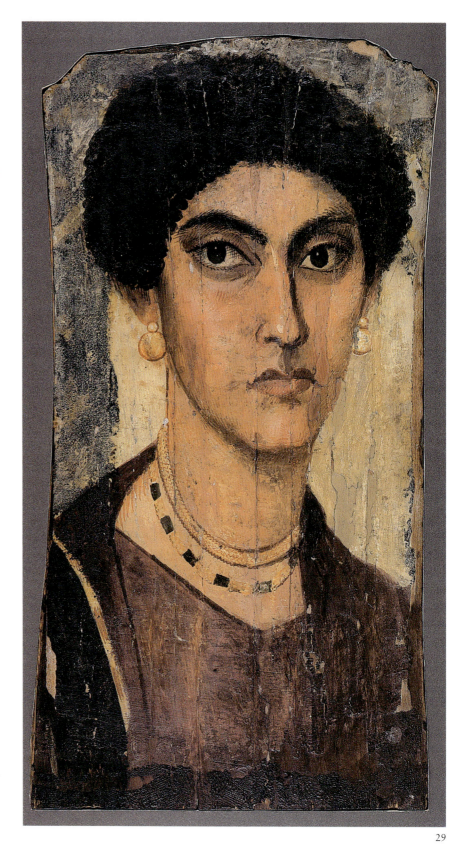

29

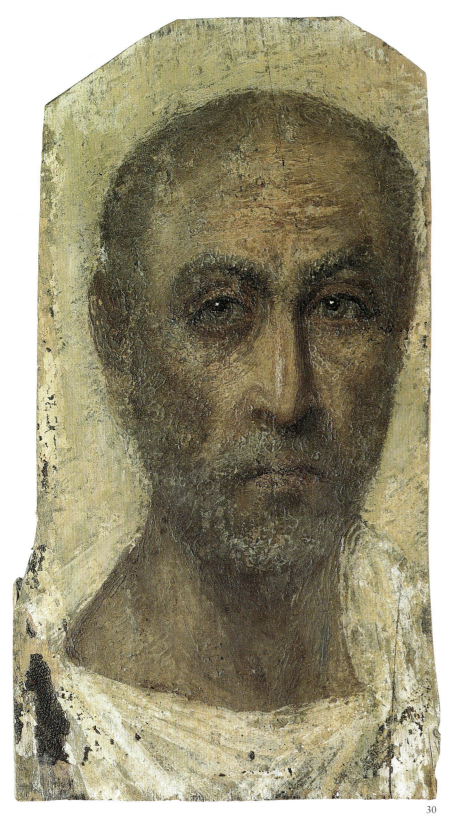

30

horizontal wrinkles across the brow gives the impression that they are raised. The result is a certain contrast between the taut, attentive area around the eyes and the lower half of the face, which is wholly relaxed. The old man's nose is straight and wide, his mouth pale red and small. His greatly receding grey hair is cut short like his beard. He wears a cream-coloured tunic, the colour of which is scarcely distinguished from that of the background. Its once-red right-hand *clavus* can be seen at the irregularly projecting lower left edge of the picture.

Its rather poor condition makes it difficult to date the portrait more precisely within the suggested period of between roughly AD 75 and 150.

U.S.

BIBLIOGRAPHY

Parlasca I, 77 no. 186 pl. 45.3; Borg 1996, 95f, 98; Aubert and Cortopassi 1998, pp. 130f no. 79; Parlasca and Seeman 1999, p. 153 no. 53.

31 Portrait of an officer in encaustic on wood with added gold leaf

About AD 110–40

H 41.5, W 19 cm

Said to be from er-Rubayat

Acquired in 1928 from the Graf Collection

Berlin, Staatliche Museen, Antikensammlung 31161/2

The upper body of this young man with a narrow, triangular face twists to the left, but he has turned his head sharply to the right to gaze at the viewer. The shape of his large, round eyes is emphasised by the clear rendering of the pouches below them. As in other portraits of the Hadrianic period (see Parlasca I, no. 189), the face is not illuminated evenly but rather structured by larger highlights on the forehead, the right cheekbone, the nose, the hollow next to the nostril, the edge of the upper lip, and the chin.

The young man wears a full beard but with only a little growth above his sensuous mouth and none at all on his chin. His hair, made up of slightly curled strands, is piled up above his forehead, leaving it completely free. In his hair he wears a funeral wreath of diamond-shaped foliage in gold leaf. His clothing consists of a white tunic under a blue-green cloak that is gathered above his left shoulder and secured with a gold fibula. Across his right shoulder and running down over his chest at an angle is a dark red sword-belt (*balteus*) ornamented with gold studs (*bullae*). The round shape between the belt and the cloak, difficult to make out, has been interpreted as either a gathering of fabric or the hilt of a sword that has been clumsily painted. In fact, such shapes seem to appear only on soldier portraits – see the panels in Windsor (Parlasca II, no. 333), Manchester (Parlasca I, no. 202) and Berlin (Parlasca I, no. 179) – so one must assume that they reflect some element of military garb.

This portrait is one of a group of male portraits generally referred to as 'officers' because of their military attributes of the sword-belt and cloak. Arguing against this interpretation is the fact that the subjects do not wear cuirasses, whereas known depictions of Roman centurions in sculpture always include them. Further, it has been pointed out that there were no significant numbers of Roman troops stationed in the Fayum in the second century AD. Both objections are dealt with if one supposes that Roman centurions served as policemen in the Fayum in this period. The suggestion that the subjects are generals (*strategoi*), that is to say high administrative officers, cannot be verified, since nothing is known of the special uniform they might have worn.

U.S.

BIBLIOGRAPHY
Parlasca II, 51 no. 334 pl. 81,1; Parlasca, *Mumienporträts* 85n, 173, 288; Doxiadis 1995, 22 pl. 15, 92, 100, 126, 188; Borg 1996, 75, 156ff, pl. 14, 1; Parlasca and Seeman 1999, pp. 39, 72, 87f n. 1, 149 no. 49.

31

32

32 Portrait of an officer in encaustic on wood with added gold leaf

AD 110–30

H 41, W 20 cm

Said to be from er-Rubayat

Acquired in 1928 from the Graf Collection

Berlin, Staatliche Museen, Antikensammlung 31161/6

The panel is cut in a semicircle at the top, and running diagonally across the lower corners are traces of mummy wrappings. To the lower right and especially in a curve circling the throat are traces of red pigment. These presumably come from a red shroud in which the mummy was wrapped (Edgar 1905, 89f, 101f).

The bearded man appears with his upper body twisted slightly to the right and wears a gold funeral wreath in his hair. He is dressed in a white tunic with a grey-violet *clavus* on the proper right side, the folds of which are rendered with lively brushstrokes in a thicker white against a thin wash background. Across his left shoulder lies a blue-green *pallium* affixed with a silver fibula. Across his right shoulder and angling across his chest is a dark red sword-belt (*balteus*) ornamented with alternating silver and gold studs (*bullae*). For the significance of military attributes, see Parlasca and Seeman 1999, 184–5 no. 86, and this volume no. 31. The subject's facial features are nicely harmonised, and their balance is emphasised by the cool colours and the ample light that falls onto the left half of the face and leaves the rest, with the exception of the right cheek-bone, in half shadow. The mouth and chin, especially, thus take on a convincing three-dimensionality.

The very carefully trimmed short beard and slightly curly hair only partially obscuring the forehead date the portrait to the Hadrianic period.

U.S.

BIBLIOGRAPHY
Parlasca I, 76 no. 179 pl. 43,2;
Doxiadis 1995, 22 pl. 16, 100, 126,

132 illus. 62, 188, 234; Borg 1996,
75, 129, 156ff; Parlasca and Seeman
1999, 12 with illus., 39, 71, 87f n. 1,
149 no. 50.

33 Portrait of a woman in tempera on wood

AD 325–50 (or second century AD; see below)

H 31, W 14.8 cm

Said to be from er-Rubayat

Berlin, Staatliche Museen, Antikensammlung 31161/49

The portrait depicts a woman turned slightly to the right. She has an oval face with round cheeks and a strong chin. Her nose is narrow and slightly curved at the tip. Her large, wide-open eyes are slightly angled. Their lids are traced in black and the lashes of her upper lids are rendered in individual strokes. Her eyebrows are only slightly curved. Her neck is short and thick. She has parted her hair in the middle and combed it back tight against the sides of her head. From the nape of the neck she has drawn it upward in a braid and fixed it in a tight bun at the top of her head with a large pin inserted from the left. The ears are covered. Her tunic and the mantle visible above her left shoulder are a pinkish red. Her jewellery consists of large hoop earrings, each of them with four white pearls, one necklace of dark oval beads alternating with white pearls, and a braided gold chain with a crescent pendant.

A portion of the rectangular panel is missing on the left. At the top a small strip was left unpainted. The flesh tone is pinkish, with darker brownish shadows around the eyes, below the nose and on the neck. The only highlights are below the right eye and above the upper lip. Parallels for the woman's coiffure are found in the time of Constantine, and as the painting style is similar to that of Parlasca III, no. 533, and Walker and Bierbrier 1997, no. 89, a date in the second quarter of the fourth century seems probable.

H.-G.F.

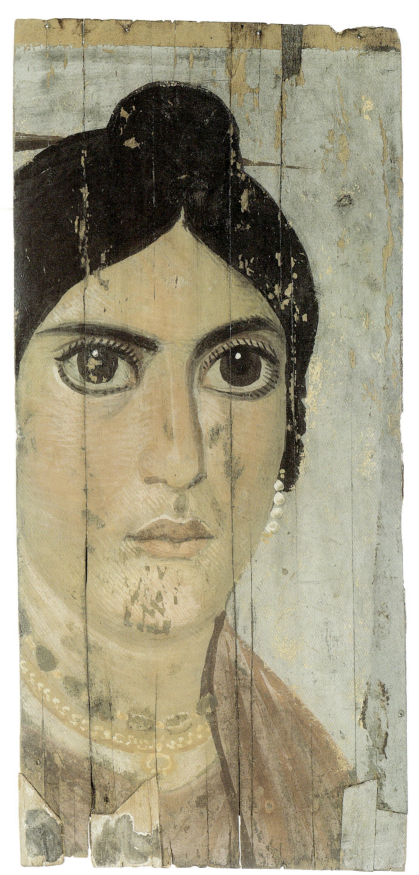

33

BIBLIOGRAPHY
Parlasca III, 61 no. 649 pl. 153,4;
Doxiadis 1995, 130 illus. SW 59, 193;
Borg 1998, 15, 37f, 171 pl. 59,1.

EDITOR'S NOTE
This painting has been placed within
a sequence of second-century-AD
portraits, as the dress, clothing and
hairstyle appear typical of that era.

34 Portrait of a woman

Shortly after AD 140

Encaustic on wood

H 35, W 18 cm

Said to be from er-Rubayat

Berlin, Staatliche Museen,
Antikensammlung 31161/9

The portrait depicts a middle-aged
woman turned slightly to the left. She
has a long face with prominent
cheekbones, a narrow chin, a long
curved nose and a well-formed small
mouth with taut lips. Her eyes, also
small, lie deeply shadowed in their
sockets, the folds leading downward
from their corners and the lighter
pouches beneath them clearly
rendered. Her neck is wrinkled. She
wears her thick black hair parted
in the middle and combed back
smoothly to the sides so that only a
triangular portion of her forehead is
visible. It is caught in a bun at the
back of her head, leaving her ears
exposed. Her tunic is white, and she
wears no jewellery.

   The lower left corner of the panel
has been broken off, and the upper
corners are cut at different angles.
The background is a bluish grey.
The painter has handled the light and
shadow with skill, rendering the signs
of age quite effectively. The coiffure
recalls that of the empress the older
Faustina; the picture was doubtless
painted shortly after AD 140.

H.-G.F.

BIBLIOGRAPHY
Parlasca II, 34f no. 270 pl. 65,3; Borg
1996, 13, 40, 93; Parlasca and Seeman
1999, 148–9 no. 48.

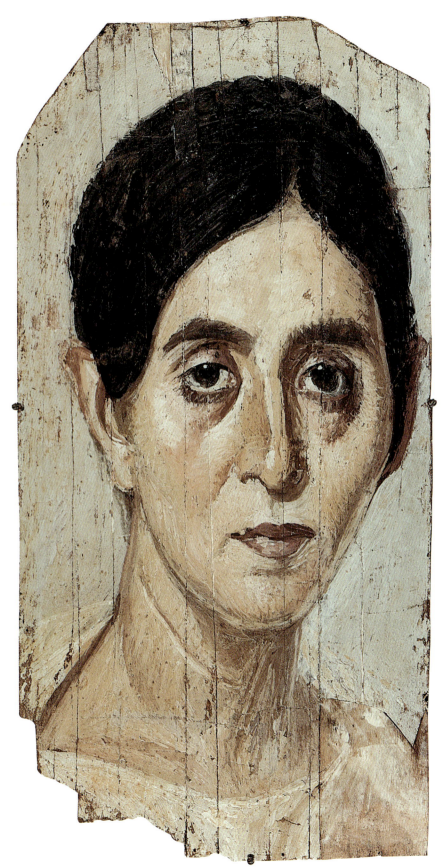

34

35 Portrait of an elderly woman in tempera on wood, perhaps sycomore fig

About AD 140–60

H 31 cm, W (max.) 18.5 cm, TH 0.6 cm

Said to be from the Fayum

Acquired by the Reverend Greville Chester

British Museum GRA 1890.9–21.1 (Painting 87)

The panel is broken at the upper right edge and in places down the right side. Traces of black paint appear on the lower right edge of the panel; where the paint has been removed to the centre left, a cream wash remains. The background is grey.

The subject wears a light terracotta tunic and a mantle, the latter draped over her proper left shoulder and around the neck. The *clavi* are painted in black on a brown ground; the left *clavus* has been misunderstood and extends over the mantle. Also misunderstood are the shoulder seams of the tunic, which appear as rows of dots on the mantle. In her hair the woman wears a band of terracotta wool, matching the mantle. The straight hair, painted in black and white on a brown ground, is parted centrally and brushed around the face and towards the back of the head in casual fashion.

The subject's face is bony, irregular in shape, sallow in complexion and marked by lines of ageing. The heavy brows are painted in black and brown. The huge brown eyes have individually indicated lashes. The long nose is highlighted in white. The thick lips are twisted, with the knotted brow giving the impression of an anxious scowl. Age lines also appear on the neck.

The painting is remarkably similar to one of an elderly man now in Vienna (KM x300, formerly in the Graf collection). They appear to be the work of the same artist and may represent members of the same family, perhaps husband and wife. Without jewellery it is difficult to

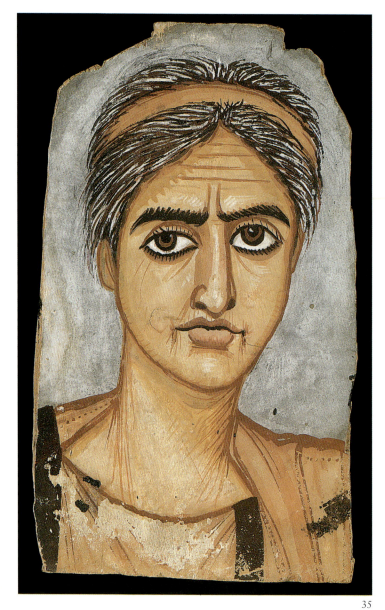

35

date this portrait, but from the hairstyle it could belong in the middle years of the second century AD.

BIBLIOGRAPHY

R. P. Hinks, *A Catalogue of the Greek, Etruscan and Roman Paintings and Mosaics in the British Museum* (1933), 58 no. 87 fig. 66; Parlasca III, 27 no. 517 (bibl.), pl. 126, 1; Borg 1996, 108, pl. 49,2; Parlasca and Seeman 1999, 180 no. 81.

36 Portrait of a middle-aged man in tempera on wood

About AD 140–60

H 35.6 cm, W 19.1 cm

Said to be from er-Rubayat

Formerly in the second Graf Collection, then in the collection of Sigmund Freud

London, Freud Museum 4947

The panel is cracked through the centre, and paint is lost from the face of the figure and the upper edge. The background is bluish grey.

Portrayed is a man of middle years, with greying curly hair and a

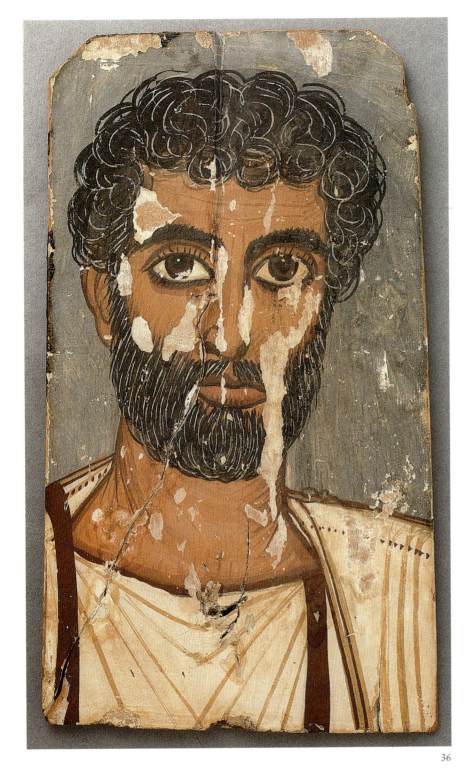

36

thick straight beard and moustache. The elongated proper left shoulder was probably intended to represent a three-quarter view.

The man wears a creamy-white tunic with yellow ochre folds and dark red *clavi*. Over his left shoulder he wears a mantle of similar hue. As in other portraits (e.g. nos 78, 79), the shoulder seams are misunderstood, appearing as a row of dots on the mantle and behind the neck on the proper right shoulder.

The lines on the brow and above the bridge of the nose are lightly drawn. The large eyes, with upper lashes indicated, are of irregular shape. The lower lip is very thick, and the skin a warm honey tone.

The hairstyle indicates an early Antonine date.

BIBLIOGRAPHY

Parlasca III, 24 no. 500, pl. 121, 4; C. N. Reeves, *Sigmund Freud and Art* (London 1989), 78–9; Borg 1996, 108, pl. 51,1; Borg 1998, 63 fig. 77.

37 Portrait of a bearded man in encaustic on wood

About AD 150–70

H 37 cm, W 21 cm

Said to be from er-Rubayat

Malibu, J. Paul Getty Museum 74.AP.11

There are slight vertical fissures in the right side of the panel, and traces of mummy wraps on all sides. The upper corners are irregularly broken. A fragment of textile is preserved at the upper left corner, and there are traces of resin and wrappings on the lower part of the panel. The background is greyish white, painted over a dark primer.

The subject wears a white tunic with a very narrow raspberry-red *clavus*. A thick white mantle is draped over his left shoulder and around the back of his neck; just above the lower right corner of the panel is a decorative woven horizontal H-motif. Traces of raspberry-red paint on the neck beside the mantle suggest an undertunic.

The hair is painted in corkscrew locks fanning out over the brow, with the frizz characteristic of later second-century portraits at the back of the head. The beard and moustache are straighter, with much growth on the lower cheeks. The arched eyebrows are painted with diagonal strokes perhaps made with a pointed graver (*cestrum*) over a solid band of paint. The almond-shaped eyes are olive brown, and the upper lashes individually indicated. The nose is long and straight, and the reddish-brown lips unusually full. The complexion is ruddy.

The hairstyle and drapery suggest an Antonine date for this expressive portrait.

BIBLIOGRAPHY
Parlasca II, 57 no. 357 (bibl.), pl. 86, 2; Thompson 42, 65 no. 6 (bibl.); Doxiadis 1995, 96 fig. 38; Borg 1996, 80, 88, 162ff; Borg 1998, 72–3 fig. 86.

38 Portrait of a bearded man in tempera on limewood with added gold leaf

About AD 150–80

H 42.1 cm, W 22 cm

Said to be from er-Rubayat

Formerly in the Graf Collection, then from 1893 in that of Dr Ludwig Mond, who gave it to the National Gallery in 1924 with no. 76

London, National Gallery 3932

The lightly arched panel is broken along the upper left edge and lower right corner, with a large piece missing from the lower left edge. There are numerous fissures through the length of the panel. A brown stain discolours the left side of the drapery; the gilded background immediately surrounding the head and neck indicates the extent of the portrait originally revealed in the mummy wrappings. The rest of the background is grey.

The subject is a mature man of forty or so years, dressed in a white tunic with crimson *clavus* just visible at the left edge of the panel, and a creamy-white mantle arranged in thick folds over the proper left shoulder and diagonally across the

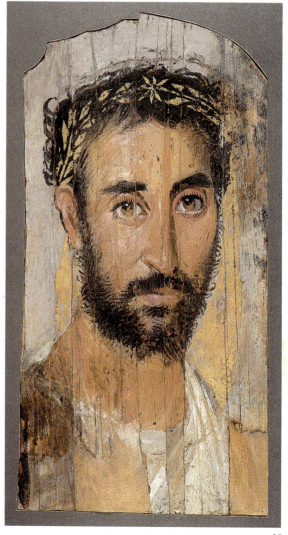

37

38

breast. The subject's dark curly hair is adorned with a wreath of applied gold leaf leaves springing from a stem, with a star-shaped flower above the centre of the brow. As is common in later second- and third-century portraits, long strands of hair fly around the edge of the head. The hair recedes at the temples. Around the face is a short beard of straight hair, rendered in bold impressionistic strokes.

The brow is high, the eyebrows unusually straight and thick, the large round eyes light brown, the nose long and the lips straight. The latter are repainted in pink and orangey red. The flesh is painted in warm tones of cream and pink; the neck has suffered from incompetent retouching.

The style of the dress with the diagonal folds of drapery over the body, the long face, curly hair and beard suggest a date in the mid- to late Antonine period.

BIBLIOGRAPHY
Parlasca II, 62–3 no. 381 (bibl.), pl. 92.1; Borg 1996, 92, 102, 121, 166, pl. 10, 1; Aubert and Cortopassi 1998, 46, 48 no. 10; Parlasca and Seeman 1999, 182–3 no. 83.

39 Portrait of a young man in encaustic on wood

AD 130–80

H 39, W 21 cm

Said to be from er-Rubayat

Acquired in 1928 from the Graf Collection

Berlin, Antikensammlung, Inv. 31161/8

The panel is trimmed in a semicircle at the top, and traces of wrapping are visible on both sides and at the bottom. An irregular diagonal strip across the lower edge was left unpainted. Here it is evident that the painter did not bother with priming, using the colour of the panel itself in his palette of brownish tones.

The young man appears unclothed in three-quarter profile. His head is turned to the right, but he does not quite fix the viewer straight in the

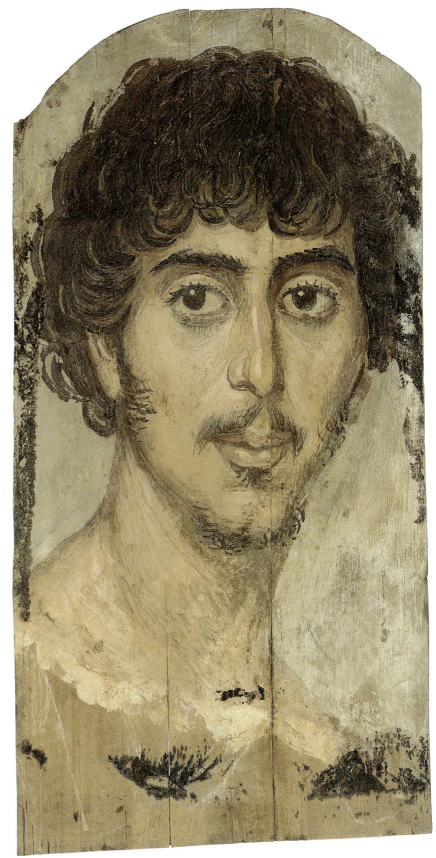

39

eye. His most striking features are his somewhat curved nose, his pointed, full-lipped mouth, and his prominent chin. His sparse beard grows only around his mouth and chin and in long sideburns, leaving his cheeks free. Long, wavy hair half covers his ears and falls low over his forehead, where the light, which illuminates the right side of his face somewhat more than the left, casts shadows of curls. The way his long hair falls low over his forehead compares favourably with portrait heads of Antinous and thus helps to date the portrait to the late Hadrianic or Antonine period. The portrait of a young woman in Berlin (Parlasca I, no. 117) is similar in style.

The masterly treatment of light and the delicate colour nuances executed in a loose style that almost completely does without contour lines give this remarkable portrait great three-dimensionality and vitality.

U.S.

BIBLIOGRAPHY
Parlasca II, 49f no. 328 pl. 79,1; Doxiadis 1995, 82f illus. 20, 193; Borg 1996, 75, 159, 192; Borg 1998, 36f illus. 42 (reversed); Parlasca and Seeman 1999, pp. 72, 171 no. 72.

40 Portrait of a military officer in encaustic and tempera, probably on oak

About AD 160–70

H 43.7 cm, W 16.5 cm

Said to be from er-Rubayat

Formerly in the Graf Collection, then from 1893 in that of Dr Ludwig Mond and later Sir Robert Mond, at whose bequest it came to the British Museum in 1939

British Museum EA 65345

The panel is split by fissures. The right side and lower left corner are restored in plain wood. The background is painted sandy brown; the lower edge of the panel is unpainted. Traces of mastic survive at the left edge. Some of the painted surface is lost.

40

Portrayed is a military officer dressed in a creamy tunic with an olive *sagum* draped over his left shoulder and around the back of the neck. Beneath it is a red *balteus* ornamented with gold. The *sagum* is pinned with a gold fibula.

The subject has brown curly hair and a full moustache and beard, grown in the style of Lucius Verus (ruled jointly with Marcus Aurelius, AD 161–9). The bushy arched eyebrows give an air of surprise. The brown eyes are round and protruding, the nose very long and the lips full. The skin was originally painted in warm tones of brown, cream and red.

This is one of a series of portraits of military officers of second-century date. The subject wears the *balteus* over his left shoulder, an unusual feature perhaps indicating elevated status, also suggested by the quality of the original portrait, which Graf believed to represent Ptolemy Soter.

BIBLIOGRAPHY
Parlasca II, 50 no. 330 (bibl.), pl. 80.1; Doxiadis 1995, 24, 118 no. 18; Borg 1996, 75f, 107, 156ff, pl. 14.1; Doxiadis 1998, 144 no. 29, pl. p. 89; Aubert and Cortopassi 1998, 144–5 no. 89; Parlasca and Seeman 1999, 184–5 no. 86.

41 Portrait of a woman in tempera on wood

About AD 160–80

H 29.2 cm, W 16.5 cm, TH 0.6 cm

Said to be from er-Rubayat

Formerly in the Graf Collection, then in that of Sir Robert Mond, who gave it to the British Museum in 1931

British Museum EA 63394

The panel is broken at the right side, with much loss of paint in the lower right corner, along the lower edge and in the flesh areas. The upper corners are clipped.

The subject is a woman dressed in a pink tunic painted with madder, an organic pigment applied with gypsum. The black *clavi* extend to the edge of the garment, but the painting is so crude and damaged that it is difficult to see whether a mantle was also shown. In her ears are triangular hoop earrings with suspended elements; only the pink outlines are preserved. Around her neck the woman wears a bead necklace and, beneath, a gold chain with a central stone or medallion.

The black hair, painted in carbon-based pigment, is drawn back in rolls from the face and wound into a plaited bun on the crown of the head. The large eyes are simply drawn in black, with no pupil and roughly sketched upper lashes. The nose is much damaged; its pillar-shaped outline is drawn in orange, with dark red nostrils. The lips are typical of paintings from er-Rubayat, with a line drawn through them in darker tone. The flesh was originally ivory, with pink cheeks.

The high-brushed hair with a bun on the crown could indicate a date in the early second century AD, but the jewellery is more typical of Antonine fashion. Similar portraits, perhaps contemporary, are published by Parlasca (III, nos 631–53).

BIBLIOGRAPHY
Parlasca and Seeman 1999, 176 no. 77 (4th century AD)

41

42 Portrait of a woman in encaustic on oak

About AD 180–200

H 33.3 cm, W 18 cm, TH 0.4 cm

Said to be from er-Rubayat

Formerly in the second Graf Collection, then in that of Sir Robert Mond, at whose bequest it came to the British Museum in 1939

British Museum EA 65343

The panel is split by a central fissure. The right edge is damaged, and the black and yellow paint of the *clavi* is largely lost, along with much of the surface in the lower right corner and patches on the face. The upper corners are painted black, as if to indicate the areas to be cut for insertion in the mummy.

The subject is a woman shown in almost frontal view. She wears a crimson tunic and a mantle of similar hue draped over her proper left shoulder. The tunic had black *clavi* edged with gold; a white undertunic is visible at the neckline. Above the lines of both shoulders and following the contours of the garments is a thick line of white paint, suggesting an additional fringed scarf or stole, or a decorative edge to the mantle.

In the ears are gold hoops threaded with three pearls. Around the neck is a necklace of blue-grey stones on a gold chain and the conventional medallion on a thick guilloche-like chain.

The black curly hair is drawn up into two wings flanking a central plait. Small strands break loose around the back of the head and around the face. The long eyebrows are almost straight, and the brown eyes, without pupils, have individually drawn lashes. The nose is long and straight, and the lips are long and full. The flesh is salmon pink, shaded in brownish ochre around the chin and neck. The eyes are carefully shaded in grey and there is an attempt to show modelling of the flesh with a hard tool, perhaps a spatula or the end of a brush.

The hairstyle and the jewellery indicate a late second-century date

42

for this portrait, which is similar in many respects to no. 91.

BIBLIOGRAPHY

Parlasca III, 38 no. 560 (bibl.), pl. 136, 1; Doxiadis 1995, 30, 191–2 no. 28; Borg 1996, 57f, 105, pl. 42, 2; Doxiadis 1998, 144 no. 30, pl. p. 90; Aubert and Cortopassi 1998, 98–9 no. 51; Parlasca and Seeman 1999, 189 no. 91 (late 3rd century AD).

43 Portrait of a woman in tempera on wood

About AD 160–80

H 34.9 cm, W 21.3 cm

Said to be from er-Rubayat

Formerly in the Graf Collection, then in the collection of Otto Benesch, Vienna

Malibu, J. Paul Getty Museum 81.AP.29

The panel is discoloured and blanched by water stains but is

43

otherwise well preserved. A grey undercoat may be seen on the bottom of the panel; the background to the figure is cream, with the upper edge unpainted and the corners irregularly cut.

The woman wears a bright pink tunic, painted with natural madder, with crudely painted dark blue *clavi*, and a mantle swathed around the upper arms, the folds indicated in impressionistic strokes of deep red. The shoulder seams over the *clavi* are obscured by patches of discolouration. Beneath the tunic a cream fringed garment is worn over the proper left shoulder. The woman wears pearl earrings with a second pearl suspended from a gold chain, and a plaited gold chain around her neck with a miniature central lunula.

Over the crown of the head some thick strokes of black paint may indicate an ornament over the parting, or may be an attempt at shading. The hair is centrally parted and rolled back from the face in a style popular in the Antonine period. It is drawn into a round bun at the nape of the neck. Wispy curls surround the face, and the back of the head has the disordered strands typical of later second-century portraits.

The large round brown eyes are heavily lidded, with individually indicated lashes and bushy eyebrows set at a rakish angle. The nose is unusually curved, and the full lips are orange in tone. The skin is sallow, with cream highlights and red shading on the nose, cheeks and eyelids. Texture is indicated with careful brushstrokes on the face and hair, but no attempt is made to reproduce the effect on the neck and drapery.

The hairstyle, jewellery and drapery point to a date in the mid- to late- Antonine period.

BIBLIOGRAPHY

Parlasca III, 59–60 no. 643 pl. 152.2; Thompson 52, 66 no. 9; Borg 1996, 15, 52f, 87, 164, 169.

44

45

44 Portrait of a girl holding a cup and a garland, in tempera on wood

About AD 190–230

H 27 cm, W 14 cm

Found at er-Rubayat in 1887; formerly in the Fouquet collection

Brooklyn Museum of Art 54.197

The panel is broken around the upper edge, the upper right side and the lower left corner. The edges were defined with a black border, traces of which remain. The background is pale, almost cream. On the back of the panel is a sketch for a portrait of a girl (*non vidi*; this is noted by Parlasca III, 54 no. 620, who identified the subject of the finished painting as a boy).

The subject on the front is to be identified from her jewellery as a girl. She is dressed in a white tunic with rose-red *clavi* curving over her shoulders and chest. At the neck an undertunic is visible, decorated at the corners with pairs of narrow black stripes. Around her neck the girl wears a gold band with a plump crescent-shaped pendant. On her wrists are bracelets of twisted bars of gold. In her left hand she holds a bound garland of rose petals, and in her right a glass *kantharos* (two-handled cup) filled with red liquid.

The girl's black hair is drawn high off the brow into a frizzy knot at the crown of the head. Her cheeks are very full, with dimples of flesh at the ends of the narrow red lips. Venus rings are drawn on the neck. The brown eyes are huge, with spiky lashes. The nose is slightly skewed.

The crescent pendant is commonly found on panel portraits of women of the later first and early second century AD, but the style of the dress suggests a date of up to a century later. This painting has been attributed to the 'Brooklyn Painter' but is likely to be by a different hand from nos 46–7.

BIBLIOGRAPHY
Parlasca, *Mumienporträts*, 23 n. 39, 25, 59 n. 5, 133, 143 n. 135, 144 n. 139, 207 n. 74, pl. F; Parlasca III, 54 no. 620, pl. 147,3; Borg 1996, 59, 94, 114, 117, 123, 125, 168–9, 194.

45 Portrait of a boy with a garland of flowers in his hair, in tempera on wood

About AD 200–30

H 30.2 cm, W 19.4 cm

Said to be from er-Rubayat

Formerly in the Graf collection

Brooklyn Museum of Art 41.848

There are some patches of paint missing from the background near the edge of the panel, which is irregularly clipped at the upper edges. Traces of resin or mastic appear on the left side. The entire surface of the panel was painted and the edges defined with a brick red line. The background is painted grey. On the back of the panel is a sketch of the boy's head. The wood has been identified as cypress (Borg 1996, 16).

The subject is a plump boy dressed in a sleeved white tunic with pale violet *clavi*. At the neck an under-tunic is shown, decorated at the corners with narrow violet bands. Around his neck the boy wears a black cord, perhaps of cloth or leather, decorated with three pendants, of which the central one resembles a *bulla*. On the little finger of his left hand is a gold ring with a broad bezel. In this hand the boy holds a bound garland of pink rose petals. In his right hand he holds a blue glass beaker filled with a red liquid. The fingers of both hands are very elongated, and neither hand is well shaped.

In the boy's hair is an elaborate garland of white flowers with pink edges and pale stems, resembling carnations. The boy's black hair is combed straight onto his brow, and tied in an untidy knot at the back of his head. His round face is painted in warm ochres and cream. The eye-brows meet over the bridge of the long thin nose. The large eyes are almond-shaped, with long upper and lower lashes. The bright red lips are pursed, with puckers of skin at each end emphasising the boy's plumpness. The chin is slightly dimpled.

This is one of a group of related paintings in tempera on thick wooden panels of small dimensions, representing children below the age of puberty. They have been dubbed the work of the 'Brooklyn Painter', but it is likely that several painters were involved in their production. One of these paintings (no. 46) is known to have been excavated at er-Rubayat (Philadelphia), and a close stylistic relationship suggests that the others are from the same site, which was explored by Theodor Graf in 1888–9.

The date of the painting has caused much discussion. The style of the dress and the drawing of the hands suggests a date in the third century AD, but the tunic, though sleeved, is not an elaborate dalmatic of the type worn in the later third and fourth centuries.

BIBLIOGRAPHY
Parlasca, *Mumienporträts*, 23 n. 39, 25, 143 n. 135, 206–7, 245 no. 9, pl. H; Parlasca III, 53 no. 618 (bibl.), pl. 147,1; Borg 1996, 15–16, 59, 94, 100, 106, 114, 122–3, 125, 128, 168, 194, pl. 52.1; Borg 1998, 90 fig. 109.

46 Portrait of a young boy in tempera on yew

About AD 200

H 26 cm, W 14.5 cm

Excavated with National Museums of Scotland, Edinburgh 1902.70, at er-Rubayat in 1901 by Grenfell and Hunt

Dublin, National Museum of Ireland 1902.4

Areas of paint are lost from the dark border and the proper left ear is restored. The upper edges of the panel are obliquely cut.

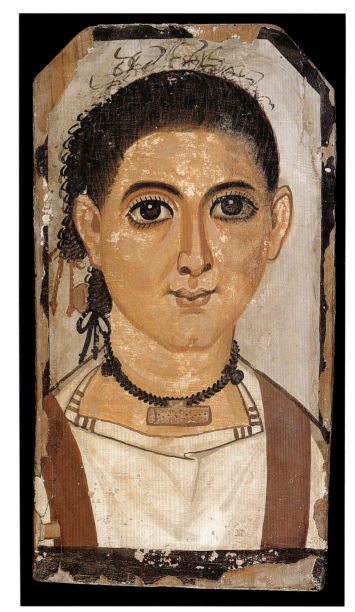

46

The portrait, almost frontal, represents a plump young boy in a creamy-white tunic with wine-red *clavi* and a white undertunic with decorative bands of red at the corners of the neck.

The boy has dark hair brushed in towards the face, but with a frizz of curls at the back of the head. On the proper right side of the head two long locks of hair are tied in red ribbons. Behind the front lock is a brown object outlined in red, perhaps a faded gold ornament. Around his neck the boy wears a brown plaited cord, perhaps of leather, with a central amulet case, the dots on it no doubt intended to represent script.

The locks of hair represent the Horus lock worn by children of both sexes and cut at puberty in a ceremony called the *mallocouria*. The boy so resembles Walker and Bierbrier 1997, 101 no. 93, in physiog-nomy that he may be identified as a member of the same family, most likely her son. The date of the female portrait indicates a late second- or early third-century date for this painting, clearly the work of the same artist.

BIBLIOGRAPHY
Parlasca III, 54 no. 621 (bibl.), pl. 147.4; D. Montserrat, *JEA* (1993), 224; M. L. Bierbrier, *Portraits and Masks*, 16–17, pl. 19, 2; S. Walker, 'Mummy Portraits in their Roman Context', *idem*, 3, pl. 2, 2; Borg 1996, 94, 106, 114, 168, 194, pl. 53, 2; Borg 1998, 91 fig. 112.

47 Portrait of a man in tempera on wood

About AD 220–50

H 34 cm, W 25 cm

Provenance unknown, perhaps from er-Rubayat

Malibu, J. Paul Getty Museum 79.AP.142

The panel, which has clipped upper corners like those from er-Rubayat, is well preserved, though with consider-able loss of the painted surface, especially to the upper right and lower left. Part of the hair and a large

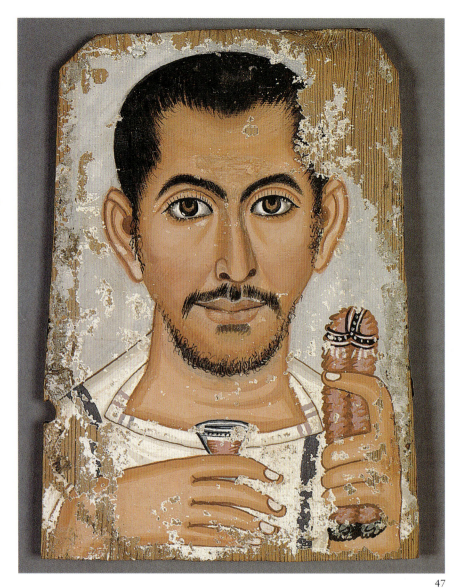

47

patch of the centre of the forehead, the moustache, the right ear lobe, the area around both lips and the lower beard are repainted. A semi-circular cutting appears on the left side of the panel (compare the Isis panel on p. 21, fig. 9); remains of textile appear on the left side and of resin on the edges. The white ground is composed of gypsum or lime, perhaps mixed with animal glue.

Portrayed frontally is a man dressed in a creamy-white tunic with lilac-grey *clavi* and an undertunic of similar hue with pinkish bands of decoration at the corners of the neck. The *clavus* on the man's left side is not carried beyond the neckline.

In his raised left hand the man holds a pink garland bound by a tripartite black band of cloth with white decoration, pink and white edging and a white fringe. In his right hand, held out over his chest, he holds a small glass vessel, decorated with dots at the rim and apparently filled with red liquid, perhaps wine. The white clothing is achieved by enhancing the ground colour; the pink is natural madder.

The man has dark close-cropped hair receding at the temples in the manner of Severan portraits. The treatment of the hair, the arched eye-brows, large eyes, long nose with nostril curled in an attempt at perspective, thick lips and high cheekbones recall the features of the subject of no. 46, but this portrait lacks the cleft chin so apparent in the other paintings, and there is no archival evidence to link it with the tomb in which it was found. However, this portrait has long been considered the work of the same artist, dubbed the 'Brooklyn painter'. The association is very likely right, at least for this painting if not for the whole group; the shared features are of stylistic rather than physiognomical significance.

BIBLIOGRAPHY

Thompson 57, 66 no. 11; Borg 1996, 15, 84, 94, 100, 106, 123, 210 cat. 10, pl. 52.2; Borg 1998, 90 fig. 110.

48 Portrait of a middle-aged man in tempera on wood

About AD 220–40

H 36 cm, W 24 cm

Said to be from er-Rubayat

Formerly in the Graf Collection, then by 1922 in that of Sigmund Freud

London, Freud Museum 4946

There is a crack in the centre and some loss elsewhere along the lower edge of the panel, as well as some surface loss above the proper left ear and in the upper part of the grey background. Traces of the mummy bands appear on the left and right edges of the panel. The upper corners are obliquely cut.

The subject is a middle-aged man, frontally portrayed, and dressed in a white tunic with broad folds indicated in light grey across the chest. The *clavi* are rose-pink, the decorative white stitching not aligned with the corners of the tunic. Around the neck is a wine-red outline, perhaps of an undertunic.

The hair is painted in black and white strokes, thin across the top of the head but bushy, even wreath-like, above the ears. The thick dark eyebrows are painted with diagonal strokes over a single arch. The close-set eyes are simply drawn, without lashes. The nose is long and pointed,

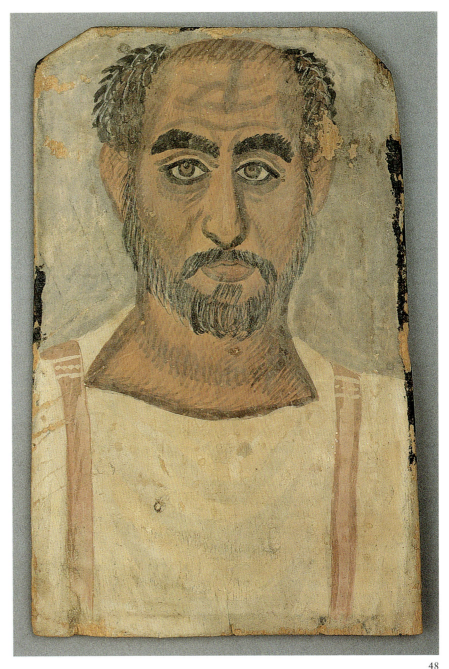

48

and the lower lip is very thick. The flesh is warm in tone, with thick diagonal brushwork suggesting shading. Lines on the brow are loosely drawn in grey, like the folds on the tunic.

A date in the early decades of the third century AD is suggested by the hairstyle, the frontality of the portrait, and the relative simplicity of the brushwork.

BIBLIOGRAPHY

Parlasca II, 88 no. 482 (bibl.), pl. 117.2; C. N. Reeves, *Sigmund Freud and Art* (London 1989), 78; C. N. Reeves, in E. Gubel (ed.), *Le Sphinxe de Vienne* (Liège 1993), 118 no. 54; C. N. Reeves, *Freud as Collector* (Tokyo 1996), 40 no. 38; Borg 1996, 122, 163; Parlasca in Bierbrier, *Portraits and Masks* 128 n. 16; Aubert and Cortopassi 1998, 94, 97 no. 50; Parlasca and Seeman 1999, 181 no. 82.

PORTRAITS FROM ANTINOOPOLIS
AND OTHER SITES

For many years the portraits from Hawara and er-Rubayat so dominated portraiture from Roman Egypt that the paintings became known as 'Fayum Portraits'. However, some of the earliest portraits to reach European collections came from Memphis, Saqqara and Thebes, and, in the earliest years of the twentieth century, excavations by Albert Gayet at Antinoopolis produced a number of portraits of outstanding quality, including a group of full-figure paintings on shrouds (no. 99). Other sites in the Nile Valley and in the Fayum basin have also produced portraits (see map, p. 8), and portrait mummies have been found in recent excavations at Marina el-Alamein, on the coast west of Alexandria.

The portraits from Antinoopolis are of particular interest for the presentation of their subjects, who are shown in austere fashion (see p. 25). The panels are consistently cut with sharply sloping edges following the lines of the shoulders of their subjects, a feature repeated in some later shroud portraits.

This section includes a group of portraits on wood and on linen shrouds acquired in 1908 by the Metropolitan Museum of Art from M. Nahman, a dealer based in Cairo. Of these, the paintings on wood have been associated with the site of Achmim, where, on grounds of their stylistic similarity, they have been assigned to a tomb of mid-late Antonine date (Parlasca, *Mumienporträts*, 41–2). However, the association with Achmim is based only on a reference in a report of 1908 made by the British scholar Seymour de Ricci to the French Académie des Inscriptions, and in the *Comptes rendues de l'Académie des Inscriptions* (1908), 802, his comment appears in the conditional tense. Close examination of the portraits reveals two groups: nos 66–9, in which the backgrounds were gilded after insertion in the mummy wrappings, and nos 70–71, ungilded and painted with a distinctly different colour palette. Another panel portrait (no. 73) does not correspond in technique or shape to any of these. The shrouds, too, are unrelated; it is suggested here that one (no. 52) comes from Antinoopolis on grounds of the style in which the subject is presented. It is furthermore likely that the portraits with gilded backgrounds date from the late first century AD through to the Antonine period. For these reasons the portraits are here treated as unprovenanced; however, the two major groups are retained on grounds of similarity of style.

In general, it may be observed that portraits from sites other than Hawara and er-Rubayat appear to represent a higher number of named individuals and that in some portraits there is clear evidence of personal religious belief. A tantalising inscription appears on the portrait of the freedman Eutyches (no. 65), a work of exceptional quality.

49 Portrait of a woman in encaustic on cedarwood with added gilding

About AD 130

H 41 cm, W 24 cm, TH 1.2 cm

From Antinoopolis

Paris, Musée du Louvre, Département des Antiquités Grecques, Étrusques et Romaines MND 2047 (P 217)

Like a pearl set in gold, this youthful face stands out against a bluish-grey background. Represented almost frontally, its perfect oval is emphasised by the regular hairline with the hair pulled back, and the semicircular braid with a gold-headed pin stuck into it. The pearl-like countenance, with pink highlights on her left cheek and the chin, is rendered with small close brushstrokes. The woman's large eyes are looking to the right, with the left eye placed slightly higher than the right. The eyelids are drawn in red under the dark arch of the thick eyebrows. The lashes are engraved with a hard tool, revealing the black undercoat. Two white dots bring the eyes to life, and a white line emphasises the ridge of the nose. The small mouth is blood-red. The ears are asymmetrical, her right ear 'crumpled' and the left shaded, but both pointed. They are decorated with earrings made of two beads framing a green stone. On the slender neck, concealed by gold leaf, is a beaded necklace. A large green gem mounted in a gold-plated oval is painted on the yellow and pink madder clothing, which is rendered with large brushstrokes.

The Greeks and Romans thought that stones or gems were endowed with prophylactic, magical and astrological powers. These green stones may be emeralds, which ranked third

49

among the most highly valued gems, behind diamonds and pearls. In the Roman period mines were exploited in Egypt, especially on Mount Smaragdus. Pearls were the favourite ornament, but also the most costly for the Roman empire. They were brought in from the Red Sea and the Persian Gulf, with those reputed to be the most beautiful coming from the island of Dilmun (modern-day Bahrain). Gold leaf was placed on the portrait upon the young woman's death. Gold, an incorruptible metal the colour of the sun, was the 'flesh of the gods' for the Egyptians; when applied to effigies of the deceased or, during the Roman period, to embalmed bodies, it was supposed to ensure immortality and divinity.

M.-F.A.

BIBLIOGRAPHY

Parlasca I, no. 139, pl. 33,2; Aubert and Cortopassi 1998, 132 no. 80; Parlasca and Seeman 1999, 277 no. 181.

50 Portrait of a young woman in encaustic on fir wood

AD 100–150

H 32 cm, W 18 cm

Excavated by A. Gayet at Antinoopolis

Paris, Musée du Louvre, Département des Antiquités Égyptiennes AF 6884

The right side of the thin wood board has been lost. The top is cut irregularly. The left side, on the other hand, has the characteristic 'shoulder' cut of Antinoopolis. There are many vertical splits along the grain of the wood, many gaps and areas of wear on the painting surface – on the clothing and the right side of the background and hair – and a horizontal crack at neck level. The wood is rough along the lower part, which was not painted. On a uniformly light-grey background the bust of this young woman is presented almost frontally. The face is oval with regular contours: lighter strokes are laid over a coat of brown paint, creating an almost pearly effect on the right side of the face. The eyes are very large with bright highlights on the upper lids and dark red circles on the lower ones. The lashes are not indicated. The ridge of the nose is marked by a beige line, and the lips are similarly drawn in a pinkish beige colour, barely differentiated from the skin colour. The very large ears stick out, and are adorned with small cluster earrings. The black hair, divided by a middle parting, is arranged into small parallel braids pulled back behind the head. The young woman is dressed in a purple tunic with dark green *clavi*, and an undertunic whose neckline is decorated with violet triangles against a white ground. The extreme severity of the very young face and the sobriety of the clothing, which are also found on other portraits from Antinoopolis, are the striking elements of this portrait.

R.C.

BIBLIOGRAPHY
Parlasca II, no. 272, pl. 66.1.

50

51 Portrait of a youth in encaustic on wood with gold leaf background

About AD 130–50

H 41 cm, W 20.2 cm

Excavated by A. Gayet at Antinoopolis in the winter of 1906/7

Acquired in December 1907

Berlin, Staatliche Museen, Ägyptisches Museum und Papyrussammlung, 17900

This panel, cut down in a semicircle at the top and reduced in size, includes a broad unpainted strip at the bottom. There and on both sides are traces of the mummy wrappings. Pairs of small holes (modern?) on all four edges possibly served to secure it. Only after the portrait was placed in the mummy was the entire exposed background covered with gold leaf, also the youth's clothing, leaving only the head and neck and the left-hand *clavus* of the tunic painted.

The rich application of gold indicates that the young man with effeminate features belonged to a wealthy family. He gazes at the viewer with large eyes. The curves of the eyebrows are taken up by the slightly curved nose. The shading above the small, full mouth suggests a first growth of beard. Light falls onto the face from the upper right, striking the middle of the forehead and proper left cheek and placing highlights on the nose and lower lip. The proper right side of the face and the neck lie in shadow, giving the depiction a distinct three-dimensionality. Thick, black ringlets frame the face in a uniform arc. In his hair the youth wears a wreath of diamond-shaped foliage in gold leaf, the two branches meeting above the centre of his forehead. A mantle lies across his neck and shoulder above a white tunic. The violet *clavus* on the proper right side of the tunic was left exposed by the gilder – apparently it was important that it remained visible. Gold, the colour of the sun, was considered protection against mortality and therefore symbolic of

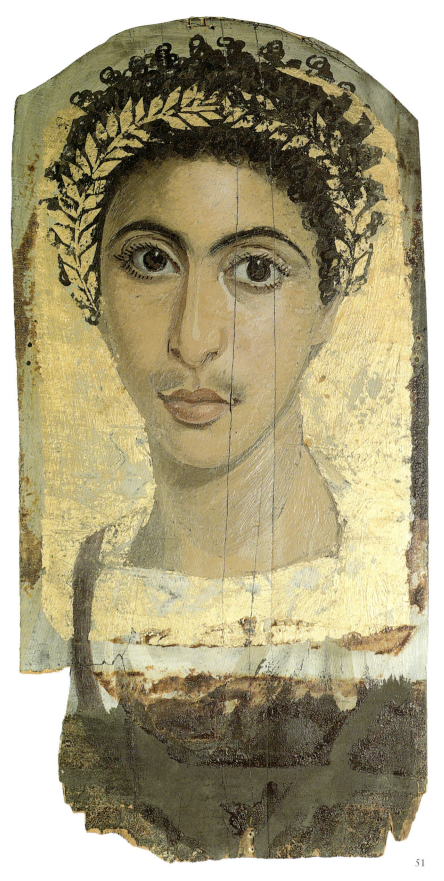

51

rebirth. The way the gilding is not only limited to the portions of the background next to the head but also covers the clothing is otherwise seen only in the Paris portrait of a woman (no. 49).

This portrait was most probably among Gayet's finds in Antinoopolis from the winter of 1907. Related to it in style is a portrait of a girl from Saqqara in London (Parlasca II, no. 306), in which the drawing of the eyes, nose and mouth is similar. The curly hair framing the forehead in a semicircle shows that this portrait of a youth was probably executed shortly after Hadrian's founding of Antinoopolis.

U.S.

BIBLIOGRAPHY

Parlasca, *Mumienporträts*, 125, 134f pl. 29,2 (with indication of origin), 135ff (on the significance of the gilding); Parlasca I, 78 no. 190 pl. 46,2 (early Hadrianic); Doxiadis 1995, 115 pl. 87, 91, 93, 99, 147, 213f with illus. (*c*. AD 138–92); Borg 1998, 26, 58 illus. 72; Parlasca and Seeman 1999, 23f, 32, 274.

52 Portrait of a woman in tempera on a linen shroud

About AD 170–200

H 221 cm, W 106 cm

Provenance unknown, but perhaps from Antinoopolis

Acquired in Cairo from the dealer Nahmann

New York, The Metropolitan Museum of Art, Rogers Fund, 1909 09. 181.8

The shroud is completely preserved but for a narrow strip down the right side. The fringed ends are unpainted, and the portrait is defined on all sides by a black line. The background is painted in a brownish tone, with an area of lighter ochre lighting the head and shoulders of the figure. To either side of the figure, at elbow level, stand the protective deities Anubis (left) and another Egyptian god (right), each carrying a *was*-sceptre.

The subject is a woman dressed in

a white tunic with narrow black *clavi* and very wide sleeves. On the woman's left arm this tunic is decorated with a purple gamma-motif. At the neck a white undertunic is visible, the edge decorated with purple triangles. The white fringe visible at the base of the tunic and the narrow sleeve at the left wrist may belong to this garment. Over the woman's right arm is draped a stole; this is carried across the front of the body, a fold of it held in her left hand. The fringed end hangs over her left arm. On her feet the woman wears red socks and black thonged sandals.

The jewellery is very rich: gold bar earrings, each adorned with triple sets of pendant pearls, and two necklaces of twisted gold, beneath which is a third necklace with a central rosette flanked by stones set in gold with small gold beads between. On both wrists are bracelets of twisted gold (four on the right wrist and two on the left) matching the upper necklaces. Two rings are worn on the third finger of the left hand; these match the rosette in the third necklace. One ring appears on the third finger of the right hand.

The black hair is tightly confined, perhaps within a net, and drawn to the back of the head. The eyebrows are lightly arched, the heavily lidded eyes almond-shaped, the nose flat with wide nostrils and the lips thick.

A recent suggestion that the portrait belongs in the first century AD is not tenable; the 'lock of hair' falling on the neck below the woman's right ear is a shadow. The jewellery suggests a date in the late second century AD. The painting is of particular interest in representing the subject dressed in a wide-sleeved tunic, apparently a dalmatic, though without the broad *clavi* typical of later third- and fourth-century examples (nos 98–9). Dalmatics rarely appear in portraits earlier than the mid-third century and literary references record them only as imperial gifts to individuals of high status. The austerely confined hair and the triangular decoration of the undertunic suggest that the shroud

52

53

The panel has suffered only minimal damage at the edges. The background is greenish grey.

Portrayed is a child wearing a white tunic with red *clavi* and a gold necklet with a pendant, perhaps of bronze. The child has dark hair neatly brushed towards the brow, and a Horus lock behind the proper right ear. The dark eyes gaze down and to the side beneath slightly arched eyebrows. There are clefts above and below a rather sullen mouth.

To the right of the panel, a painted Greek inscription identifies the subject as a girl named Didyme, aged seven years: Διδύμη ἐτῶν ζ. Iconographically, however, the subject appears male, and it is not out of the question that the unusual addition of the inscription indicates that the portrait, intended for a boy, was unexpectedly used for the sudden death of a girl.

The cut of the panel with 'shoulders' suggests that this painting originates from Antinoopolis, and in general style and presentation it compares well with Parlasca 174–5, portraits of a boy and a young man from Antinoopolis, now in the Louvre.

BIBLIOGRAPHY

Parlasca, *Mumienporträts*, 81 no. 16 with n. 144; J. Bourrieau, *JEA* 69 (1983) 151 no. 726 pl. 19, 4; Borg 1996, 152d, 209, cat. 1; Aubert and Cortopassi 1998, 56, 58 no. 17; Parlasca and Seeman 1999, 285 no. 185.

54 Portrait of a man in encaustic on limewood

AD 150–200

H 38 cm, W 24 cm

Perhaps from Antinoopolis

Paris, Musée du Louvre, Département des Antiquités Égyptiennes AF 6883

Three fragments of the thin wooden board have been preserved, with many vertical cracks along the grain of the wood. The wood was not painted along the lower part, and is rough over about two centimetres.

comes from Antinoopolis.

BIBLIOGRAPHY

Parlasca I, 31–2 no. 20 (bibl.), pl. 6,1; Berger and Creux 1977, 216 with fig. 6; Corcoran 12; Parlasca and Seeman 1999, 226–7 no. 135.

53 Portrait of a child in encaustic and tempera on sycomore fig wood

About AD 180–200

H 34.8 cm, W 19.2 cm, TH 1.5 cm

Perhaps from Antinoopolis

Formerly in the collections of A. B. Cook and C. Seltman

Cambridge, Fitzwilliam Museum E5.1981

The left side has the characteristic 'shoulder' cut of portraits from Antinoopolis. The painting surface shows signs of wear, particularly under the ear.

The portrait is characterised by a dark palette with cold tones; the background is an unusual dark grey. The man is shown in three-quarters profile, his face very long and thin. The bone structure, particularly the forehead and cheekbones, is emphasised by the juxtaposition of strokes. The skin is weather-beaten, with reddish brown spots in the centre of the cheeks. The shape of the nose – short and irregular – is marked by the play of highlights; two deep wrinkles begin at the nostrils.

The eyes are without lashes and are drawn with a brown line, possibly kohl. The hair is very short, forming a clear outline all around the head. The hairline forms a point, leaving the temples bare. A fine moustache is attached to a close-cropped beard, which emphasises the angular chin and the elongated face. The right ear, the only one surviving, sticks out but is small. The thin neck with notably dark skin contrasts with the whiteness of the tunic. The painter has even accentuated this contrast with a fine line of pure white at the corners of the neckline. The purple *clavi* are the only decoration on the clothing, which was painted with broad, rapid strokes.

R.C.

BIBLIOGRAPHY
Parlasca II, no. 301, pl. 7.15; Parlasca and Seeman 1999, no. 183.

55 Fragmentary portrait of a woman in tempera on limewood

About AD 140–60

H 30.9 cm, W 7.4 cm, TH. 0.1 cm

Provenance unknown

Formerly in the Sams Collection and acquired in 1834

British Museum EA 5619

Only the central part of the panel is preserved, with a fissure through the length of it and minor cracks to either side and through the lower lid of the proper right eye. The background is creamy grey.

The woman wears a white tunic and mantle with sandy-beige shading indicating the folds. The neck is drawn in brownish red. Curved over her left breast is a broad lilac *clavus*. At the crown of the head is a painted gold hairpin, outlined in brownish red. By the proper left cheek is a pearl, probably the innermost of a series suspended from a bar earring. Around the neck is a painted gold chain, again drawn in brownish red.

The black hair is looped around the face in mid-Antonine fashion, with three short corkscrew locks hanging from the centre parting; a similar style appears on a marble bust of a woman from Alexandria. The line of the finely drawn arched eyebrow is continued to a prominent bony nose. The lips are thin and of a refined appearance. The surviving eye is enormous, with a brown pupil on a cream ground, and individually painted lashes. The complexion is pinkish ochre, with shading in strokes of red and ochre; the

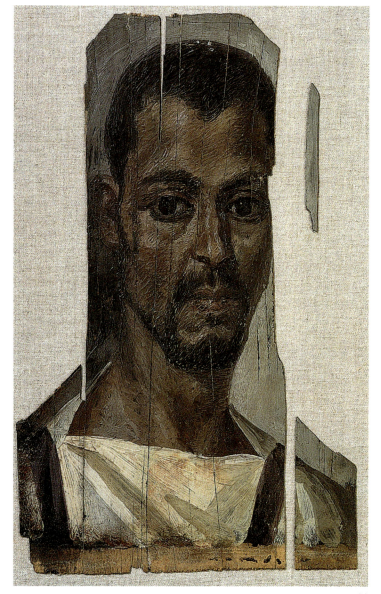

54

55

diagonal strokes are repeated in the hair.

The hairstyle and jewellery suggest a mid-Antonine date for this portrait, which closely resembles a portrait in the Louvre (P. 200) said to be from Memphis, and also registered in 1834. This painting came from the collection of Louis Philippe and was formerly in the collection of the Comte Louis de Laborde, who is said to have excavated the portrait in Memphis in 1827.

BIBLIOGRAPHY

Parlasca I, 92 no. 246 (bibl.), pl. 60 5; Borg 1996, 15, 104f, 108, 171, pl. 46.2; Parlasca and Seeman 1999, 228 no. 138.

56 Shroud for a young man in tempera on linen

About AD 170–80

H 185 cm, W 130 cm

Site of discovery unknown, presumably Memphis

Acquired in 1892 as a gift from the publisher Rudolf Mosse

Berlin, Staatliche Museen, Ägyptisches Museum und Papyrussammlung 11651

This cloth, exquisitely preserved except for the slightly trimmed edges and slight abrasion of the surface in spots, depicts a group of three figures standing on a boat. In the centre is the deceased, dressed as in life in a tunic and mantle. He is flanked by two Egyptian gods, on the right by the jackal-headed Anubis, characterised by his black skin as the god of the underworld. He guides the deceased toward the left, where the mummiform Osiris stands facing directly forward. The deceased, a young man with a short beard, steps toward Osiris, to whom he offers a libation from a small flask. In his left hand he holds a small garland, a common sepulchral attribute. Behind this group is the suggestion of a tomb facade. The actual background is further enriched by several detailed motifs. Next to or on top of the cornice on the right we can see a weighing scene and in the centre

Anubis embalming a mummy. Most interesting is the vignette at the upper left edge of the picture. Here the dead man is drawing water from a well (*shadûf*). He is joined by souls of the dead rendered as stick figures: the one at the bottom drinks water from the bucket, the other two disport themselves on step-like structures possibly meant to suggest a pyramid. The whole illustrates the motif of the thirsting dead, which is commonly encountered in funerary texts. The head of the deceased is rendered as a portrait. The way he wears his hair and beard suggests a dating in the later Antonine era.

In the first publication of this shroud Siegfried Morenz offered another interpretation that occasioned heated discussion in the scholarly literature. Recalling the well-known notion that in death every person takes on the very essence of Osiris (the deceased as 'Osiris' followed by their own name), Morenz maintained that here and on similar shrouds the deceased is depicted twice – in the centre as a living person and on the left after he has been transformed into Osiris. However, the compositional scheme clearly follows another pictorial tradition. Anubis, like the Greek Hermes 'Psychopompos' (conductor of souls), is leading the deceased into the underworld or to judgment. Also, the deceased would hardly – as would be the case here – offer a libation to himself!

K. P.

BIBLIOGRAPHY

Parlasca, *Mumienporträts*, 39 n. 154, 154, 170, 173, 292; Parlasca II, 49 no. 325 pl. 78,2 (portrait); S. Morenz, *Forschungen und berichte [Berlin]* 1 (1957), 52ff illus. 1–4 (= S. Morenz, *Religion und Geschichte des alten Ägypten* [Berlin 1975], 231ff, illus. 3–6); K. Parlasca in *Enciclopedia dell'Arte Antica* 7, 1966, s.v. 'Sudario', col. pl. after p. 546 (reversed); K. Parlasca in *Les syncrètismes dans les religions grecques et romaines. Colloquium Strassburg 1971* (Paris 1973), 95ff (interpretation); Ch. Desroches-Noblecourt in J. Leclant, *Ägypten 3. Spätzeit und Hellenismus*

56

(*Universum der Kunst*) (Munich 1981), 218, col. endpaper; I. Müller in K.-H. Priese, *Ägyptisches Museum Berlin* (Mainz 1991), 216 col. illus. 132; Parlasca and Seeman 1999, 260–1 no. 165.

57 Portrait of a girl in encaustic on limewood with added gilt

About AD 50–70

H 28.7 cm, W 19.3 cm, TH 0.4 cm

Provenance unknown

Given to the National Gallery in 1943 by R. G. and T. G. Gayer-Anderson and presented to the British Museum in 1994

British Museum EA 74719 (formerly National Gallery 5399)

The wooden panel is cracked in several places. Much of the greyish background is lost. There are impressions of textiles on the nose and brow of the figure. Traces of the mummy wrappings appear as a diagonal line at the lower right corner. Laboratory analysis indicates that the pigment is consistent with Roman work, despite certain compositional difficulties which raise doubts over the antiquity of this painting. It is likely that the painting was retouched in recent times, especially in the area of the mouth and neck; the former feature does not relate well to the nose and eyes, and in both areas paint was found within the cracks in the wood.

The young girl wears a dark red tunic and bluish-green mantle and perhaps a bluish-black scarf with bobbles resting on her proper right shoulder. Traces of a violet *clavus* appear on the tunic to the right of this garment. Around the neck is a brownish red thong, perhaps of leather (no trace remains of gilding), with pendant crescent.

The hair is cut close to the head with locks perhaps extending down the neck behind the proper left ear. A gilded wreath on red-brown ground with lozenge-shaped leaves appears in the hair across the crown of the head.

The eyes are very large, with prominent upper lashes and fine arched eyebrows. Much of the surface colour is lost; warm peach and pinkish tones survive. The lips are orangey red and were most likely repainted. It is, however, likely that the original painting is Claudian or Neronian work, as Parlasca proposed.

BIBLIOGRAPHY

Parlasca I, 33, no. 27 (bibl.), pl. 7,6; Borg 1996, 32, 91; Parlasca and Seeman 1999, 215 no. 122.

57

58 Fragmentary portrait of a woman in tempera on wood, inscribed in Greek 'Sarapi[as]'

AD 100–20

H 4.5 cm, W 17 cm, TH 0.1 cm

Acquired from the Fayum by the Reverend G. Chester who presented it to the British Museum

British Museum GRA 1890.8–1.2 (Painting 86)

Only the left edge of the panel is preserved with sand and mastic on the back. Visible are the proper right ear, the lower lid and part of the pupil of the right eye, the nose from bridge to nostril and part of both cheeks. In her pierced ear the woman wears a gold hoop earring threaded with pearls, of which two are visible.

58

Above them two corkscrew locks of black hair hang in front of the ear. The flesh is warmly tinted in tones of cream, apricot and rose pink with an ochre-green shadow by the nose. The nostrils are drawn in dark red.

To the left of the face is inscribed Σαραπί(α) (Sarapi[as]), painted in creamy-white letters 2.3 cm (max.) and 1.5 cm (min.) high. The sigma is lunate; the alphas have dropped bars. The background is bluish grey.

The corkscrew locks indicate a date in the very early years of the second century AD, also appropriate for the hoop earrings. The name Sarapi(as), unknown in other mummy portraits, is well attested, for example in six papyri naming members of the 6,475 descendants of the Greek settlers in the Fayum.

BIBLIOGRAPHY

R. P. Hinks, *A Catalogue of the Greek, Etruscan and Roman Paintings in the British Museum* (1933), 58 no. 86 fig. 65; Parlasca, *Mumienporträts* 30 n. 93, 81 no. 13; Borg 1996, 152m, 210 cat. 6; Parlasca and Seeman 1999, 220 no. 127.

59 Portrait of a man in tempera on fir

About AD 160–80

H 31.2 cm, W 18 cm, TH 0.9 cm

Excavated by Petrie in 1912 at Kafr Ammar, Tomb 340

University College London, Petrie Museum UC 14768

The panel, broken on all sides, is in three fragments, of which two are now joined. Much of the painted surface is lost, and the proper left

side of the face is missing. The background is chestnut brown.

Portrayed is a plump man dressed in a white tunic outlined in ochre. A violet *clavus* appears by the extreme left edge of the panel and, nearby, some indication of decoration – perhaps a tendril or possibly part of the fringed garment that appears on the proper left side of the neck. Beside the latter appear the folds of a mantle drawn in ochre.

The curly hair is, unusually, drawn in black and red, the latter also used to outline the face. The man has beetling arched eyebrows, a moustache and a stubbly beard immediately below the lower lip and around the chin and cheeks. Corpulent flesh is indicated by deep shading at the ends of the lips and in a deep dimple on the round pink chin; two further folds of flesh are drawn below in red.

A date in the mid- to late Antonine period is suggested by the rendering of the hair and facial features. The tomb also contained a wicker-covered pottery jar; the burials were disturbed.

BIBLIOGRAPHY

Petrie and Mackay, *Heliopolis, Kafr Ammar* (London 1915); B. Ramer, 'The Technology, Examination and Conservation of the Fayum Portraits in the Petrie Museum', *Studies in Conservation* 24 (1979), 1–13, esp. 6.

60 'Isidora': portrait of a woman in encaustic on wood, set in a painted linen shroud

About AD 100–10

Portrait H 33.6 cm, W 17.2 cm; cartonnage H 46.4 cm, W (top) 21.6 cm (below) 36.8 cm

Probably from el-Hibeh (Ankyronpolis)

Malibu, J. Paul Getty Museum 81.AP.42

The shroud is formed of seven layers of cloth, the uppermost sealed with a resinous substance into which the panel is set. The panel, once covered with bitumen, is perfectly preserved. Beneath the wrappings the panel appears trimmed, its lower edge projecting below the painted cloth, with a large patch of resin on it. The panel and wrappings were here cut through to remove them from the mummy.

The panel was prepared with a grey ground, visible at the base and used as a background to the portrait, with added lilac on the right side. Represented is a matron dressed in a lilac tunic and mantle, the black *clavi* with gilt edges added to the wrappings with the mantle, the latter appearing red rather than lilac on the orange-painted cloth. Indeed, it is clear that the wrappings were painted after the panel was inserted, as some orange paint has spilled onto the panel.

In her hair, set in the plaited bun at the crown, the woman wears a gold pin with an acorn-shaped head, and, lower down, a large silver pin. Above the curls around the brow is a gold-leaf wreath with a central feathered crown. In the ears are gold bar earrings, unusually with four suspended pearls and a single pearl above the bar. Around the neck are three necklaces, graduated in weight. The uppermost is of small emeralds, pearls and gold beads. The second is an elaborate set of small gold plaques. The lowest is composed of large rectangular emeralds and gold elements. In the centre is an amethyst in an elaborate gold setting incorporating a bust in a pharaonic wig. Like the acorn-shaped pin, the gold of the

59

60

necklaces and earrings was originally painted in ochre, but after the panel was inserted the neckaces and earrings were further embellished with tiny lozenges of gold leaf, replicating the decoration of the wrappings around the panel.

The black hair, apparently at least in part a wig, is worn in typical Trajanic fashion, with curls around the face and corkscrew locks before the ears, and a large plait wound into a bun on the crown of the head.

The deep-set brown eyes with shadows beneath suggest mortal illness, as does the pallid skin. The nose is very long, the lips small and regular; Venus rings indicate a fleshy neck.

The hairstyle, dress and jewellery point firmly to a date in the very

early years of the second century AD for this portrait of Isidora, whose name is painted in Greek in black ink on the left side of the cartonnage, towards the back: Ισιδώρα.

BIBLIOGRAPHY
Thompson cover, 32, 64 no. 1; Doxiadis 1995, 1996, 164, 218 no. 102; Corcoran 11 no. 18, 40, 43–4, 63, 66, 158; Borg 1996, 45, 88, 121 129, 149, 152, 170ff, 210 cat. 11 (bibl.).

61 Portrait of a boy in encaustic on wood

About AD 150–200

H 20.3 cm, W. 13 cm

Said to be from Oxyrhynchus

Malibu, J. Paul Getty Museum 78. AP.262

The rectangular panel was apparently cut to the unusually small format from a larger size. The lower edge is unpainted. Traces of the wrappings may be seen on the other edges. The centre of the panel is cracked and repaired; some filling and repainting has also been carried out on the right side of the panel.

The boy wears a creamy-white tunic with a narrow purple *clavus*. Over his left shoulder is a mantle of similar hue, decorated with a horizontal H-motif. On the neck beside the mantle is a pinkish white undergarment with a brown border, the latter carried along the edge of the tunic. Around his neck the boy wears a band, perhaps of leather, from which is suspended a gold amulet.

The boy's head is shaven, with a Horus lock on the proper right side, and two tufts of hair above the brow (compare the complete shroud portrait of no. 116). In the Horus

lock is a gold pin set with miniature garnets; its design matches that of the amulet-case worn around the neck. The huge eyes of irregular form have shadows beneath them, with the pallor of the skin suggesting mortal illness. The lower part of the neck is shaded with diagonal brush-strokes, echoed in the shading of the drapery folds.

The style of the drapery and of the shaved head suggest a date in the later second century AD.

BIBLIOGRAPHY

Parlasca II, 67 no. 674 (bibl.), col. pl. F; Thompson 40–1, 65 no. 5; Doxiadis 1995, 37, 224 no. 7; Borg 1996, 107, 114, 119, pl. 19, 2; Borg 1998, 68–69 fig. 81.

62 Portrait of a woman in encaustic on limewood

AD 100–50

H 33 cm, W 20 cm

Formerly in the Salt Collection

Perhaps from Thebes

Paris, Musée du Louvre, Département des Antiquités Égyptiennes N 2733 (P 212)

The support is composed of a thin piece of wood glued to a modern board. A recent restoration has eliminated the newer additions on the sides and upper corners, which were designed to make the portrait rectangular, and has thus restored its original shape, with the top corners cut off. No priming coat was applied. The grey background is composed of two coats of the same colour, one on top of the other. The painting surface is well preserved, except along the edges, where the grey background has partly disappeared. There are vertical splits along the grain of the wood.

The young woman is depicted in three-quarters profile, her head slightly to one side. Only her right ear, completely uncovered, is visible; the left is barely indicated. The face is delicate and triangular. The skin is rendered with fine close brushstrokes that follow the curve of the cheeks, nose and forehead. On the first ochre coat increasingly lighter strokes have been added to build volume. The first ochre coat remains visible all along the hairline of the forehead and under the chin. The ridge of the nose and the upper lip are drawn with white highlights. The irises are brown and the pupils black, with impasto to indicate the brilliance of the whites of the eyes. The lashes are drawn individually with brown strokes. The thick eyebrows are rendered with small black and brown strokes.

61

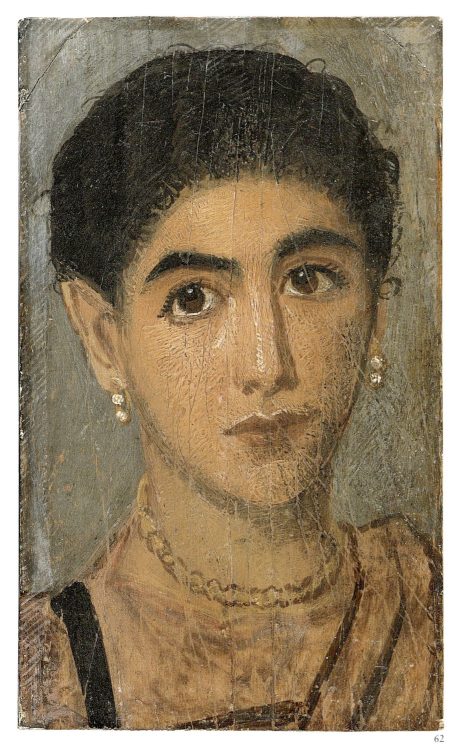

62

The hair is painted black, forming a compact cap from which wispy little curls stand out against the grey background and the forehead. The young woman is wearing hoop earrings with two beads highlighted in pure white, and a necklace composed of a simple chain of yellow and brown links. She is dressed in a pink tunic, decorated with a simple black *clavus*, and a mantle, also pink, placed over her left shoulder, with brown folds extending across the chest. The rapid, fluid treatment of the clothing contrasts with the meticulous detail of the face.

R.C.

BIBLIOGRAPHY

Parlasca I, no. 220, pl. 54.4; Borg 1996, 95–6, 185; Parlasca and Seeman 1999, 346–7 no. 237.

63 Portrait of a woman in encaustic on limewood

AD 200–50

H 30.2 cm, W 18.8 cm

Formerly in the Salt collection

Paris, Musée du Louvre, Département des Antiquités Égyptiennes N 2733 (P 211)

The support is composed of a thin piece of wood glued to a modern board. A recent restoration has eliminated newer additions at the upper corners, which were designed to give a rectangular shape to the portrait; the portrait has thus recovered its original arched shape. There are vertical cracks along the grain of the wood, and zones of wear are visible on the clothing.

The grey background consists of a single coat of paint. The female bust is represented almost frontally. The face is chubby and the chin round and prominent. The eyelashes are painted in single strokes all around the two eyelids, the irises are brown, the pupils are black and the whites of the eyes have white highlights. The thick brows, which meet at the top of the nose, are drawn with crosshatching. The nose has a round and fleshy tip. The modelling of the face is constructed on a reddish brown background to which areas of yellow ochre were applied, and sharpened by yellow hatching.

Two deep wrinkles are drawn in the same way on the forehead. The hair is uniformly black. Curls are represented by black loops that stand out against the grey background all around the head. Small black curls fall over the forehead, accompanied by grey strokes indicating shadows. The woman is wearing earrings made of three beads, and a large necklace with an oval pendant. The white tunic has two purple *clavi*. The mantle covers her left shoulder and falls across the chest in deep folds indicated by rapid brushstrokes. A binder, probably with a wax base, was used on the painting surface, which is very smooth and deposited in thin coats with no impasto. The technique is similar to that normally used for tempera.

R.C.

BIBLIOGRAPHY
Parlasca II, no. 393, pl. 97.1; Borg 1996, 20, 65–6, 98–9, 102–3, 168, 187, pl. 44.2; Parlasca and Seeman 1999, 348–9 no. 238.

64 Portrait of a man with grey hair in encaustic on sycomore wood

About AD 95–105

H 32.5 cm, W 15.4 cm

Unknown provenance; entered Goucher College, Towson, Md (inv. no. 1895.1), with the founder John Franklin Goucher (d. 1907)

Baltimore, Walters Art Gallery TL (temporary loan) 1990. 28.1

The portrait is fragmentary, the right side lost and the upper and lower edges cut as if to follow the area exposed within the mummy wrappings. Three fragments have been joined together, of which the central piece is cracked horizontally and vertically beside the subject's mouth and chin. The other fragments have vertical cracks, and larger areas are missing at the neck, the brow, the crown and the left of the head.

63

The damage indicates the rough removal from the mummy wrappings of a portrait perhaps already damaged on the right side but rightly considered to be of sufficient quality to save. The surviving areas present a finely executed portrait of a mature man with strong features and grey hair. He is dressed in a white tunic, a mantle passing over his left shoulder. The silver-grey hair is painted in impressionistic style on a dark ground. The eyebrows are bushy at the centres; the limpid hazel eyes are highlighted. The face is dominated by the long nose, with a deep fold in the skin beside the proper right nostril. The lower lip is very full, and the neck and brow are wrinkled. The skin is tanned, with a warm glow of peach and pink, and judicious use of white highlights. The man is beardless, but with the shadow of a moustache above his mouth.

The hairstyle and physiognomy of the subject and the finely executed veristic style of the portrait suggest a date around the time of the Emperor Nerva (AD 96–8) or in the early years of the reign of his successor Trajan (AD 98–117).

BIBLIOGRAPHY
Parlasca I, 68 no. 150; Borg 1996, 16, 74, 105, 107.

65 Portrait of a boy in encaustic on limewood, inscribed in Greek with his name 'Eutyches'

About AD 100–50

H 38 cm, W 19 cm

Provenance unknown

New York, The Metropolitan Museum of Art, Gift of Edward S. Harkness, 1918 18.9.2

The upper right edge of the panel is damaged, and there are some vertical fissures in the wood. The panel has been mounted on a wooden board. There has been minor retouching of the painted surface to the right of the proper left ear; the upper and lower margins of the panel are unpainted,

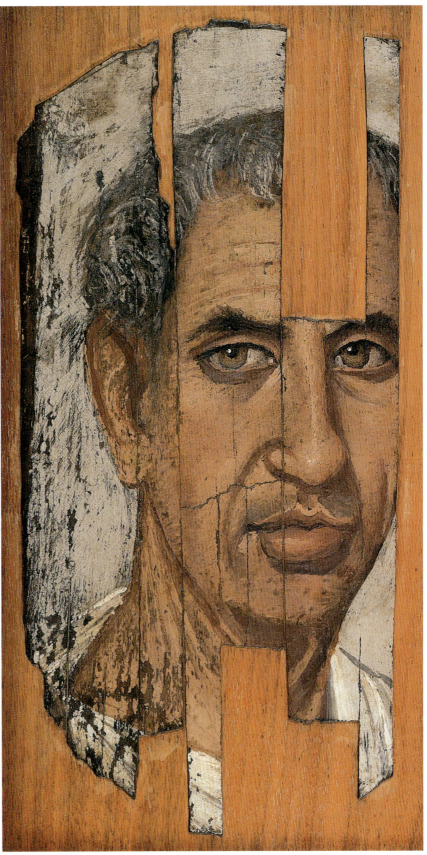

64

and there are marks of mummy bands at the base. The background is painted light olive.

The boy is portrayed in three-quarter left view, his head turned to face the viewer. He is dressed in a white tunic, the folds painted in olive, grey and creamy yellow. Over his right shoulder is a narrow purple *clavus*. A mantle the same colour as the tunic is draped over his left shoulder. The three-line text is written below the neck of the tunic.

The boy's hair, a rich shade of brown, is neatly arranged around his head, with short locks brushed to either side above the centre of the brow. The features are painted naturalistically in thick wax; both flesh and drapery are carefully lit from the left. The face is quite fleshy, and squarish in shape; the skin is tanned a golden brown.

Much debate has ensued on the date of this painting. Parlasca dated it to the Hadrianic period in his corpus, but recent opinion has favoured a Severan date, as did U. Schädler in Parlasca and Seeman 1999, 233 no. 141. The comparisons cited, a marble bust of Elagabulus and a painting of a young soldier from Tanis, now in Oxford (see here no. 73) are not convincing; indeed, the closest comparison for the style of the dress, the proportions of the features within the face, and the lighting of the portrait is offered by a portrait of a boy from Hawara now in Norwich, dated to AD 90–120 (Walker and Bierbrier 1997, no. 31).

The inscription has proved equally controversial. Translated by Parlasca as 'Eutyches, freedman of Cassianus Heraclides', the text was amended by Clarysse in Doxiadis to read 'Eutyches, freedman of Cassianus son of Heraclides'. An alternative reading was proposed by Bagnall and Worp, who saw another name 'Evandros' and the verb 'signed'. According to their reading, the Greek text is as follows:

Εὐτύχης ἀπελ(εύθερος) Κασιανοῦ Ἡρακλειδ( ) Εὐανδ(ρο) σεσημ(είωμαι)

The translation reads: 'Eutyches freedman of Kasianos', then either 'son of Herakleides, Evandros' or 'Herakleides, son of Evandros' followed by 'I signed.'

It is not clear whether the act of signing referred to the manumission of Eutyches, an unexpected reference on a mummy portrait, or to the completion of the portrait. As Borg noted, the verb can also be translated as 'to pay honour to', a sense that could be accommodated in the context of Herakleides or Evandros ordering and paying for the portrait of Eutyches and the accompanying funerary ritual. A second inscription σεσεμ occurs on the back of a first-century portrait from Hawara, now in Berlin (no. 7). In an addition to a footnote in a recent paper by the late Jan Quaegebeur, Professor Willy Clarysse notes that the text on the portrait of Eutyches and that on a mummy label in the Louvre collections that appears to be related to the portrait (no. 65A) probably both originate from Philadelphia in the Fayum and are of second-century date.

BIBLIOGRAPHY

Parlasca, *Mumienporträts*, 61, 80 no. 8 pl. 29.3; Parlasca I, 72 no. 167 pl. 40,2; R. S. Bagnall and K. A. Worp, *Bulletin of the Egyptological Seminar* 3 (1981) 23–4; D. Montserrat, *JEA* 79 (1993), 215–16; Doxiadis 1995, 32, 37, 126, 192, pl. 30; Borg 1996, 12, 84, 92, 151, 154, pl. 86.3; J. Quaegebeur in Bierbrier, *Portraits and Masks*, 72–3 with n. 17, 75–6; Borg 1998, 40, 48, 54, 61, fig. 60.

65A Mummy label in the name of Eutycheion, written in ink on wood

Second century AD

H 4 cm, L 12.6 cm, D 1.1 cm

Provenance unknown

Paris, Museé du Louvre, Departement des Antiquités Égyptiennes, AF 12541

This mummy label has the customary shape of a rectangle whose two left corners have been worn away; a hole was made in the left margin, which allowed the label to be attached to the corpse. The lower part has disappeared but, given the module of letters, there was probably no loss of text. The three lines were written in black ink, in careful handwriting characteristic of the second century AD. Εὐτυχείων | θρεπτὸς | Κασιανῶ (Κασιανου) ('Eutycheion, "adopted son" of Kasianos').

The name 'Eutycheion' is not found elsewhere in Egypt, except perhaps in the form 'Eutychion' on another label in the Louvre (Boyaval, 1976, no. 1405), dating to the third to fourth centuries AD; it is, however, very well attested throughout the Greek region, particularly in Asia Minor. The name 'Kasianos', which corresponds to the Latin 'Casianus', is abundantly represented in the papyrological and epigraphic documentation of Egypt, principally in the second and third centuries AD.

The parallels offered by papyri and inscriptions suggest that *threptos*, 'adopted son', more specifically means a 'slave reared in the house' (see A. Cameron's essay in *Anatolian Studies Presented to W. H. Buckler* [Manchester, 1939], pp. 45–84).

J. Quaegebeur (in Boswinkel and Pestman 1978, 239) was the first to link this label to a portrait in The Metropolitan Museum of Art representing a young boy (no. 65), with an inscription telling us he was 'Eutyches freed [*apeleutheros*] by Kasianos'. The Belgian scholar proposed that Eutycheion and Eutyches were a slave and a former slave, respectively, of the same Kasianos, and that they may have been buried together. The date suggested for this portrait would not contradict the association.

On the basis of Quaegebeur's study Boyaval has gone a step further (1979, 225–6); he proposes that the two names refer to a single individual. He does not believe that the differences between the two title-holders present any obstacle, and to respond to the difference in the ending of the two names, he counters with the example of another label (Boyaval, 1976, no. 145), where the name of the deceased is written 'Kolanthos' on one side and 'Kolanthes' on the other. As for the

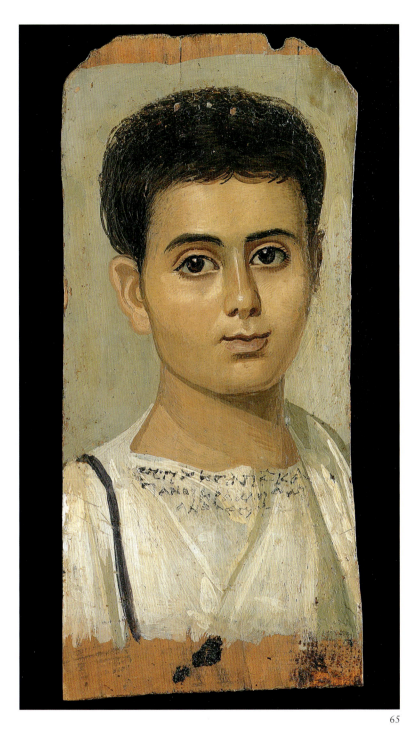

65

other titles of the dead man, *apeleutheros* defines his legal status at the time of his death, while *threptos*, an affectionate and therefore less precise designation, might very well apply to a slave brought up in the house who had been freed before his death.

In the absence of other evidence, the validity of that hypothesis cannot be determined. One would also have to explain why the mummy was accompanied by a label that contained no more information than the inscription on the portrait fitted into its bandages. It is a pointless duplication, of which no other examples are known. Normally, when there is a label as well as an inscription on a mummy, it is because the label gave the place where the body was to be sent, which was not specified on the inscription on the shroud or portrait, as in the case of Diogenes at Hawara (Boswinkel and Pestman 1978, 229–30). Are we to think that, during the transport of the mummy, the portrait was protected to avoid any possible damage, which made the information inscribed on it inaccessible, and that this information was then reproduced on a label that was left visible?

J.-L.F.

BIBLIOGRAPHY

F. Baratte and B. Boyaval, 'Catalogue des étiquettes de momies du Musée du Louvre', *Cahiers de Recherches de l'Institut de Papyrologie et d'Égyptologie de Lille* 3 (1975), 206 no. 465; B. Boyaval, *Corpus des étiquettes de momies grecques* (Lille 1976), 70 no. 892; E. Boswinkel and P. W. Pestman, eds, *Textes grecs, démotiques et bilingues*, Papyrologica Lugduno-Batava (Leiden 1978), 239; B. Boyaval, 'CEML 465', *Zeitschrift für Papyrologie und Epigraphik* 33 (1979), 225–6; B. Boyaval, 'Le transport des momies et ses problèmes', in F. Hinard, ed., *La mort au quotidien dans le monde romain* (Paris 1995), 109–15 (esp. 111).

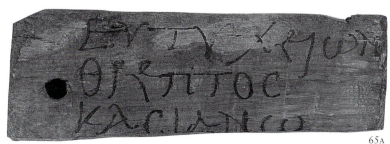

65A

66 Portrait of a young woman with a gold wreath, in encaustic on limewood

About AD 90–120

H 41.3 cm, W 21.5 cm

Acquired in Cairo in 1909 from the dealer M. Nahman

New York, The Metropolitan Museum of Art, Rogers Fund, 1909 09. 181.6

The painting, apparently executed on a very thin panel of wood, has been mounted on a back panel. The three major vertical fissures have been filled. A little paint has been lost from the background, but generally the portrait is remarkably well preserved. The panel is not painted at the upper and lower edges; indeed, the unpainted lower margin is substantial, indicating that the painting was intended for no other purpose but insertion in the mummy wrappings, as Barbara Borg has observed (1996, 192). Traces of gold remain on the dull grey background, showing that gilding was applied after insertion, as on the other paintings in this group.

The woman wears a dark red tunic with a black *clavus* curving over her right breast, and a mantle of similar hue. In her hair is a simple diadem of gold leaves without a stem. Her hoop earrings strung with pearls were also gilded, as probably too was her chain necklace, which is painted a very dull ochre.

The woman wears her hair in a mass of loose curls piled high on the crown of the head and extending down the back of the neck on her left side. The heart-shaped face, of great beauty, is brilliantly lit, the neck left dark. The lightly arched eyebrows and long eyelashes are painted in impressionistic strokes, giving energy to an otherwise calm, gentle expression. The skin tone is cream, warmed with reds and yellows at the edges of the face. The nose is long and slender and the mouth full, with a dimple below the lower lip.

On the grounds of its association with other portraits said to be from Achmim and acquired through Nahman, this painting has been

66

66

dated to the mid-second century AD. However, Parlasca admitted difficulty in finding comparable hairstyles, and it is perhaps better considered Flavian or early second century in date. A date in the late first or very early second century would be appropriate both for the jewellery, and the colour and style of the dress. The portrait, especially in its hair-style but also in its capture of a sense of youthful exuberance, echoes the coquettish appearance of some portraits in stone and bronze of Flavian women.

BIBLIOGRAPHY
Parlasca II, 43–4 no. 308 (bibl.); Berger and Creux 1977, 216; P. Dorman, *Egypt and the Ancient Near East in the Metropolitan Museum of Art* (1987), 86–7; Doxiadis 1995, 153–4 with pl. 97; Borg 1996, 192.

67 Portrait of an elderly woman with a gold wreath in encaustic on limewood

About AD 100–25

H 36.5 cm, W 19.7 cm

Acquired in Cairo in 1909 from the dealer Nahman

New York, The Metropolitan Museum of Art, Rogers Fund, 1909 09.181.5

The thin panel has been mounted on a wooden board. There are three large vertical fissures; the left side and upper edge are broken in places. The panel is left unpainted at the upper and lower edges. The grey background has been gilded; traces of a line of gilding across the chest represent the extent of the mummy wrappings, and show that the gilding was applied after the panel had been inserted in the mummy wrappings.

The woman is turned slightly to her right. She wears a reddish tunic, shaded in violet and decorated with a broad black *clavus*, and a violet mantle. In her hair is a simple wreath of gilded leaves (with no stem). Her hoop earrings are also gilded, and are threaded with two pearls interspersed by a small black bead. Like other elderly women represented in the corpus of mummy portraits, the woman wears no other jewellery.

The woman's hair is grey, and painted in loose curls which are quite unrelated to imperial court fashions. Her skin, especially on the neck, is rendered in very dark tones of terracotta shaded with grey. Her face is strong and bony, with wrinkled brow, arched eyebrows, a long hooked nose and deep lines running to either side of the large mouth. The deep-set hooded eyes are painted with grey highlights; one eyelid falls lower than the other.

Recently an Antonine date has been proposed for this portrait, but the facial physiognomy and the style of the hair echo male portraits of the Trajanic period (for instance no. 11). The form of the earrings, and the colour and style of the tunic and mantle may be compared with other early second-century paintings: indeed, the colour of her tunic and

67

the style of the painted *clavus* is very similar to no. 66, here dated to the late Flavian period. The portrait is of some interest in its rendering of a woman of advanced age as strong, with masculine features, her sex nonetheless clearly signalled by her clothes and jewellery.

BIBLIOGRAPHY

Bulletin of the Metropolitan Museum of Art V (1910), 56, 71 fig. 7; Parlasca, *Mumienporträts*, 42, nn. 172 and 175, pl. 27.1; Berger and Creux 1977, 216, fig. 4; Parlasca II, 44 no. 310 pl. 73.3; Doxiadis 154, pl. 95; Borg 1996, 160, 186, 192; Parlasca and Seeman 1999, 339 no. 233.

68 Portrait of a young woman with a gilded wreath

About AD 120–40

H 39 cm, W (base) 19 cm

Said to be from the Fayum

New York, The Metropolitan Museum of Art, Rogers Fund, 1909 09.181.7

The wafer-thin panel has been mounted on a wooden board. Four vertical fissures and minor cuts have been filled. There is considerable loss of paint in the hair and around the earrings. The panel is not painted beyond the margins exposed on the mummy; traces of varnish from the wrappings appear at the lower left corner of the painting.

The background is covered in gold leaf. This is also used for a simple wreath of leaves, with no band, and for the second necklace, a band with suspended lunate pendant. The gold background is continued around the base of the painted area to frame the portrait.

The subject is a young woman dressed in a dark cyclamen tunic and mantle, somewhat crudely shaded with dark purple paint strokes. Her black hair is tightly wound into plaits at the crown of the head. Around the brow are corkscrew locks. She wears hoop earrings threaded with pearls, and, above the gilded band, a necklace of long emerald beads interspersed with large pearls.

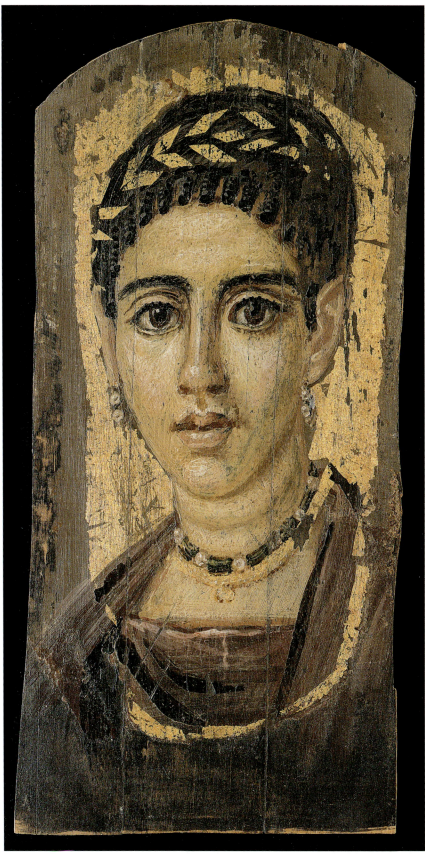

68

The skin is thickly painted in cream, much heightened with pink on the cheeks, nose and around the eyes. As Doxiadis notes, the shades are built up from a dark ground, in a technique later used by painters of Byzantine icons, to which this portrait bears some resemblance. The eyebrows are long and barely curved, the eyes round with thick upper lashes, the nose long and straight and the thick lips almost closed. The use of highlights on the nose, proper left ear and around the mouth and chin is particularly skilled. The cheeks are full, and the neck plump, with Venus rings.

A date for this portrait in the reign of the Emperor Hadrian is suggested by the hairstyle, which appears on a number of portraits of late Trajanic to early Antonine date (Borg 1996, 44ff). The corkscrew locks are a local or individual variation. The jewellery is compatible with a Hadrianic date, as are the style and colour of the tunic and mantle.

BIBLIOGRAPHY
Bulletin of the Metropolitan Museum of Art V (1910), 56, 70, fig. 6; Parlasca, *Mumienporträts*, 42 nn. 172 and 177, 135, pl. 27 (2); Parlasca II, no. 309; Berger and Creux 1977, 216, fig. 5; Doxiadis 153–4, pl. 96 and p. 218; Borg 1996, 44ff, 186.

69 Portrait of a thin-faced man with strands of hair falling on his brow, in encaustic on limewood

About AD 140–70

H 42 cm, W 19 cm

Acquired from the dealer Nahman in Cairo in 1909

New York, The Metropolitan Museum of Art, Rogers Fund, 1909 09.181.3

The painting, which has several vertical cracks, has been mounted on a wooden board. The right side is broken off at the level of the lower earlobe. The lower edge of the panel is unpainted. Traces of the mummy wrappings obscure the drapery below the neck. The grey background is

69

gilded to the edge of the area exposed on the mummy, and was thus applied after the panel had been inserted in the wrappings.

The subject is a man dressed in a white tunic and mantle, both heavily shaded with grey, the mantle draped high on the neck. His receding dishevelled hair falls in strands onto his brow. On his head is a wreath of gilded leaves, displaced on his right side and without a stem.

The man is very thin, with bulging brow, slightly open mouth and eyes staring almost in surprise beneath short bushy eyebrows. Below the eyes bags of flesh are suggested with streaks of pink paint, feathered below his right eye. Pink is also used on the brow and to highlight the area beside the nostrils. He has a full moustache and quite a thick beard, through which his chin is barely visible. The thick lips are painted red, and the face is thrown into relief by the dark skin on the neck.

An Antonine date is suggested by the length of the face and the form of the beard. This appears to be the latest of the gilded portraits acquired from Nahman.

BIBLIOGRAPHY

Bulletin of the Metropolitan Museum of Art V (1910), 56, 70, fig. 6; Seymour de Ricci, *CRAI* 1908 802, fig. 3; A. Strlkov, *Fajumski portret* (Moscow-Leningrad 1936) 84, fig. 5; Parlasca, *Mumienporträts*, 41 n. 172, 42, n. 177, pl. 2 [4]; Parlasca II, no. 311; Berger and Creux 1977, 216; *Bulletin of the Metropolitan Museum of Art* Winter 1983/4, 55, pl. 55; P. Dorman, *Egypt and the Ancient Near East in the Metropolitan Museum of Art*, N.Y. (1987), 87; Doxiadis 1995, 153–4, 219 with pl. 98; Borg 1996, 186 n. 25

70 Portrait of a man with a mole on his nose, in encaustic on limewood

(illustrated with no. 71 overleaf)

About AD 130–50

H 41.8 cm, W 21 cm

Acquired in Cairo through the dealer Nahman in 1909

New York, The Metropolitan Museum of Art, Rogers Fund, 1909 09.181.2

The panel, mounted on a wooden board, has split into thin strips, giving an irregular appearance to the upper edge. There is some paint loss, but generally the condition of the painting is very good. The upper and lower edges of the panel were left unpainted, and traces of the mummy wrappings survive in the centre of the lower edge. The grey background is arched over the head.

The subject, a thin-faced mature man with a long moustache and thin beard, is turned from a three-quarters-right pose to face the viewer. He is dressed in a thick white tunic and mantle, both heavily shaded with grey to give the impression of thick cloth. On his left shoulder just below the mantle a thin pink *clavus* is visible. His curly black hair is cropped quite close to the head, and recedes slightly at the temples. It forms a straggly beard around the jaw, fuller beneath the chin, with a full moustache above the mouth, and slight growth below.

The subject's gaze is arresting, an effect achieved by highlighting the enormous brown eyes, of which the upper and lower lids are further emphasised with pink paint. Pink is also used to shade the long nose, which, unusually, has a mole or wart above the proper right nostril. The tone of the skin on the face is a warm peach, lit on the brow, nose and above the prominent cheekbones with white, and contrasting with the neck, which is painted a ruddy terracotta.

This painting is very similar in the shape of the panel and the colour palette employed by the artist to no. 7, a young man with a hairstyle

recalling the Emperor Lucius Verus. Here, the drapery is more naturalistically shown. The hairstyle and beard seem more typical of Hadrianic and early Antonine portraits, and have rightly been compared with the features of an unprovenanced portrait now in Chicago (Parlasca II, no. 373, and Borg 1996, 186 with pl. 24).

BIBLIOGRAPHY

Parlasca, *Mumienporträts*, 41–2; Parlasca II, 45 no. 312 (bibl.), pl. 74.1; Doxiadis 1995, 153–5, 219 with fig. 97; Borg 1996, 79, 186; Parlasca and Seeman 1999, 339 no. 232 (bibl.).

71 Portrait of a thin-faced bearded man in encaustic on limewood

About AD 160–80

H 40 cm, W 22.4 cm

Acquired in Cairo in 1909 from the dealer Nahman

New York, The Metropolitan Museum of Art, Rogers Fund, 1909 09.181.1

The broken upper edge and any other cracks have been consolidated and the painting mounted on a wooden board. The lower margin of the panel is unpainted. There are traces of the mummy wrappings at the right side, the upper left corner and below the painted area in the centre of the panel. The background is a bluish grey; the upper right corner of the panel is unpainted, showing that the background was arched over the head.

The subject of this portrait, a work of outstanding quality, is a man mature but not advanced in years, dressed in a white tunic with a narrow pink *clavus*. His white mantle, worn over the proper left shoulder, is indicated with vertical lines (compare no. 21).

The bushy black hair stands far out from the head, emphasising with the thick beard the emaciated form of the subject. The rounded eyes are wide-set beneath lightly arched brows. The nose is straight and prominent over a thick moustache; the lips too are thick. The manipu-

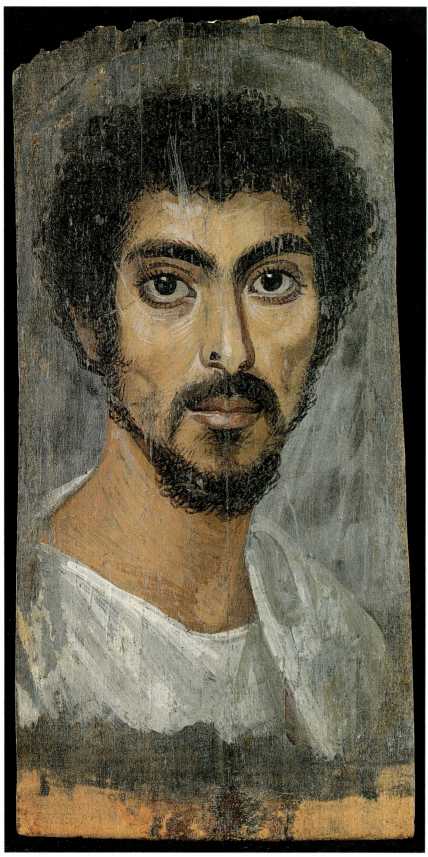

71

lation of light and shadow in this painting is highly skilled. The nose is highlighted in white, with lighter pink areas around the other features. In contrast, the neck is painted a ruddy pinkish brown.

Though very similar to no. 70, the style of the hair and beard suggests a slightly later date, in the reign of Lucius Verus (AD 161–9).

BIBLIOGRAPHY

Parlasca, *Mumienporträts*, 41–2; Parlasca II, 45 no. 313, pl. 74.2; Doxiadis 1995, 153–4, 163 pl. 99, 219; Borg 1996, 79, 166 n. 119 (drapery), 186; Parlasca and Seeman 1999, 337 no. 231 (bibl.).

72 Portrait of a bearded young man in tempera on a linen shroud

About AD 120–50

Preserved H 96 cm, W 67.8 cm

Acquired in Cairo in 1908 from the dealer Nahman

New York, The Metropolitan Museum of Art, Rogers Fund, 1909 08.202.8

The shroud is broken all around; the top was decorated with a winged sun-disc, of which the remains of feathers survive in the upper left corner. Ladders of vignettes have been lost from the sides (only one is partially preserved on the left side of the shroud, showing a dark-skinned deity with a blue crown and pink collar, the proper left arm outstretched). The original width was about 90 cm; the portrait is life-sized, and the height of the shroud must have come close to 2 m with upper and lower borders. A second fragment of this shroud, wrongly joined to the major piece, has been removed. This comprises a part of the lower tunic with two narrow violet *clavi*. There is considerable paint loss in the centre of the large fragment and at the sides. There are several holes in the shroud and an ancient patch has been sewn to the shroud just below the subject's right shoulder.

Above the portrait is an unpainted area with a strip of hieroglyphic text painted in black on yellow ochre, the latter simulating gold. The hieroglyphs have been translated as follows: 'The Bahdetite, great god, lord of heaven, he of the variegated plumage, who goes forth in the horizon, foremost (in) the two shrines of upper Egypt in…'

The portrait is set against a dark grey background, the area immediately around the head painted a lighter grey. The subject is a young man with curly black hair, a thin beard and faint moustache above and below the lips. His eyebrows are lightly arched, the brown eyes large and rounded, the nose long and hooked, the smallish pink lips closed. The skin is painted pink, with lighter highlights on the nose, brow and cheeks.

The young man wears a white tunic and mantle with the folds indicated in green. The mantle is drawn up from the subject's right hip over his left shoulder, where a thick

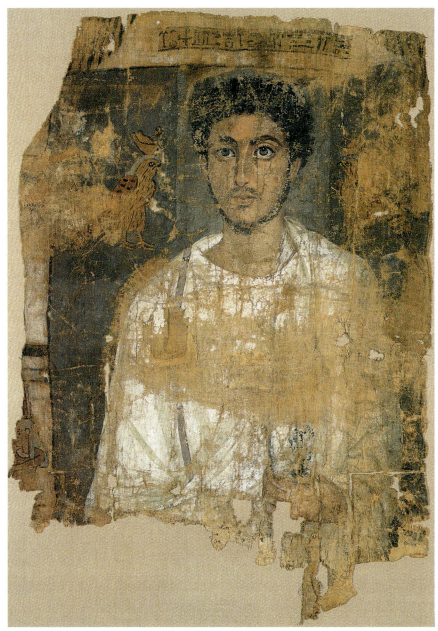

band of cloth may still be seen. The lilac *clavi* are thin, the shoulder seams painted as white dots. Beneath his left shoulder may be seen a fringed undergarment in pinkish white. In his left hand the young man holds a bunch of foliage, perhaps myrtle rather than a rose-petal garland as no trace of pink paint remains.

To either side of the young man's head are falcons bearing the crown of upper and lower Egypt.

The portrait has recently been dated from the hairstyle and beard to the Hadrianic/early Antonine period. Some resemblance can be seen with a double-sided portrait of a man, excavated at Hawara and now in Manchester (Doxiadis pl. 35: late Trajanic/Hadrianic), and with another Hawara portrait of a beard-less youth (no. 14: late Flavian/ Trajanic). The faint moustache indicates the subject's youth, and the beard could be his first (compare Berlin 13277, shroud of Dion). The manner of draping the mantle is seen on sculptured portraits of second-century date.

BIBLIOGRAPHY

Parlasca, *Mumienporträts*, 184–5 (Severan); Parlasca 1, 84 no. 216 (early Antonine); Corcoran 12, no. 5; Parlasca and Seeman 1999, 227 no. 136 (bibl.).

73 Portrait of a youth with a surgical cut in one eye, in encaustic on limewood

About AD 190–210

H 35.9 cm, W 18.8 cm

Acquired from the dealer Nahman in Cairo in 1909

NewYork, The Metropolitan Museum of Art, Rogers Fund, 1909 09.181.4

The painting has been mounted on a wooden board. Around the irregu-larly arched upper edge of the ancient panel the wood has split into narrow strips. The lower edge of the panel is slightly damaged, but in other respects the painting is in good condition. The background is painted a warm mushroom grey, and there are traces of the mummy wrappings

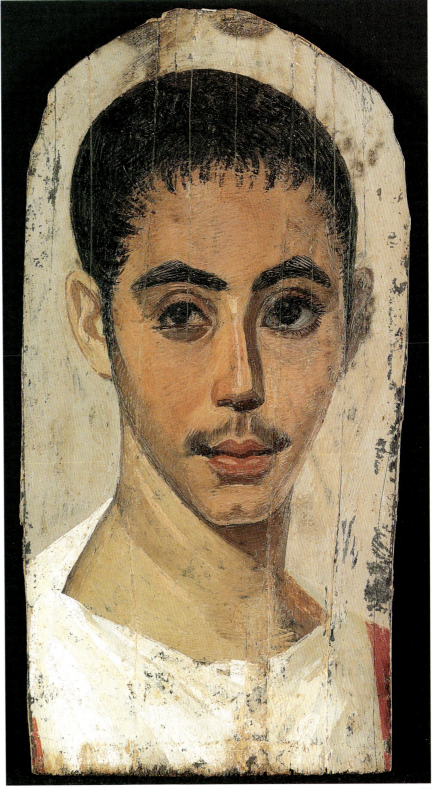

73

at the sides of the panel and over the youth's clothing.

The youth is dressed in a creamy white tunic with olive and yellow ochre shading respectively on his left shoulder and on the underside of the tunic. The *clavi* are bright magenta. He wears no mantle. His hair is brushed across the crown of his head, not unlike that of several youths painted in tempera (e.g. nos 45, 46), but here individual strands fall onto the high brow. A downy moustache is painted over the thick pink lips. Most remarkably, the youth's right eye appears to have been cut across the lower edge, the lower lid painted as a greyish fold of skin with no lashes. The regular cut appears to be the result of surgery. Although in the foreground of the painting, the youth's right cheek is less fleshy than his left, suggesting a congenital lesion for which surgery would have improved vision and facial appearance. The other eye, in contrast, is round and very large, with long lashes. The nose is very long, with a highlight on the left side. The cheekbones are very prominent and the jaw narrow. The neck, shaded under the chin in the conventional terracotta, is painted olive on the left side with pink highlights. Evidently the painter was interested in recording the exact age of the subject, shown by the faint moustache and perhaps too by the strands growing out of a haircut given to younger boys (see nos 45 and 46).

Much discussion has been engendered by the date of this painting. Most recently it has been pushed as late as the reign of Gallienus (AD 253–67), but this view does not accord with the style of dress affected by the subject. Borg has dated the portrait well into the third century on the grounds of the similarity of the hairstyle to the portraits of Alexander Severus (AD 222–35). However, the style has strong local overtones, with strands of hair falling onto the brow in a manner not seen on metropolitan Roman portraits; it compares well with the portrait of a youth

excavated by Grenfell and Hunt at Tanis, now in the Ashmolean Museum, Oxford (Parlasca III, no. 469; Borg 1996, pl. 40,1). This too has been dated to the late Severan period, but the style of the clothing of both portraits suggests a late Antonine or early Severan date: that of the New York portrait may be compared with the painting of a bearded man named Sarapas found by Petrie at Hawara (Cairo CG 33259).

This painting differs considerably from the other panels purchased for the Metropolitan Museum from Nahman. The panel is smaller, with a more pronounced arch, and no areas are left unpainted. The colour palette is much brighter than that used for the two bearded men (nos 70 and 71), and there is no gilding. The comparable paintings are both from the Fayum, and an origin in the Fayum for the painting now in New York should also be considered.

BIBLIOGRAPHY
Bulletin of the Metropolitan Museum of Art V (1910), 56, 68 fig. 4; M. H. Swindler, *Ancient Painting from the Earliest Period of Christian Art* (New Haven and London 1929), 319 ff, fig.513; MMA. *A Handbook of the Egyptian Rooms* 1911–22, fig. 59 (left); Drerup 1933, 42, 61 n. 24, pl. 15a; V. Müllerin, *Cronaca d'Arte* 5 (1940), 74, pl. 24; M. Cagiano d'Azevedo, *EAA* III (1960) 332 s.v. 'encausto' with figs 403–4; Parlasca, *Mumienporträts*, 42 n. 172, 132, 253; Berger and Creux 1977, 216; Parlasca II, 85 no. 470, pl. 114.2; Parlasca, *El-Fayyum* (1985), 110 (for revised date of c. AD 160); Doxiadis 1995, 153, fig. 56 p. 219; Borg 1996, 84, 161; Borg 1998, 26, fig. 30; Parlasca and Seeman 1999, 342–3 no. 235.

74 Fragmentary portrait of a man in tempera on a linen shroud

AD 300–400

H 59 cm, W 44 cm

Provenance unknown

Paris, Musée du Louvre, Département des Antiquités Égyptiennes N 3408

Painted on very fine linen, the man is dressed in an immaculate tunic decorated with a purple band, which is set off by two white lines. The drawing of the hands, with the nails indicated by a red stroke, is unusually elegant. The right hand is holding a glass, whose top is painted as a dark oval with a white stroke circling it, in an attempt to render its volume. Its transparency is indicated by the pinkish tint of the wine with a zone of blue and white hatching above it. The left hand, emerging from the fringed sleeve, is wearing two gold signet rings, one on the first joint of the index finger, the other on the first joint of the little finger. (Heavy gold signet rings adorned with cartouches were found in the same position on the gold-plated fingerstalls on Tutankhamun's left hand.) The left hand holds the garland of roses of the deceased favourably judged by Osiris, with a myrtle branch and a *volumen* (scroll) made of papyrus or parchment. It is rolled around an *ombilicus*, a wood or bone cylinder, whose 'horned' ends, extending beyond the *volumen*, have been gilded. The *ombilicus* was glued onto the last sheet of the scroll to make it stiff. Magical formulas might have been inscribed on this *volumen* to ensure immortality or, in accordance with the Roman fashion, to signify that the deceased was a poet or writer.

The chalice shape of the glass is unusual and dates to the end of the fourth century AD. The wine that it contains – a potion of immortality – identifies the deceased with Dionysus-Osiris. A painting found in Herculaneum and housed in the Naples Museum depicts a bust of Dionysus, accompanied by a Maenad and holding a *kantharos* filled with

74

75 Full-length portrait of a boy in tempera on a linen shroud wrapped around his mummy and placed in a painted wooden coffin

About AD 230–50

Mummy H 85 cm, W *c*.21.5 cm, TH 18.5 cm; coffin L 95.5 cm, W *c*.32 cm

Provenance unknown

Formerly in the third collection of Henry Salt; acquired in 1835

British Museum EA 6715

There are some patches of discolouration, but otherwise the shroud is well preserved. The boy is frontally portrayed, his right hand raised with palm out-turned, his left holding a branch of myrtle. He wears a white tunic and mantle, the folds indicated in sandy yellow. The mantle is drawn across the chest in the band of folds (*contabulatio*) popular in the third century AD. The trapezoidal neckline is also characteristic of later portraits; the pink above it is probably intended for flesh rather than an undertunic. On his feet the boy wears white slippers with a black sole and heel and a thick strap around the ankle.

On the crown of his head the boy wears a wreath of rosebuds. His hair has been shaved, the outline preserved in reddish pink in a cut typical of the second quarter of the third century AD, with four tufts of black hair left above the brow (compare no. 109). The eyebrows are black and bushy, the large brown eyes deeply hooded, the nose long and the lips small. The ears are low-set and project at an angle from the head. The flesh tones are predominantly pink, with ochre and cream.

As with many of the panel portraits, the background is grey but here is bordered with two wine-red bands, framing a central band of brick-red ground. This is decorated with a loosely intertwined grey and wine-coloured cable interspersed with cream flowers. The inner wine band, edged in white, is painted with

wine. In fact, Dionysus was the patron of artists and poets, who were grouped together in a single category. That iconography became very common at the end of the third century AD and throughout the fourth century: see, for example, the so-called portrait of Ammonios (housed in the Louvre Museum) and the casing covering mummies from Deir el-Bahri (see no. 98).

M.-F. A.

Unpublished

EDITOR'S NOTE
This fragment has been placed with third-century works as the dress does not appear typical of fourth-century fashions as seen on nos 98 and 99. Closely comparable dress is shown on a stone relief from Oxyrhyncus (Parlasca and Seeman 1999, 327 no. 224).

cream leaves; the outer band is undecorated.

The mummy rests in a shallow wooden coffin set on two battens. C.A.T. scans of the mummy suggest an age at death of eight to ten years. The interior of the coffin is painted in black and pink with a chain-like garland and a representation of a goddess, probably Nut, painted full-face.

BIBLIOGRAPHY

Dawson and Gray 37 n. 70 pl. 18d; Parlasca II, 71 no. 413 (bibl.), pl. 102, 3; Doxiadis 1995, 95, 225 no. 36; J. Filer, 'If the Face Fits…', in Bierbrier, *Portraits and Masks*, 123, pl. 45, 3, 4; Borg 1996, 160, 165, pl. 87, 2; Borg 1998, 50 fig. 62.

76 Portrait of an elderly bearded man in tempera on sycomore fig wood

About AD 250

H 38 cm, W 22.5 cm, TH 2 cm

Unknown provenance; acquired in 1944 from the collection of A. Gallatin

New York, The Metropolitan Museum of Art, Rogers Fund, 1944 44.2.2

The panel is almost bell-shaped, curving around the head and shoulders. It is pierced with five holes, one at the centre of the top, two at each side and two at the base. These, larger than the nail-holes found in encaustic panels (e.g. no. 21), indicate that this panel, much thicker than those designed for insertion, was intended to be tied to a mummy or coffin, rather than inserted within the wrappings. Indeed, the shape roughly reflects that of a wrapped mummy or cartonnage coffin, and the spread of the portrait over the entire width and almost the full height of the panel indicates that it was never intended for insertion. The surface of the painting is damaged below the proper left shoulder, and in a long crack, now filled, running from the neck to the centre of the base of the panel.

The subject is an elderly man dressed in a voluminous tunic with

75

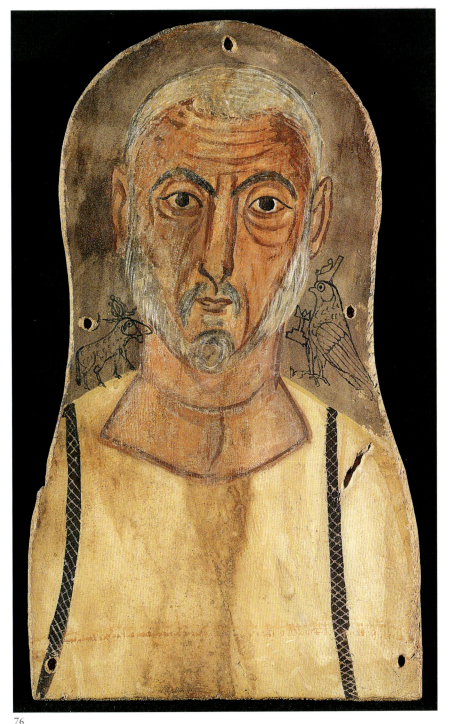

76

narrow *clavi* of rather irregular form, decorated with a white net pattern on a dark brown ground. The tunic itself is off-white, the splayed neckline drawn in reddish pink, a colour also used to delineate his features; there is no sign of an undertunic.

The man has straight greyish-white hair, receding at the temples with a tuft remaining above the centre of the brow. His skin, well tanned on the face, is heavily wrinkled on the brow, with prominent bags below the eyes and deep lines beside the mouth. The eyebrows are strongly arched, the almond-shaped eyes relatively small, the pupils undifferentiated and lacking highlights. The nose is narrow, very straight and long; the mouth small, with thin, pink lips, above which hangs a pair of moustaches. The beard is worn quite long at the sides of the jaw, but clipped round on the chin, leaving an area of skin exposed. In contrast to the face, the neck is painted in pink tones.

On the man's right shoulder is sketched in black outline a ram wearing an *atef*-crown; above his left shoulder is the falcon-god Horus before a horned altar, wearing the crowns of Upper and Lower Egypt. The significance of the deities has been discussed by Borg (1996, 127–8).

A mid-third-century date is suggested by the hairstyle, clothing and frontal pose. As has been observed by U. Schädler in Parlasca and Seeman 1999, 239, the portrait is close to that of the Emperor Trajan Decius (AD 249–51). Borg notes that the panel is not comparable to others in the surviving corpus, and may therefore have originated in an otherwise unexplored cemetery.

BIBLIOGRAPHY

Parlasca, *Mumienporträts*, 69, 126 n. 14, pl. 28,3; Parlasca II, 79, no. 444, pl. 109.1; Borg 1996, 127–8, 149, 192; Borg in Bierbrier, *Portraits and Masks*, 27 n. 18; Borg 1998, 74; Parlasca and Seeman 1999, 239 no. 147.

PORTRAITS OF TECHNICAL INTEREST

This short section is devoted to two unusual paintings which illustrate technical aspects of the commissioning and painting of portraits. Of exceptional interest is the panel from Tebtunis (no. 77) with a sketched portrait accompanied by instructions written in Greek for the artist. The finished version may be represented in another panel from the same site (the latter is not exhibited). The sketch is sufficiently detailed to suggest a date within the middle years of the second century AD. The section also includes a commemorative portrait of a girl named Tekosis (no. 78), painted on panels of wood joined by pegs.

77 Sketch portrait of a woman on wood, perhaps sycomore fig, with instructions for the artist in Greek

About AD 140–60

H 36 cm, W 24 cm

Excavated in cemetery VII or VIII at Tebtunis by B. P. Grenfell and A. S. Hunt in 1899–1900

Given by Mrs Phoebe Hearst

Berkeley, University of California, Phoebe Apperson Hearst Museum of Anthropology 6/21378b

77 (6/21378a)

77 (6/21378b)

The panel is damaged by insects at the top, and is broken through the right side. In antiquity it was used on both sides (a, b). Sketched in black ink on one side is a woman in almost frontal pose, dressed in a tunic with a mantle over the proper left shoulder, with a line around the base of the neck evidently representing a necklace. The hair is dressed with a central parting and a high chignon in Antonine fashion (compare the Cyrenaican marble bust in Walker and Bierbrier 1997 no. 264). The eyes, nose and mouth are carefully drawn; the eyes very large, with arched eyebrows; the nose long; the mouth small, with a cleft below; and the face round with a straight thick neck.

To the left of the neck is written, in the same ink as the drawing, the word πορφύ|ρα (purple), perhaps a reference to the colour of the *clavus* that appears on her right shoulder.

The text above is illegible. Above her left shoulder is written, ἀλύσιον ἔχαι ὂιά|χληρον ('she wears a green necklace', the qualifying word ὂιά meaning either completely or interspersed with 'green'. Above, a less legible inscription concerns the eyes, τοὺς|ὀφθαλ|μούς, with which the instruction ends. To the right of the chignon appears the word παχή (thick) with an illegible line below. In the upper left corner of the painting is written χρῶρα δύο, apparently a reference to two colours.

From the very clear details of the hairstyle, the sketch is unquestionably Antonine. Recent archival research (Bierbrier 1997) has shown that eleven portraits from Grenfell and Hunt's excavations in cemetery VII and VIII at Tebtunis are to be identified with those in the Phoebe Hearst Museum (as indeed is clear from the museum records, but the portraits were mistakenly identified

by Parlasca as originating from various Fayum sites). Now that their context is clear, a visual assessment of the group may be made. On grounds of similarity of physiognomy and hairstyle, it is suggested here that this sketch is for Phoebe Hearst Museum 6–21375 (illustrated below) and that the painting on the reverse could be a preliminary version of a portrait of a woman named Thau(b)arion, Phoebe Hearst Museum 5/21376 (Parlasca 433), illustrated in an archival photograph by Bierbrier 1997, pl.19,1. Both finished paintings are apparently in encaustic and appear to be of superior quality to the other members of the Tebtunis group. It could, however, be the case that the preliminary painting on the reverse was replaced or rejected because of the poor quality of the wood; traces of primer, gesso and colours surviving on it along with residue of resin used in mummification show that it was actually used before being discarded. Alternatively, 6/21378a and 5/21376 may be by the same artist, perhaps representing members of one family.

BIBLIOGRAPHY
Parlasca II, 76–7 no. 432 (bibl.); Doxiadis 1995, 89 no. 31; M. L. Bierbrier, 'Fayum Cemeteries and their Portraits', in Bierbrier, *Portraits and Masks*, 16.

Phoebe Apperson Hearst Museum 6–21375

78 Portrait of Tekosis, daughter of Harunis, in tempera on two dowelled cedarwood panels

About AD 180–200

H 25 cm, W 33 cm, TH 2 cm

Brought from Egypt in 1909 by Walter Dennison, who purchased the painting from the dealer Nahman; said to come from near Assyut (Lycopolis)

Swarthmore College, Dennison 375

Two panels of this painting are preserved, with considerable loss of paint, especially to the background. The upper right corner appears to have been charred. It is clear from the back and lower edge of the

78

painting that a third panel was originally joined to the lower edge by two wooden pegs, which now project from the base of the lower panel. The central and right pegs joining the surviving panels were remade in modern times. There are two fractures, one at the right end of the join, the other at the girl's forehead. Analysis of the pigments conducted during conservation of the painting in 1970 revealed the use of paratacamite (a natural chloride of copper, used for the green necklace); calcium carbonate mixed with gypsum for the white background; orpiment for the yellow earring; hematite; black iron oxide; and anhydrous ferric oxide for the black and reddish brown beads.

The painting was evidently designed to be openly displayed rather than inserted into mummy wrappings. There is no evidence that it was framed, and the fact that the thick cedarwood was cut cross-wise rather than vertically may suggest that the painting was unframed (however, the surviving suspension hole is modern). Unusually, the subject is named as Tekosis, daughter of Harsunis, eleven years old; the inscription appears in four lines of black ink to the left of the girl's head.

The subject is portrayed frontally. She is dressed in a red tunic with broad crimson *clavi*. Over her head is a white veil with a red fringe, perhaps a mantle worn in this way for ceremonial purposes (Tekosis wears no mantle over her tunic).

Her hair is elaborately coiled into large locks which project from the head. At the sides of the head, the locks are outlined in ink, which is also used to draw tiny curls around the brow. Around the crown of the head, the tips of the locks are decorated with gold discs, three of which also adorn the centre of the coiffure from the crown to the brow. Beside the six discs flanking the centre are projecting gold ornaments, possibly pins or, less likely, gold versions of the snakes drawn in black at the sides of the portrait (they have been identified as *uraei*, but the tips do not resemble snake-heads and the necks are too thin for cobras).

In her ears Tekosis wears gold hoop earrings from which are suspended pyramidal clusters of gold drops, resembling bunches of grapes. She wears seven necklaces: the upper two are of small beads, the first emerald and gold, the second a coral-coloured bead interspersed with gold. Beneath these is a heavier necklace of large black beads with H-shaped gold spacers. Below this is a silver band decorated with black lines, and beneath that a necklace of very large black and gold beads, painted with bold white highlights, with gold spacers, one perhaps in the form of a vessel. There follows a gold band with suspended medallion (the lower part is lost, so it is not clear whether the medallion was circular or lunate: probably the former); beneath this is a necklace of large red beads with gold spacers.

The black brows are strongly drawn, the large eyes are rounded, with brown iris and black pupil and only the hint of a highlight. The pink lips are drawn into a pout; the face is full and rounded, the neck thick.

This portrait has been published as an image of a priestess of Isis, of fourth-century-AD date (Thompson 1981). However, it was admitted that the identification of the objects to either side of the portrait was problematic, and no comparable material was known within the Isiac regalia.

To the left of the inscription is a gilded object with silver interior, the latter carefully highlighted. Above it are traces of another gold object, no longer recognisable, and of curling black lines. Two straight vertical black lines join the gold and silver object to a gold sphere placed immediately above an *unguentarium* (perfume-flask). To the side of the vessel is another curling black line, in this instance with a thickened head resembling a serpent. Two similar creatures may be seen by the vessel to the right of the figure; a third wriggles over the top of the sphere.

It may be suggested that the objects and the veil represent not so much the world of the initiate of Isis as the *mundus muliebris*, the world of married women which Tekosis would never experience due to her premature death. The object in the upper left corner may be a hinged case, perhaps holding a mirror (hence the strong highlighting and silver colour). Indeed, it is possible that the gold sphere is a mirror that fitted into the case, or it could be a sponge, like the sponge in a hinged lidded case on a contemporary stone relief commemorating a priestess of Eleusinian Demeter at Kalyvia, near Sparta, illustrated as no. 14, fig. 4, pl. 52 in S. Walker and A. Cameron (eds), *The Greek Renaissance in the Roman Empire. BICS Suppl. 55* (London 1989). Traces of bluish green pigment on the right-hand *unguentarium* suggest that the vessels were glass. *Unguentaria* and mirror cases are represented on tombstones and commemorations of women in the eastern provinces of the Roman empire, numerous examples of which are recorded in M. Waelkens, *Die kleinasiatische Türsteine* (Mainz 1982).

The radiating curls of hair might suggest an early second-century date, and the earrings are a type known from Hadrianic Antinoopolis. However, the hair falls low behind the ears, and the facial features are drawn in a manner reminiscent of late second- and early third-century portraits from er-Rubayat (nos 44–7). The silver band resembles necklaces worn by male and female children in second-century portraits and may signify a status at death below the age of puberty or marriage.

Thompson notes the similarity of names on the portrait with those listed in *P. Oxy III*, 170–72, no. 482, a document of AD 109 naming Tekosis, daughter of Harthonis, in a property receipt. There is, however, no direct evidence to link the document and the portrait, the latter evidently a record of a child lost to her parents' hopes of a successful and prosperous marriage.

BIBLIOGRAPHY
D. L. Thompson, *AJA* 85 (1981), 88–92; Borg 1996, 112–13, 211 Cat. 15.

PAGAN ICONS

While mummy portraits were unframed and painted on boards so thin as to make them unsuitable for use outside the mummy casing, framed panel paintings on much more substantial boards were also known in Roman Egypt. A few portraits survive in this genre showing half-length figures (see no. 78), but of greater interest are over thirty paintings of sacred subjects which can only be termed 'icons', for their purpose was clearly cultic. Four of these have been included in the present exhibition.

In construction, composition, iconography and in their cultic use, these works anticipate the early Christian icons of two or three centuries later. They are framed paintings, using tempera rather than encaustic, and they present non-narrative subjects: one or a few figures, either full-length or half-length, usually in frontal poses with haloed heads. Most of them come from Egypt, chiefly from the Fayum, where they were commonly found in homes.

The pagan veneration of panel paintings is poorly documented in classical authors, but both Pausanias and Pliny refer to panels, *pinakes* in Greek or *tabulae* in Latin, that showed individual gods in non-narrative settings. On the other hand, Christian authors who witnessed the rise of the Christian cult of icons, consistently compared it with pagan practice in which icons of the ancient gods were venerated at home with garlands of flowers and candles. Clement of Alexandria (d. *c.* AD 215) even refers to an icon of the adulterous couple Ares and Aphrodite which his contemporaries venerated in their bedrooms (*Exhortation to the Greeks*, 4).

The subjects of the surviving icons give an interesting profile of religion in late Roman Egypt. Among the gods of higher rank Isis is the most common, as might be expected; but one also finds Serapis, Sobek, the nude Harpocrates, the ithyphallic Min as well as Fortune and Nemesis. In a lower rank we find a proliferation of military gods. Heron is the most common, but a camel god, patron of caravans, and a number of equestrian figures also appear. These were the 'saints' from whom the Egyptians sought protection for themselves and their homes.

T. M.

79 Heron (not exhibited)

About AD 200–25

H 41 cm, W 25.5 cm

Excavated in a private house in Tebtunis in the Fayum

Berlin, Staatliche Museen, Ägyptisches Museum und Papyrussammlung 15979

While along the top and right side the reserved edge gives evidence of the panel's framing, the other broken edges indicate that the panel was originally a good deal larger. The appearance of the soldier's leather cuirass at the bottom implies that the figure was shown full length, and the serpent-entwined lance along the break on the left side gives evidence of the inclusion of a second military figure. The full dimensions must have been around 60 × 50 cm.

The surviving military figure stares boldly at us, his dark hair set against a bright halo. He wears a garland in his hair, and holds a spear in his left hand and a serpent-coiled pine bough in his right. A medusa head protects the fastening of his mantle on his chest.

Two other occurrences of this two-figure composition have been found, indicating that it had attained a kind of fixed canonical status. One is in Brussels Musées Royaux d'Art et d'Histoire (E7409), the other in a private collection in Étampes. In these instances, however, the serpent and pine bough are given to the figure on the left, who also brandishes a double axe in his right hand, while the figure on the right holds a *patera* with which he makes an offering at a diminutive altar.

On the basis of inscriptions on frescoes from Theadelphia and on a relief in Berkeley (Phoebe Apperson

79

Hearst Museum of Anthropology 6–20309), Nachtergael has identified a military god making an offering before a serpent on a tree or bough as Heron. Heron is one of a throng of obscure military divinities in the Late Antique world for whom we lack narrative myths. He first appears in Thrace, generally on horseback, sometimes with a companion bearing a double-headed axe, an ancient symbol of lightning and thunder. His serpent, sometimes a cobra, is a source of blessings. Otto Rubensohn's discovery of this panel in a domestic context in Tebtunis in 1901 is important evidence for Late Antique religion; military figures were later to become a popular theme in Christian icons.

T.M.

BIBLIOGRAPHY

Otto Rubensohn, 'Aus Griechische-römischen Häusern des Fayum', *Jahrbuch des Deutschen Archäologischen Instituts* (1905), 1–25; Georges Nachtergael, 'Trois dédicaces au dieu Hèrôn', *Chronique d'Égypte* 71 (1996), fasc. 141, 129–42; Ernest Will, 'Hèron', *Lexicon Iconographicum Mythologiae Classicae* v, 1 391–4.

80 Heron with attendant donor, Panephrimmis

About AD 300

H 58.1 cm, W 48.7 cm (without frame H 52.4 cm, W 42.5 cm)

First known in a private collection, Cairo; purchased on the art market in 1959

Providence, Museum of Art, Rhode Island School of Design, Museum Works of Art Fund, no. 59.030

For its excellent preservation this is one of the most important of the Egyptian icons. The panel is comprised of five boards within a carefully constructed frame of grooved pieces interlocked at the corners, demonstrating the ancient Roman technique of framing. Three similarly framed icons are known (Alexandria Graeco-Roman Museum, inv. no. 22978; Brussels Musées

Royaux E7409; and a destroyed panel formerly in Berlin). The iconography relates to that of the previous entry: a soldier god in purple mantle, with laurel crown and halo, makes an offering at an altar before a tree entwined with a serpent. The serpent in the tree identifies the military figure as Heron.

Behind Heron in miniature scale a dark-skinned donor gives a poignant personal note to the icon. He offers flowers and incense beneath a column supporting the griffin of Nemesis, the vindictive force of divine wrath whom one venerated in the hope of being spared its justified reprisals (see the following entry.) An inscription in the upper right refers to the human donor by name, ῾Υπερ Πανεφρυμμιο ἐπ ᾿ἀγαθῶι ('on behalf of Panephrimmis, for a favour'). The language is characteristic of votive offerings and may be interpreted either as thanks for a past favour or as a petition for an expected favour. Christian icons included similar miniature donor figures.

T.M.

BIBLIOGRAPHY

Franz Cumont, 'Un dieu supposé syrien associé à Hérôn en Égypte', *Mélanges syriens offerts à M. René Dussaud* (Paris 1939), 5; Rolf Winkes, *Roman Paintings and Mosaics: Catalogue of the Classical Collection* (Museum of Art, Rhode Island School of Design 1982), 68–9; Georges Nachtergael, 'Trois dédicaces au dieu Hèrôn', *Chronique d'Égypte* 71 (1996), fasc. 141, 138–9.

81 Nemesis

About AD 200

H 25.5 cm (as reconstructed), W 23 cm

Purchased in Egypt in 1934–5, perhaps from Dr David Askren

Ann Arbor, Kelsey Museum of Archaeology 88723

Nemesis, the personification of retributive justice, was the reverse of Tyche, or good fortune. This unpublished panel, made of a single board with edges reserved for a frame, has suffered several vertical

80

81

breaks and is missing a narrow segment right of centre. The fearful eagle-lion holds the swift wheel of fortune in her claw. The beast inhabits a temple with lotus capitals, with a damaged and undeciphered medallion (a male bust?) in the pediment.

The subjects of icons generally turn their gaze directly and beneficently on the viewer, but significantly Nemesis is shown in profile against a deep blue ground; should the goddess turn to face us, her evil eye would certainly destroy us. Nemesis was the agent of the divine wrath against those who presumed too much, and she had to be turned aside to assure

the course of one's good fortune. On the other hand, she could be invoked for vengeance against one's enemies, the wheel being an instrument of punishment and torture. The circumstances of the discovery of this piece are unfortunately unknown (see the figure of Nemesis in the preceding entry).

T. M.

BIBLIOGRAPHY
Elizabeth Riefstahl, 'Nemesis and the Wheel of Fate', *Brooklyn Museum Bulletin* 17, no. 3 (1956), 1–7; Charles M. Edwards, 'Tyche at Corinth', *Hesperia* 59, no. 3 (1990), 529–42.

82 Enthroned figure

About AD 200

H 30 cm, W 26 cm

Purchased in Egypt in 1934–5, perhaps from Dr David Askren

Ann Arbor, Kelsey Museum of Archaeology 88617a–m

Prominent in the corpus of Egyptian icons are representations of enthroned gods, especially Isis and Sobek. This unpublished figure, however, remains unidentified and may represent a mortal in his divinised state after death. The fragments of this panel, with conspicuous lacunae in the upper right and lower left, have been remounted. Most of the surface remains intact, however, including the reserved edge for the frame. The painting is warm and vibrant with a lively palette and firm, confident modelling in the face.

We are confronted by a young male with a ribboned laurel crown and a bright yellow halo. He is dressed in a white mantle and a floor-length tunic appropriate to gods, priests and ordinary men in their funerary portraits on shrouds. He wears sandals, and he sits on a great gilded throne draped in purple. In his left hand he clutches a wreath; his right hand holds a cup, or *patera*, behind which we see a jointed sceptre. The proffered cup may be a gesture of worship or, in the case of gods, an offering of blessings to the viewer.

T. M.

BIBLIOGRAPHY
Erika Simon, *Opfernde Götter*, Berlin, 1953

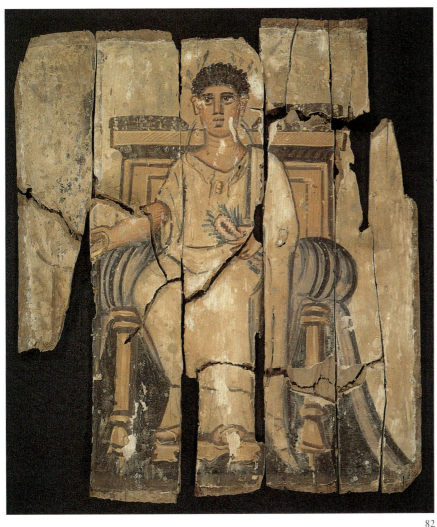

82

PORTRAITS ON PAINTED PLASTER MASKS

In Roman Egypt funerary portraiture was not limited to mummy portraits: an alternative genre developed where a portrait mask of painted clay or plaster was extended to form part of the lid of a wooden coffin, on which the deceased appeared to recline as if on a bier, the hands folded on the chest and the head slightly raised. Sometimes elaborate masks were attached to mummies, as in the remarkable mummy of Artemidora (no. 85).

The painted plaster masks derived from pharaonic traditions, in the sense that the mask served as a substitute for the head of the deceased and a means of elevating him or her to immortal status, often reflected in the paintings and texts written on the mantle surrounding the head (e.g. nos 84–5, 91). However, like the two-dimensional panel and shroud portraits, the masks exhibit a strongly individualised appearance. Many masks were painted and gilded; Roman fashions in hairstyles, jewellery and dress were followed, but a wide range of physiognomies and skin pigmentation may be observed. Despite the individuality of the masks, most faces were made in a mould, the eyes and ears added separately (the former often inlaid in glass or stone) and the distinguishing details worked in plaster with a spatula or knife, then painted or gilded.

Like the gilded masks, the painted plaster masks appear to date from the earliest years of the Roman occupation of Egypt. However, like the two-dimensional portraits, they continued in use for a much longer period, running well into the third century AD. From the second century AD, the heads were modelled in the round and raised high above the coffin lid (e.g. nos 90–91).

Little is known of the provenances of the masks, though some dealers' groups may be reconstructed from surviving documentation. The masks seem to have been especially popular in Middle Egypt, notably, the sites of Meir and Tuna el-Gebel.

83 Painted plaster mask of a boy with inlaid glass eyes

About AD 55–70

H 22.7 cm, W 17.2 cm, TH 15 cm

Excavated by Petrie at Hawara

University College London, Petrie Museum UC 19615

The mask is broken at the sides of the head below the ears; the neck is restored from a joining fragment. Part of the supporting mantle survives at the back of the head.

Only two red bands of decoration survive on the proper right side of the mantle. The youth's hair is painted black and behind the ears is worked with a fine point. The front is chiselled into two rows of straight strands, which fall onto the brow in a slight wave reminiscent of portraits of the Emperor Nero. A tapered strand of hair falls in front of the ears.

The ears project in the style of Roman portraits of Julio-Claudian date. The eyes are inlaid in glass, the

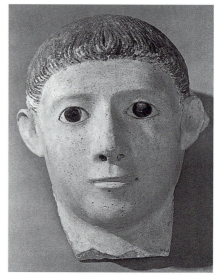

83

pupils and irises appearing as solid
black. Traces of red paint appear in
the nostrils and lips. The latter are
very thin; in general, the features
appear refined.

The lack of Egyptianising features
in this portrait may be due to the
disappearance of much of the painted
surface. Nonetheless, the Romanised
appearance of the youth is very
striking and appears to represent a
development from the slightly earlier
portrait, Walker and Bierbrier 1997,
no. 133.

BIBLIOGRAPHY
Grimm, *Mumienmasken*, 73, 120,
pl. 20, 2.

84 Painted plaster and cartonnage mummy mask of a woman with a jewelled garland

About AD 60–70

H 53 cm, W 33 cm, L 63 cm

Provenance unknown, but likely to be
Meir

New York, The Metropolitan Museum
of Art, Rogers Fund, 1919 19.2.6

The complete mask is preserved, with
the support for the head. Two holes
are pierced at the lower corners of
the mask, the left hole containing
cord with which the mask was
attached to the mummy. Several
small spots of paint are lost from the
woman's tunic, and her left hand is
scuffed, but in other respects the
mask is in excellent condition.

The woman is represented as if
lying almost flat upon her bier. She
wears a black wig which cascades in
tight waves onto her shoulders. The
wig appears to be made of flax,
papyrus and other plant fibres dyed
with carbon black mixed with a
binding medium. Across her brow is
a row of corkscrew locks apparently
made of the same fibres and of the
same thickness as the cord used to
attach the mask to the mummy. Both
the wig and the front locks were
glued to rough unpainted plaster.
Attached to the wig is a thick garland
of white rose petals, edged in pink,

84

set between banks of leaves, the central tiers of which are gilded on the outside and painted in yellow ochre on the back. A very similar mask in Berlin is described as having hair made of cotton (Wildung 1990, 206 fig. 1).

The face and hands are pale ivory, the long feathery eyebrows painted black on a blue ground. The eyes are outlined in greenish grey and black. The pupils and irises are black, with small white highlights. The ears project strongly, with well-defined lobes. The lips are painted bright red, matching the woman's tunic. Venus rings are lightly drawn on the neck. The fingernails and joints are indicated in the red paint used for the tunic.

In the centre of the garland is painted a red stone, the same shade as the lips and tunic. The setting is gilded. Attached to her earlobes by cords are small rectangular wooden blocks with a painted green square;

these represent earrings, no doubt once gilded and set with green stones. Strung from a peg high on the neck is a necklace of jet beads, interspersed with rectangular beads painted green to represent emeralds, and gilded globular beads. On the woman's neck lies a ridged gold band, rendered in gilded plaster, with a centrally mounted crescent pendant and small gold beads suspended from the band. On her wrists are gilded snake bracelets with two heads, and on the third and fourth fingers of her left hand are gilded rings with, respectively, blue and red stones, the blue matching that of the earrings.

The woman wears a bright red tunic with black *clavi*, outlined in the same greenish grey used to define the eyes. No mantle is shown.

The back of the head rests against the support, on which there is a gilded wreath with a disc at the top flanked by four dots. To either side are leaves and berries, including vine

and perhaps myrtle. The wreath is tied at the base with a bow. Within the wreath is a gilded scarab (a placement first attested about 900 BC in the Pharaonic Period), encircled by a green and pink striped and dotted border, and set against a red, blue, black and white chequered ground, which matches the kilt worn by Osiris in the scene below. The wreath itself is set against a red, blue and white net, the customary dress of the mummy of Osiris, worn in the scene below by Nephthys, who appears to the left of Osiris.

The panel with the wreath is divided by a conventional striped and dotted border from scenes in two registers at the sides of the mask. The upper register comprises four *tit* knots and three *djed* pillars, the knots decorated with vertical stripes, the central *djed* pillar with horizontal bands and the flanking pillars with nets, the latter replicated in the dress worn by some of the deities below.

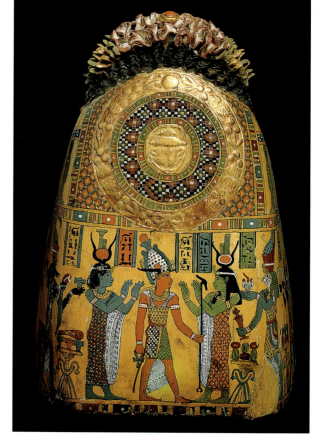

84

84

This register is topped with a band of white stars or petals set against a dark blue ground.

In the lower register Osiris, facing right and centrally placed below the crown of the woman's head and the panel with the wreath, carries an *ankh* and a *was*-sceptre; tucked into the waistband of his kilt is an animal tail, a sign of royal status. He also wears a decorated corselet, a gold collar and a mantle. On his head is the *atef*-crown. Osiris is flanked by Isis (right), her flesh painted green and wearing a gold collar and a pink and black net dress, and by Nephthys (left), painted blue and wearing a red and blue net dress. Both goddesses raise their arms to Osiris in worship. On their heads are horned sun-discs, on which rest the hieroglyphs of their names. Four deities process towards the central group on the mask's left side, each bearing offerings and each identified by a column of hieroglyphs in front of the figure. From left to right they are Seshat, mistress of writings, with stylus and tally sheet; a single personification with cobra and vulture headdress of the two deities Wadjet and Nekhbet, representing Upper and Lower Egypt; next the lion-masked Tefnut; and at the head of the group, the jackal god Anubis. On the other side the procession is led by Horus, followed by Amun-Re, king of the gods; Thoth, master of secrets; and the sun-god, Re-Harakhty. Many of the deities wear white mantles with dot, bar and zigzag decoration reminiscent of the clothing on cartonnage coffin portraits from Akhmim.

This remarkable mask is very like two others now in Cairo Museum, which were excavated at Meir in Upper Egypt (Cairo, Egyptian Museum CG 33130, 33131, illustrated by Wildung 1990, 220 fig. 33). Estimates of the date of these masks has varied from the mid-first to the early second century AD. In recent years the Egyptian Museum, Berlin, has acquired four masks of closely related but not exactly similar form; one of these, a gilded male mask, has a demotic inscription. It has been argued that the Romanised portraits on masks of this type were inspired by the visit to Aswan of Germanicus Caesar (Wildung 220). However, the New York and Cairo masks, all commemorating women, are slightly less ornate, with jewellery of a type found in mummy portraits of later Julio-Claudian date. In particular the gold necklace with the crescent pendant and miniature suspended globes may be compared with jewellery worn by women with Neronian hairstyles in painted panel portraits (e.g. nos 1–4), while the disc and dot motif on the gilded wreath recalls the jewelled armbands on some mid-first century gilded masks (e.g. Manchester Museum no. 1769, excavated by Petrie at Hawara). Grimm notes Italian influence in the dress of the women portrayed on the masks from Meir; however, unlike the men, and unlike women portrayed on gilded masks, their hair is dressed in Egyptian style.

BIBLIOGRAPHY

E. Grebaut, *Le Musée Égyptien*, vol. 1 (Cairo 1890), pl. 32; G. Maspero, *Art in Egypt* (New York 1912) 277, fig. 532; Williams 1924, 108 and N. 134; M. Davenport, *Book of Costume* I (New York 1948), 33 pl. 100; Parlasca, *Mumienporträts*, 120 and 148, n. 168 and pls 2,1 and 3,2; Grimm, *Mumienmasken*, 51, 62 pl. C2; D. Wildung, 'Geheimnisvoller Gesichten', *Antike Welt* 21 (1990), 206–21.

84

85 Mummy of a woman named Artemidora, with a gilded and painted plaster mask and gilded appliqué decoration

About AD 90–100

Mummy L 2.05 m; mask H 71.5 cm, L 78 cm, W 46.5 cm; footcase H 102.5 cm, W (top) 46 cm

From Meir

New York, The Metropolitan Museum of Art, Gift of J. Pierpont Morgan, 1911 11.155.5

Mask
Both hands are chipped, with the thumb and first finger of Artemidora's right hand lost. Flecks of paint are lost from the surface of the tunic. In other respects mask and mummy are in remarkably good condition. Two holes are pierced at the front end of the mask to attach it to the mummy, but the cord is lost.

The mask portrays a young woman, her hair arranged in tiers of snail curls above the brow, the curls studded with small gold squares. In front of this coiffure, fashionable in Rome in the last decade of the first century AD, is a row of moulded corkscrew locks. Behind the tiers of curls flows a black Egyptian wig, the long locks of hair bound with narrow bands of gold in Pharaonic fashion.

The eyebrows are painted in feathery style. The glass eyes are set in lapis and the pupils engraved. The skin tone is very dark, the neck painted with Venus rings. The nose is long and straight, the thin lips slightly smiling, and the small chin is prominent.

Artemidora wears gold ball earrings, a gold necklace with pendant triangles decorated with small balls of gold at the apexes, and an elaborate gilded necklace set with six stones and a large flat disc with rays resembling the sun positioned low between the breasts. On her wrists are gilded snake bracelets, and a gold ring adorns each of the index, third and fourth fingers of her left hand. She is dressed in a dark red tunic, scooped at the neck below the first necklace. The *clavi* are black, edged in gold.

At the back of the head the mask support is divided into two zones of decoration. The upper zone, topped by a feather pattern and frizzy hair emerging from beneath the wig, is an ornamental *kheker* frieze with figures including Anubis, realised in gold appliqué on a green ground. In the centre of the register, below the crown of the head, is an elaborately decorated winged scarab holding a disc in its forelegs and a *shen* ring of turquoise and glass in its rear legs. Its body is made of lapis, the wings painted on gilded ground. Beneath the scarab are Osiris with Nekhbet (left) and Wadjet (right). The lower register, in gold appliqué on a red ground, is divided from the upper by the customary band of stripes and dots, and a band of gold stars. A procession of deities attending Osiris decorates the lower frieze. Each is identified by a hieroglyphic inscription. From left to right they are described as The Eye of Horus; Nut; Anubis, son of Osiris, divine son, Eldest of the Gods; Nephthys;

85

85

Osiris, the great Ba, Lord of Burial; Isis; Osiris the [...] of Re; Hathor; Western Ba.

The portrait mask may be dated to the final years of the first century AD by the hairstyle and the gold ball earrings, the latter not apparently worn in the second century. The form of the necklaces, narrow finger rings, single-headed snake bracelets and the gold-edged *clavi* also suggest a date in the first century.

Mummy

Across the centre of the body of the mummy, which is encased in a plain wrapping of linen dyed red, are six strips of gold decorated with red triangles. These are flanked by two gold bands of hieroglyphs running from shoulder to ankle, the texts of which refer to epithets of Osiris, such as 'Great God, Lord of the Sky, Greatest Sovereign of the Gods and Goddesses'. Beneath the bands, on both sides of the mummy, are isolated gold appliqués of Osiris with Isis and Nephthys. On top of the feet Isis and Nephthys appear again, wearing discs on their heads and kneeling beneath a winged solar disc. No mention of the deceased is made in any of the texts described above, nor does she appear with the deities. Instead, she is identified in a conventional Greek funerary inscription, set within a *tabula ansata* on the base of the footplate, above a figure of Anubis. The text reads: Ἀρτεμιδώρα Ἁρ|ποκρά ἀώρος Λκζ|ἐυψύχει ('Artemidora, daughter of Harpocras, died untimely, aged twenty-seven. Farewell.') The letters are applied in gold on a red ground. Recent C.A.T. scans of Artemidora suggest the body of an adult woman of an age (twenty-five to thirty years) commensurate with that offered by the text.

BIBLIOGRAPHY

Williams 1924, 108 and N. 134; MMA, *A Handbook of the Egyptian Rooms* (eds. 1911–22), figs 60–61; Ahmed Bey Kamal, *Annales du Service des Antiquités de l'Égypte* XIV (1914), 62ff; *Art and Archaeology* V (January 1917), 6 no. 1; *American Journal of Philology* XXXIV, 197; George F. Kunz, *Rings for the Finger* (New York 1917, reissued

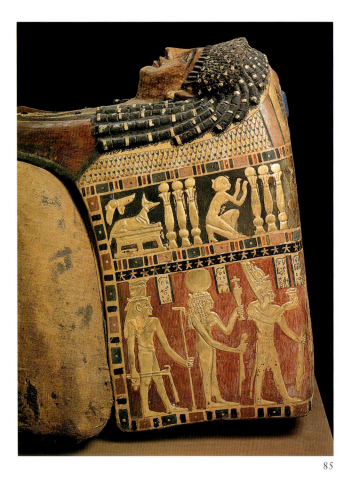

85

85

85

85

by Dover Press), pl. opp. p. 52; Parlasca, *Mumienporträts*, 120, 148, pl. 2,2; Grimm, *Mumienmasken*, 14 (n. 6), 64, 77, 82, 108, 120, 134 C2, Tafel C1; R. S. Bianchi, 'Egyptian Mummies: Myth and Reality', *Archaeology* 35, no. 2 (March/April 1982), 28.

86 Painted plaster mask of a woman

First century AD

H 24.5 cm, W 18 cm

Provenance unknown, bequeathed by Albert Marquet, 1976

Paris, Musée du Louvre, Département des Antiquités Égyptiennes E 27152

The mask is broken just under the chin, but the face, both ears, and part of the head have been preserved. The polychromy of the skin is completely lost, with the exception of a few

85

86

traces of red at the corners of the lips. By contrast, the black colour of the hair is well preserved. The face is typically Greek: the perfect oval, the very straight nose, the barely smiling lips, the dimple on the round chin and, especially, the characteristic arch of the eyebrows link this mask to Hellenistic sculpture. The eyes are inlaid with white and black glass. The ears, uncovered and placed very high, are adorned with hoop earrings with three beads. The hair, styled into parallel waves, forms a sort of cap, which ends on the forehead with a band of small frizzy locks. A single ringlet survives behind each ear, but traces of three others are visible above the left ear. Two curls, one shorter than the other, fall in front of each ear.

R.C.

BIBLIOGRAPHY

Aubert and Cortopassi 1998, 141 no. 86.

87 Painted plaster mask of a woman

About AD 110–20

H 20 cm, W 19 cm

Site of discovery unknown, presumably Tuna el-Gebel (Hermopolis West)

Acquired in 1912 in Cairo by L. Borchardt from the estate of the antique dealer Michel Casira

Heidelberg, Ägyptologisches Institut der Universität, Inv. 7

Plaster masks were generally mass-produced, and only a few examples are distinguished by artistic qualities, among them the present one. It was partly executed with the help of moulds and consists of porous plaster whose fine slip surface has been painted. The edges are somewhat chipped. Where the edge is preserved, as in the central area of the mask, its profile shows that the mask was attached to a neck section, presumably made of wood. A similarly shaped edge in the neck area is found in a Hadrianic mask in Paris (Louvre, Inv. E 12177), in which the wooden insert beneath the face is also preserved (Grimm, *Mumienmasken*, 71 n. 106, 80, 121 pls 31,4, and 131,3.4).

The manner in which the mask was produced prohibited the development of a true portrait. A dimple in the chin, and earrings with two round pearls nevertheless lend the work a certain individuality. The impression that this is a specific individual is further enhanced by the extremely carefully worked coiffure. The woman's reddish brown hair forms a triangle-shaped projection above her forehead. On the back of the head is a wreath of braid into which a hairpin of some other material was inserted. Especially noteworthy is the structure of the front section of the hair consisting

87

87

of small corkscrew curls. This is a local variant of a Flavian fashion that presumably required artificial hair. In this particular form the hairstyle reflects a fashion stage late in Trajan's reign.

K.P.

BIBLIOGRAPHY

Grimm, *Mumienmasken*, 83, 108 pl. 77,1.2; M. Bergmann in E. Feucht, *Vom Nil zum Neckar* (Berlin/Heidelberg etc. 1986), 131 no. 288.

88 Painted plaster mask of a woman

About AD 100–20

H 34.5 cm, W 20 cm, TH 28 cm

Provenance unknown; acquired in 1897

British Museum EA 29477

The mask is broken at the back of the head. The painted surface is lost in places, notably on the nose and brow and the proper right cheek.

At the base of the neck the folds of a red tunic appear. In the woman's ears are double hoop earrings of gold, strung with three beads. Below the ears hang two matching chains of oblong beads separated by groups of one square bead flanked by two small round beads. All the jewellery is rendered in yellow ochre paint, some perhaps modern.

On her head the woman wears an elaborate wreath of rosebuds, originally pink but now faded. In front of the wreath the hair is arranged in three tiers of corkscrew curls, brushed back over the ears, behind which fall corkscrew locks, of which only one survives complete on either side. Behind the wreath the hair is painted black with carbon pigment.

The eyebrows are carefully drawn, the upper lid of the eye outlined in black, the pupil and iris crudely painted in black and brown. The skin, including the whites of the eyes, is covered with a pinkish-brown wash. The long neck is as if divided in tiers by Venus rings. The physiognomy of the face also suggests a fleshy appearance.

The mask may be dated by the jewellery, hairstyle and sober, rather matronly appearance to the early years of the second century AD.

BIBLIOGRAPHY

Grimm, *Mumienmasken*, 28, n.47, 34, 63, 77, pl. 71, 4.

88

89 Painted plaster mask of a woman

AD 100–150

H 18 cm, W 19.5 cm

Perhaps from Akhmim; acquired in 1899

Paris, Musée du Louvre, Département des Antiquités Égyptiennes AF 2128

Made of stuccoed and painted plaster, this mask consists of the part of the face and neck to which the hairpiece, veil or mantle fragment, and perhaps ears were attached. At the back a broad, flat, intermediate partition, with a small opening in the centre, bears the imprint of wood grain, which suggests that this mask was fixed to a coffin, like that of Teuris (Amsterdam, Allard Pierson Museum, APM 7069).

The face, with an ochre tint, is modelled free-hand: the cheekbones are prominent, and character lines begin at the straight nose and surround the thick-lipped mouth, which is slightly open, displaying the teeth. The eyes and eyelids are painted black; the ears are half concealed by the wavy black hair. A space has been provided for the wreath of roses, attribute of the deceased favourably judged by Osiris. Crowning the skull is a 'pretzel' braid, a hairstyle worn by Sabina, the wife of Emperor Hadrian. The neck displays three Venus rings.

This work is one of the rare examples of realistic portraits executed in plaster, a medium more often used for mass production. The slightly open mouth showing the teeth is a characteristic of Hellenistic portraits. An intense life emanates from this face without beauty and marked by age, which could link it with the portrait painted on wood of Klaudiane (Dijon, Musée des Beaux-Arts, GA 5), that of an elderly woman (no. 67) or that of a woman (no. 34). This type of realistic portrayal is inherent in the Egyptian tradition of the Old Kingdom and was sometimes even taken to the point of caricature, as is evident in the Alexandrian 'grotesques', ranging from the Fourth Dynasty portrait of Vizier Hemionu (Hildesheim, Romer-Pelizaeus Museum) to that of the priest Hor from the Ptolemaic period (40–30 BC) in the Cairo Museum (CG 697). It persisted in funerary portraits of the Roman period.

M.-F. A.

BIBLIOGRAPHY
Parlasca, *Mumienporträts*, 231; Grimm, *Mumienmasken*, 66 no. 64, 83, 107, pl. 82.3; Walker and Bierbrier 1997, 142 no. 155.

90 Painted plaster mask of a woman

Late second or early third century AD

H 21 cm, W 13.5 cm

Perhaps from Akhmim; acquired in 1899

Paris, Musée du Louvre, Département des Antiquités Égyptiennes AF 6705

Made from fine and homogeneous plaster, this is more a head than a mask, a round head whose back part is missing. It is joined to a breastplate on which the remains of a veil survive. This veil still bears the imprint of cloth, which indicates that the breastplate was still wet when it was placed on the shroud enveloping the mummy. The neck is concealed and the barely modelled face is chubby. Below the once-painted eyebrows, the eyes, looking askance, are inlaid with opaque white and black glass; the upper lids are drooping. The nose is small with dilated nostrils; the mouth is large, and the lower lip recedes behind the upper. The ears are Y-shaped. The youthful hairstyle appears on the surface of the skull itself, and was probably rendered by passing a comb

89

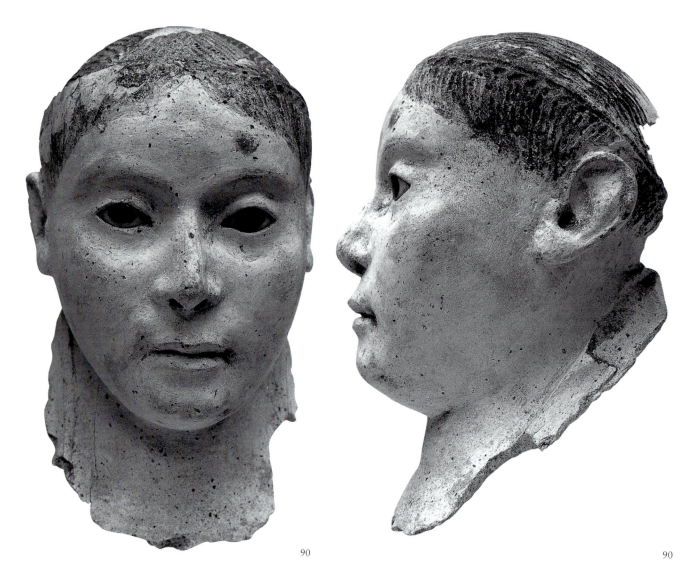

90

90

of sorts across the still-wet plaster. The black hair, only slightly wavy, was formed into a braid and pulled back to form a chignon, now lost. At the front the hair is pulled up and divided into thin braids that extend back to the nape of the neck. The median part is covered by a larger braid that forms a triangle above the forehead. This hairstyle reproduces in graphic terms a Roman model from the first century AD, as depicted in a sculpted portrait in the Louvre Museum (AGER MA 3445).

This work of art belongs to a family of funerary portraits with identical characteristics, denoting an Egyptian style: the eyes looking askance, the drooping eyelids, the mouth with upper lip larger than the lower, and the Y-shape of the ears. They have Roman-style haircuts, either feminine or masculine with beard and moustache, and they were manufactured in Tuna el-Gebel from the mid-second century AD. They are linked in style to the masks found in Mirgissa dating to the Middle Kingdom, which culminate in the 'bubbleheads' of the fourth century AD, and in their extreme simplicity they oddly evoke Buddhist heads.

M.-F. A.

Unpublished

91 Painted plaster portrait mask of a youth in a tunic and mantle

About AD 140–90

L 55 cm, H (max.) 32 cm, W (base) 28 cm

From Tuna el-Gebel

New York, The Metropolitan Museum of Art, Rogers Fund, 1912 12.182.46

Some paint flecks have been lost, especially from the hair and garland, and cracks have opened up at the top and base of the garland. The lower right corner and part of the adjacent side are unpainted. Two holes are pierced at the front ends of the mask for attachment to a mummy or coffin.

The youth is dressed in a white tunic with *clavi* painted in rose madder, a colour also used to define the upper edge of the garment. Unusually for a portrait mask, a white mantle is also shown, the curved folded edge moulded in relief, with a horizontal H-motif below his left hand. In his right hand he holds a garland of rose petals and leaves.

The youth's black hair is roughly combed into thick strands reminiscent of the romantic barbarian-style portraits fashionable in the Greek-speaking eastern provinces in the middle and later years of the second century AD. A similar hairstyle appears on a marble head of a boy from Athens (NM 343), dated to the early Severan period by K. Fittschen in S. Walker and A. Cameron (eds), *The Greek Renaissance in the Roman Empire. BICS Suppl.* 55 (1989), 108–13, pl. 36 fig. 6. Both the eyebrows and the upper arch of the orbit are defined with scribbled lines. The eyes are set in lapis, the pupils and iris of glass. The eyelashes are painted with short straight strokes. The nose is long; the lips painted with rose madder are long, thin and smiling; the cheekbones are high; and the chin is small and prominent.

91

Rose madder is also used to outline the hands; the fingernails are painted white, and the skin a warm pinkish terracotta.

The youth's head is raised on a support decorated with Egyptian motifs. Flanking the neck are banks of three golden *uraei* painted in schematic but lively style on a green ground. Behind them, divided from the *uraei* by a vertical band, Quebesennef and Duamuref, two mummiform sons of Horus, flank the falcon-god Re-Harakhty. All three creatures have elliptical bodies, the lower part encased in a net.

This mask offers an interesting mixture of archaising Egyptian and Greek features. Apart from the painted support, more expansive than is the norm, the face with its archaising smile and eyes inlaid in lapis is also reminiscent of earlier work. In contrast, the slightly wild hair is also found in romanticised Greek portraits of the period, and the clothing is certainly suggestive of the Greek man of culture.

BIBLIOGRAPHY

Parlasca, *Mumienporträts*, 92, 120, pl. 3.3; Grimm, *Mumienmasken*, 102 n. 6.

91

92 Portrait of a woman on a painted plaster coffin lid

About AD 190–220

H 34 cm, L 62 cm, W 26 cm

Excavated by A. Gayet at Antinoopolis

Paris, Musée du Louvre, Département des Antiquités Égyptiennes E 21360

This mask, consisting of several fragments glued back together into a single piece, has a face perpendicular to the breastplate, which indicates a relatively late date. A recent restoration has eliminated modern plaster plugs, especially on the right side of the skull. Two holes were made along the edges at shoulder level, to attach the breastplate with fasteners to the mummy. The polychromy is well preserved, despite numerous gaps.

The portrait is of a young woman with a bloated face, the position of her head accentuating her double chin. The hairstyle is sober: the hair is divided by a middle parting and gathered into a braid forming a spiral chignon, held together by a pin. A second pin, now lost, was located near the first. The eyes are painted, with a depression in the plaster to indicate the pupil. There is a dimple in the chin. The clothing consists of a blue tunic with purple *clavi*, which emphasises the shape of the small pointed breasts. A mantle rises from behind the neck and falls over the shoulders. It is decorated with a dark L-shaped motif. The woman is wearing numerous pieces of jewellery, all in relief, which were originally gilded on an ochre-coloured undercoat, and all are set off by a red line painted below them on the pink flesh, indicating the shadow and reflection of gold on skin. The earrings are shaped like bunches of grapes attached to horizontal clasps; two chains and a beaded necklace with three round pendants adorn the neck. The left hand sports three rings, including a double ring that joins the middle and ring fingers. Each wrist once bore two heavy, solid bracelets, one of which is now lost. Two of these bracelets are thick, twisted gold cords, decorated with a round cabochon and a bead in the centre. The long, delicate hands are placed flat on the belly. The right hand holds the wreath of rose petals of the deceased favourably judged by Osiris. In the left hand are stalks of wheat and poppies, once gilded, which were associated with the cult of Demeter, who had been assimilated to Isis.

Behind the head, on the support, the deceased is represented as Osiris, her arms crossed over her chest, with the attributes of that god. The head is drawn within a square. On either side of the mummiform body of the god, a rectangle, suggesting a stela or label, bears letters, perhaps Greek. Part of a black serpent is preserved on the left; the serpent on the right has been almost completely effaced. The space allocated to the representation of Osiris is delineated by a red band on the right and left sides.

The contrast between the sober and severe hairstyle and face and the rich jewellery is certainly the most striking element of this breastplate mask.

R.C.

BIBLIOGRAPHY

Grimm, *Mumienmasken*, 88, 154, pl. 95,1; Walker and Bierbrier 1997, no. 164; Aubert and Cortopassi 1998, no. 42.

92

STONE FUNERARY STELAE

In simpler burials an image of the deceased was sometimes provided on a stela placed with the body. Comparison of the stelae from the northern and southern parts of Egypt reveals interesting differences in iconography. Those from the north, exemplified by specimens from Kom Abu Billo, are classical in style, showing the deceased in Hellenistic dress and pose, frequently framed by architectural details of classical type and with an inscription in Greek. Their only concession to Egyptian belief is the inclusion of a small jackal deriving from the image of the god Anubis. The carving of the figures in very high relief on several stelae is also uncharacteristic of Egyptian sculpture.

The stelae from the south (here represented by examples from Abydos) are purely Egyptian. The traditional pharaonic lunette at the top contains a winged solar disc, and the main scene (usually in low relief) represents the gods Osiris, Isis and Anubis, with the deceased either as a mummy on a bier or as a living individual being presented to Osiris. Here, only the deceased's costume is classical in type, and the scenes as a whole recall the designs painted on the mummy shrouds of the same period.

93

93 Limestone funerary stela showing Anubis presenting a man and a woman to Osiris

Perhaps first century BC

H 60 cm, W 53 cm, TH 12.5 cm

Provenance unknown, possibly Abydos

Acquired in 1837 (d'Athanasi Collection)

British Museum EA 189

The two figures representing the deceased are escorted by the jackal-headed Anubis, who is apparently shown twice. The first of the pair to be presented is the man, who wears a long tunic and a mantle with a thin overfold draped over his left shoulder; his hair is cut short in Ptolemaic fashion. The woman beside him also has a Ptolemaic hairstyle, brushed back from the face. She wears a long tunic and a mantle draped over her left shoulder (the latter hidden by her companion).

Osiris wears a tall crown and is seated on a throne, his head awkwardly turned to face the viewer. To his right stands Isis, wearing a horned disc on her head. All the deities wear broad collars; Isis and Osiris wear long tunics with either a border above the hem or a second tunic beneath; the escorting deities wear short tunics. The scene takes place on a ground-line; a narrow arch frames the top of the relief.

The hairstyles and dress of the mortal figures suggest a date in the later Ptolemaic era. Similar scenes also occur on shrouds and stone reliefs of Roman date; no. 105 comprises a painted shroud perhaps of comparable date but with a later inserted portrait bust. Most recently, the relief has been ascribed to a local workshop of the first century AD.

94

95

BIBLIOGRAPHY
A.Abdalla, *Graeco-Roman Funerary Stelae from Upper Egypt* (Liverpool 1992), 76, no.186, pl.58; Parlasca and Seeman 1999, 326–7 no. 223.

94 Inscribed limestone funerary stela of Tryphon with a praying youth flanked by jackals

About AD 55–70

H 29 cm, W 20.5 cm, TH 10 cm

Provenance unknown; acquired in 1924

British Museum EA 57358

The stela is well preserved, with traces of red paint on the boy's hair and towards the base of the scene. The background has a brown deposit which may represent a wash or coating of the stone.

The youth is shown frontally in the centre of the stela, his arms raised with palms out-turned in a gesture often associated with prayer (*orans*), but also intelligible as a sign of joy at acceptance by Osiris in the afterlife. He is dressed in a short-sleeved pleated tunic that reaches to his ankles, and a pleated mantle drawn across the lower body, folded at the waist, and taken over his left shoulder. His feet are bare. His hair is cut straight in Roman fashion, with a wave at the front recalling the style of the Emperor Nero.

The youth is flanked by two jackals, each seated on a plinth and turned to watch him. They represent the gods Anubis and Wepwawet. The scene is set within an architectural frame, perhaps intended to represent the tomb. The columns are monolithic shafts, with exaggerated entasis, set on bases moulded with an upper and lower torus only. The capitals are also shown with simplified mouldings, as if roughed out.

Immediately above them is a pediment with a central (broken) acroterium and concave sides, as if it were made of more flexible material than stone. Beneath the scene is an inscription crudely carved in two lines of Greek: Τρύφων Lδ ἄωρος| – = ᾽Αθυρ ιβ ('Tryphon who died young, aged four. Year 6, 12th of Athyr.')

The hairstyle, physiognomy and clothing suggest a Julio-Claudian date for the stela, most likely in the reign of Nero.

BIBLIOGRAPHY
Parlasca and Seeman 1999, 256 no. 161 (second century AD).

95 Sandstone funerary stela with a reclining woman

About AD 100–20

H 38.1 cm, W 27.3 cm, TH 9 cm

Provenance unknown

Bequest of Sir Robert Mond in 1939

British Museum EA 65337

There is some loss to the surface of the stela, and any trace of paint has now vanished. Otherwise the stone is well preserved but for the subject's damaged right eye.

A woman dressed in a tunic and mantle, the latter draped over her hips, rests on three cushions piled onto a bed. She sits up, her face turned to the viewer. In her out-stretched right hand she holds a libation dish (*patera*); in her left, a scroll. On her right wrist is a thick bracelet. Her hair is parted centrally, and arranged in tiers of curls with long locks falling behind the ears and onto the shoulders. The face is oval, the surviving proper left eye almond-shaped. The drapery is carefully carved to suggest a voluptuous figure.

Beside the woman on a shelf is a reclining jackal, representing the god Anubis, companion and protector of the dead. The bed and shelf are set within an architectural frame, perhaps representing the tomb. The setting comprises monolithic column shafts, set on bases which rest on rectangular plinths; lotus capitals with imposts; and an epistyle with moulded cornice supporting a moulded pediment.

The woman's Egyptianising hair-style is also found on painted portraits and plaster masks of the very early second century AD (e.g. nos 111, 141–3), a likely date for this stela.

BIBLIOGRAPHY

J. Pelsmaekers, 'Studies on the Funerary Stelae from Kom Abu Billou', *Bulletin de l'Institut Historique Belge de Rome* LXV (1995), 5–12, esp. 10–12.

96 Limestone funerary stela with hieroglyphic inscriptions and scenes showing the deceased being led by Anubis towards Osiris

About AD 90–150

H 34 cm, W 32 cm, TH 4.5 cm

Excavated by John Garstang at Abydos in 1907

Liverpool School of Archaeology, Classics and Oriental Studies E.89

The lower left corner of the stela is lost, and the upper surface of the left side has been hacked off. All traces of paint are lost.

The scenes are incised in panels, the borders of which have been cut down to leave the figures in relief. In the arched top of the stela is carved a winged sun-disc; one pendant *uraeus* survives. In the scene below, the deceased, wearing a tunic and mantle, the latter draped over the proper left shoulder, is protected from behind by Nephthys, and led by Anubis towards the mummy of Osiris. In front of Osiris is an offering table piled with food, perhaps loaves. Behind Osiris, who wears the white crown and carries the crook and flail, stood Isis, now lost but for the hand on Osiris' left shoulder. Columns of hieroglyphic text are set above the figures, recording that each of the deities spoke, but not giving the content of their speech. Above the deceased is part of a name not recorded elsewhere in sources later than the Twentieth Dynasty. In the hieroglyphic text beneath the figured scene is part of a speech by Ra, Thoth and Horus-in-Pe: 'Come [or give] the revered one...'

A date in the late first or early second century AD is suggested for the figure of the deceased, who in general bears some resemblance to panel portraits of that date. Though of Romanised appearance, he wears his mantle in a style that is not matched in other representations. The quality of the carving of this stela is markedly superior to other work from Abydos and, with the Egyptian content, suggests some

96

interest on the part of local elites in traditional Egyptian culture (see also the mask, perhaps contemporary, of Titus Flavius Demetrios, no.74).

BIBLIOGRAPHY

A. Abdalla, *Graeco-Roman Funerary Stelae from Upper Egypt* (Liverpool 1992), 56 no.131, pl. 50.

97 Inscribed limestone funerary stela of Petemin

About AD 160–240

H 44.5 cm, W 29 cm, TH 8 cm

Excavated by John Garstang at Abydos in 1907

Liverpool, School of Archaeology, Classics and Oriental Studies E.3

The stela is slightly damaged along the lower edge; no traces of colour survive on the surface.

The stela is divided into three registers by pairs of incised lines. In the arched upper register is the familiar winged sun-disc with pendant *uraei*. Beneath, Anubis attends the mummy of the deceased, laid on a bier supported on legs decorated with lions' heads and paws. Behind the bier stands Isis; at its foot appears Osiris, wearing the *atef*-crown, holding a flail and a sceptre. Both Anubis and Isis raise their right hands towards Osiris in a gesture of adoration. The mummified Petemin has the short hair typical of portraits of children of later second- or early third-century date.

The Greek inscription is incised between guidelines in the bottom register: Πέτεμιν Ἐχοίσιος Εἰμούθου | ἄωρος ἐβίωισε ἐτῶν ιζ̅ It may be translated 'Petemin, son of Ekois, son of Imouthis [or Petemin Ekoisios son of Imouthis], who died before his time. He lived seventeen years.' Though there are some orthographical errors, the quality of the carving of the figured scenes is unusually high.

BIBLIOGRAPHY

A. Abdalla, *Graeco-Roman Funerary Stelae from Upper Egypt* (Liverpool 1992), 20–1 no. 15 (bibl.), pl. 8A.

97

PORTRAITS OF THE LATER THIRD CENTURY AD FROM DEIR EL-BAHRI AND ANTINOOPOLIS

The Metropolitan Museum of Art is one of a number of institutions to have conducted excavations at the site of Deir el-Bahri on the west bank of the Nile at Thebes. Working in 1924–5 by the site of a Coptic monastery built in front of the shrine of Anubis in the Temple of Queen Hatshepsut, the excavator H. Winlock discovered a number of late Roman burials, some in reused coffins. A small number of the mummies, wrapped in plain cloth, had elaborately painted plaster masks. The complete mummy presented here (no. 98) allows the unusual opportunity of seeing how the mask was attached to the mortal remains. The portrait mask shows an individual dressed in a sleeved tunic with broad *clavi* and a mantle with decorative woven patches (*orbiculi*), quite a different style from the subjects of the panel portraits. A sleeved tunic with a decorated stole is worn by the woman portrayed in much more refined style on a shroud excavated by Albert Gayet at Antinoopolis (no. 99). These representations date respectively to the later third and fourth century AD, when sleeved tunics with broad *clavi* and other woven decoration had become fashionable enough to rate thirty-three entries in the Edict on Maximum Prices issued by the Emperor Diocletian in AD 301.

By this period, very few panel portraits were being produced, and it is likely that the wealthiest families had left the settlements of the Fayum for more secure accommodation in the larger urban centres of the Nile Valley such as Thebes and Antinoopolis.

98

98 Mummy of a woman with a painted plaster and linen mask

About AD 270–80

L 1.54 m, W 28 cm, TH 25 cm

Excavated in a shallow grave in the Mentuhotep forecourt at Deir el-Bahri, West Thebes in 1923–4, Roman Burial IVA

New York, The Metropolitan Museum of Art, Rogers Fund, 1925 25.3.219

This is one of two complete mummies surviving from excavations undertaken by the Metropolitan Museum of Art at Deir el-Bahri. The moulded face mask of painted plaster rests on a wooden block supported by a straw stuffing, and is attached to a longer panel of reinforced and painted linen, which is sewn to the plain linen mummy wrappings with large stitches and cords at the top and base. The face was reconstructed, and the nose lifted and realigned with other facial fragments in 1983/4.

A red line, thought to have solar significance, separates the three zones of the painting and provides a border for the mask. The woman is portrayed lying on a gold pillow with white decoration. Her elaborately braided black hair is drawn up at the back of the head and rolled onto the crown. She wears a garland of jewels, perhaps intermixed with flowers. The large black eyebrows almost meet, the huge black eyes are outlined in black and shaded in brown, and the nose is shaded with a pink line down the centre. The dark lips are very thin, with a very small lower lip. The cheeks and chin are rouged. The chin and neck are stained brown.

On her ears elaborate drop earrings are represented. Around her neck are four necklaces, of which the first is a plain gold collar, and the second a rope of pearls and red stones, perhaps garnets interspersed with gold discs. Below this is a necklace of long emerald beads and small pearls, and then a heavy necklace of large gold plaques, alternately circular and lozenge-shaped, the latter set with emeralds and the former with pearls. A gold band hangs from the central pearl of the third necklace, passing beneath the central disc of the fourth necklace to end in a disc set between the small conical breasts. On each wrist the woman wears two gold bracelets, the outer plain and the inner ribbed with a central bezel set with a pale blue stone. On the third finger of her right hand the woman wears a double gold band, on her left thumb and forefinger a double ring set with an intaglio, and on the little finger another ring with a setting.

The woman is dressed in a white tunic with broad purplish-black *clavi*, the shoulder seams indicated with a row of dashes flanked by two rows of dots. She is wrapped in a white fringed shawl edged with a plain band and decorated with green *orbiculi*. In her right hand she holds a footed goblet of green glass with one handle; the white T-shaped shading perhaps indicates the transparency of the vessel, which contains a red liquid. In her left hand she grasps a small bouquet, probably of myrtle.

Below the portrait – a fashionably three-quarters-length presentation of the sort found in contemporary marble sculpture – a rich garland of petals and leaves flanking a yellow disc forms the second zone of decoration. Beneath it is the conventional but well-designed scene of the barque of Sokar, attended by two jackals with keys around their necks, apparently a local motif.

98

99

Recent work on the dress worn by the subjects of shroud portraits from Antinoopolis and the masks from Deir el-Bahri suggests that both types of portrait should be dated to the later third or fourth century AD. The relative simplicity of the dress (if not the jewellery) of the Deir el-Bahri portraits indicates a date fairly early within the sequence, within the third century AD. Though sketchily rendered and partly obscured by the elaborate garland, the shape of the hair bears comparison with portraits on Roman sarcophagi and other stone memorials which have been dated to the post-Gallienic period, about AD 270–80 (see M. Bergmann, *Studien zum römischen Porträt im dritten Jahrhunderts nach Christus* [Bonn 1977] 194, pl. 58.1–2).

BIBLIOGRAPHY
H. E. Winlock, 'The Museum's excavations at Thebes', *Bulletin of the Metropolitan Museum of Art Part II. The Egyptian Expedition 1923–1924*, fig. 38 (centre); Winlock, *Excavations at Deir el-Bahri 1911–1931* (New York 1942), pl. 95 (r.); Parlasca, *Mumienporträts*, 208 n. 84; Grimm, *Mumienmasken*, 143 B 1, pl. 112, 5.

99 Portrait of a woman in encaustic and tempera on a linen shroud

Fourth century AD

H 166 cm, W 85 cm

Excavated by A. Gayet at Antinoopolis

Paris, Musée du Louvre, Département des Antiquités Égyptiennes AF 6440

This shroud fragment reproduces the pattern of pharaonic coffins, but with Roman iconography. The frame is drawn in bright red, coupled with a garland of leaves and flowers. Of the vignettes framing the effigy of the deceased, only two have survived: two birds (peacocks?) drinking from the jar of life, a theme of Eastern origin common in Roman tombs. The deceased woman is represented in a full-length portrait. Her face, with an ivory skin tone, stands out against a grey background. She is dressed in a purple dalmatic and a purplish red stole, decorated with a grape-leaf foliated scroll coloured yellow in imitation of gold. At neck level a white line suggests an undertunic. A large label of the Roman *tabula ansata* type is painted on the deceased's body. The incomplete inscription in Greek mentions her name and age (forty-five years old) with the formula 'Take heart!' It is located above an openwork net in the pharaonic style; the two feet, which extend beyond the netting, are wearing ankle boots made of soft hide, held together with gold fasteners that cross at the ankle. These shoes are called *calcei mullei* and were worn only by patricians.

In fact, this is the portrait of a patrician woman from head to toe, with her noble features and subtle accessories: a gold net circling her dark hair, which is divided into two masses and pulled up into a soft braid at the back of the skull, following the fashion of the fourth century; earrings made of three pendants attached to clasps; and a chain concealed by the neckline of the dalmatic. There are no rings on the fine white hands. The raised right hand, its palm open, replicates Isis's gesture to Osiris, a gesture of both protection and veneration; the left hand holds an *ankh*, in this case a circle surmounting a cross. Two other *ankh* crosses, painted yellow on a red ground, are located on either side of the dead woman's feet, in place of the usual Anubis jackals.

Purple was highly valued from the Hellenistic period. It is the colour of the sun and of blood, and became a symbol of power and immortality in the Roman period; emperors wore it, as does Christ on a painting in the Louvre where he is represented with Abbot Mena. Within the pharaonic funerary context the grape-leaf foliated scroll is a symbol of rebirth: it was appropriated by Christians, for whom it became a favourite decorative motif, since wine was the blood of Christ. The gesture of protection and veneration was adopted for the iconography of saints and martyrs. The pharaonic *ankh* amulet, or *crux ansata*, signifies eternal life. Here it is repeated three times, increasing its efficacy for the afterlife of the deceased tenfold. Because of its magical power, it became a Christian symbol equivalent to Christ's cross.

With its ambiguous iconography – the theme of the vignettes and their horizontal orientation, indicating that the deceased is lying down and not standing in the manner of Osiris; the purple and gold; the gesture of the right hand; and the *ankh* – this shroud perfectly illustrates that the fourth century was an interface or period of transition between paganism and Christianity.

M.-F. A.

BIBLIOGRAPHY
Parlasca II, no. 419, pl. 104.1; Walker and Bierbrier 1997, no. 180; Walker in Parlasca and Seeman 1999.

THE CULTURAL AND ARCHAEOLOGICAL CONTEXT

This section includes artefacts which illustrate or help to date features of the portraits. Jewellery reveals a development from fashions current in first-century AD Italy, such as gold ball earrings (nos 100–101), represented on many early mummy portraits, to the hoop and bar earrings of the second and third century (nos 104–8), which reflect a more regional, east Mediterranean trend. Magical amulets (no. 113) and snake-jewellery (no. 103) reflect the need to protect the deceased in their vulnerable state of transition to the afterlife.

Of particular interest and poignancy are the rare papyri which record the arrangements for travelling painters to pay a licence fee (no. 114); the letter from Senpamonthes to her brother Pamonthes recording the transport of their mother's mummified and labelled body to a family tomb (no. 115); and the accounts for a funeral (no. 116), which cost the equivalent of two years' income, a sum surely affordable only by the wealthier families.

Jewellery

100 Gold ball earrings

Later first century AD

(a) H 3 cm, D (of ball) 2.2 cm, wt 3.8 g
(b) H 2.9 cm, D (of ball) 2 cm, wt 3.7 g

From Pozzuoli, Italy

British Museum GRA 1872.6–4.1109 (Jewellery 2618, 2619)

Earrings of the standard gold ball-and-disc type. The ball elements, forming less than a hemisphere, are made of two sections with a very neat vertical join. At the back they are finished with a flange 4 mm wide. A vertical supporting wire is attached at the back of the ball, and the end of the recurved hook is coiled around the end of it; the hook then runs up the back of the domed disc, about 9 mm in diameter, which is attached to the top of the ball. The join is concealed by a row of four gold grains.

A very similar construction may be seen on an earring in Mainz (Deppert-Lippitz 1985, no. 48,

Taf. 19). For the appearance of similar earrings in the portraits, see nos 1–4.

C.J.

BIBLIOGRAPHY
Marshall 1911, nos 2618, 2619; Parlasca and Seeman 1999, 246 no. 152.

101 Gold ball earrings

First century AD

(a) H 2.8 cm, D (of sphere) 1.8 cm, WT 4 g; (b) H. 2.8 cm, D (of sphere) 1.8 cm, WT 7.5 g

Provenance unknown

Franks Collection

British Museum GRA 1899.12–1.4, 5

A closely matching pair of disc-and-ball earrings, with thick S-curved hooks terminating in a small knob. The ball element is a complete sphere and is very well made, without any visible trace of joins other than a small 'lid' at the top of each, through which the wire hook is attached. Each ball also has a small chevron-shaped cut in the back. The hook is soldered to the back of the disc element, which is 1.1 cm in diameter. Three small gold grains decorate the join of disc and ball.

Earring (a) has suffered some damage, and the ball is slightly torn and crushed in places; (b) is in

100, 101

excellent condition and is very much
heavier, presumably because it still
contains a filling material of some
kind.

C. J.

102 Gold necklace with crescent pendant

First to second century AD

L (chain) 38.8 cm, W 6 mm,
W (pendant) 2.9 cm, WT 34.7 g

Provenance unknown

British Museum (GRA 1917.6–1.2719
(Jewellery 2719)

The necklace consists of a strap of
four loop-in-loop chains linked. The
ends are clamped into neat tongue-
shaped terminals ending in a ring; the
actual clasp elements are lost.
The terminals have a border of
beaded wire and are decorated with a
stylised *uraeus* 7 mm long.

The crescent pendant hangs on a
ribbed ring. Soldered to the ring is a
uraeus matching those on the
terminals and a tiny gold disc bearing
a rosette of seven gold grains,
matching another pair soldered to the
tips of the crescent. The arms of the
crescent have a lozenge-shaped cross-
section and taper slightly.

Necklaces with crescent pendants,
often interpreted by modern scholars
as a sign of fertility, appear on
painted panel portraits of women of
the later first and very early second
century AD, from Hawara and other
sites in the Fayum (see illustration,
right). Crescentic pendants were
frequently associated with chains
which fasten with a wheel-shaped or
domed-disc clasp, possibly indicating
a combined lunar/solar symbolism.
The type was still current in the
province of Britain as late as the
middle of the second century:
a jeweller's workshop hoard from
Snettisham (Norfolk), consisting of
locally made silver jewellery, includes
crescent pendants and both wheel-
shaped and domed clasps (Johns
1996, 92–4; Johns 1997, nos
317–23, 326–8). The deposition of
this hoard is dated by the coins to
AD 154/5 or later. Compare also a

102

Detail of
no. 68.
Girl with
necklace as
described in
no. 102.

necklace from the Fayum, now in Baltimore, in which a chain with a Medusa-head medallion also carries a small crescent and two Isis busts: it is likely to be of late second-century date (Stefanelli 1992, no. 145, fig. 198).

Though the necklace described here is unprovenanced, the use of the *uraeus* as a decorative detail is a strong indication that it was made in Egypt.

C.J.

BIBLIOGRAPHY
Marshall 1911, no. 2719; Higgins pl. 55 B; Stefanelli no. 126.

103 Five gold snake-rings and three snake-bracelets

First century AD

New York, The Metropolitan Museum of Art

(a–c) 10.130. 1509-1511. Three gold snake-rings. Unprovenanced. Gift of Helen Miller Gould, formerly Murch collection, 1910.
(a) a coiled snake. D 2.3 cm. *Bulletin of the MMA VI* (1911), fig. 21.
(b) a coiled snake. D 1.9 cm.
(c) a coil with both ends terminating in snakes' heads. D 2.3 cm.
(d) Rogers Fund, 1924, 24.2.9. Ring formed of a single plain band with a snake's head and tail coiling to form bezel. D 2.1 cm, Unprovenanced.

Lansing, *Ancient Egyptian Jewellery* (1940), pl. 19.

(e) Rogers Fund, 1924, 24.2.10. Ring formed of a double plain band ending in two snakes' heads coiled once around each other to make the bezel. D 2 cm. Unprovenanced.

(f–g) Rogers Fund, 1918, 18.2 19-20. Two bracelets in the form of a snake with a large head, the mouth opened to show a protruding tongue. The tail is bent into the form of a slithering small snake. D 9.1–9.3 cm. From Lower Egypt.

(h) Rogers Fund, 1920, 20.2.26. Bracelet in the form of a flat-headed scaly serpent with bent tail. D 7.3 cm. Unprovenanced.

Snakes became a popular motif in jewellery during the Hellenistic period, and continued to be fashionable throughout the Roman Empire during the first and second centuries AD. In addition to the suitability of the slender and sinuous form of the snake for the design of finger-rings and bracelets, the reptiles had a wide range of benevolent symbolic connections, above all with the healing god Asclepius.

The stylized form of the *uraeus*, the venomous Egyptian cobra (*Naja haje*) with its ancient royal

103

103

associations, continued to appear on some Egyptian-made jewellery, but the type of snake represented in Classical serpent jewellery, even that made and worn in Egypt, is the Asclepian snake, *Elaphe longissima*, a species that is not poisonous in spite of its impressively large size.

Various typologies of a Roman serpent jewellery have been devised, all based on a primary distinction between a design formed of a single, more or less realistic snake, with its head at one end and tail at the other (Johns Type A), and one in which a penannular ornament terminates with a serpent-head, realistic or highly stylized, at each end (Johns Type B).

Though regional variations existed, the two main types are broadly contemporary: both are represented in surviving Ptolemaic and Roman-period Egyptian jewellery, and in depictions of jewellery in wear seen on cartonnage mummy-cases and painted on mummy base-boards and in some mummy portraits.

C. J.

BIBLIOGRAPHY
A. Henkel, *Römische Fingerringe der Rheinlande und der benachbarten Gebiete* (Berlin 1913), 231–4; H. Guiraud, 'Un aspect de la bijouterie romaine; les bagues serpentiformes', *Pallas* 22 (1975), 82–6; Johns 1996, 37–8, 44–7; Johns 1997, 34–7.

104 Loop earring with pearls

Second century AD

H 2.5 cm, WT 1.4 g

Provenance unknown

British Museum GRA 1872.6–4.602 (Jewellery 2679)

An S-shaped loop earring is made from a single wire finely tapered at both ends, one forming the point of the suspension hook, the other wound around the body of the wire to create the beaded ring. The decoration on the front of the loop consists of nine white pearls, all of somewhat irregular shape and graduated in size, the largest with a

104–8

Detail of earrings in no. 68.

diameter of roughly 4 mm at the top. A tiny gold bead acts as a stop beneath the last pearl.

Such earrings are commonly found on mummy portraits of women from Hawara and other Fayum sites, ranging in date from the early to late second century AD (see illustration p. 152 right).

C. J.

BIBLIOGRAPHY
Marshall 1911, no. 2679.

105 Loop earring with beads

Second century AD

H 2.9 cm, WT 2.1 g

Provenance unknown

British Museum GRA 1917.6–1.2680 (Jewellery 2680)

A single tapered S-shaped wire with a small knob at the tip is finished in front with a neat coiled-wire join. On the front of the wire a central cylindrical dark blue glass (?) bead is set between two small emeralds. Separating the stones are two small reel-shaped gold beads. The wire thickens immediately below the beads to hold them in place.

C. J.

BIBLIOGRAPHY
Marshall 1911, no. 2680; Higgins pl. 54 F.

106 Pendant earrings

Second to third century AD

(a) H 3.5 cm, W 1.9 cm, WT 2.0 g
(b) H 3.4 cm, W 1.8 cm, WT 1.8 g

Provenance unknown

Franks Collection

British Museum GRA 1917.6–1.2672, 2673 (Jewellery 2672, 2673)

The earrings are in a pale gold and are fairly crudely worked. The upper part of the ornament is a crescentic plaque with a symmetrical series of volutes below, formed of repoussé-gold sheet. An S-shaped hook is soldered to the back and the wire runs up to support a bead within the horns of the crescent. Hanging from

three loops, which are attached behind the volutes, are wires covered by narrow cones of sheet gold, and terminating in beads.

One of the suspended beads on (a) and the bead within the crescent on (b) are hollow glass. The other beads appear to be pearls.

C. J.

BIBLIOGRAPHY
Marshall 1911, nos 2672, 2673.

107 Earring with pearl and emerald pendant

Third century AD

H 3.4 cm, WT 1.1 g

Provenance unknown

British Museum GRA 1872.6–4.583 (Jewellery 2588)

The earring consists of a simple gold penannular ring with overlapping ends, each finishing in a small knob; from this is suspended a gold element incorporating a very small, round/oval box-setting, tapering to a wire on which is threaded a pearl. The box-setting contains an emerald, and between this and the pearl is a single reel-shaped gold bead, now somewhat crushed.

C. J.

BIBLIOGRAPHY
Marshall 1911, no. 2588.

108 Earrings with pearl pendants

Second century AD

(a) H 2.5 cm, WT 0.8 g
(b) H 2.5 cm, WT 0.9 g

Provenance unknown

British Museum GRA 1872.6–4.1493, 1494 (Jewellery 2540, 2541)

A closely matching pair of earrings consist of small hoops closing in front with a hook-and-loop fastening which is partially concealed by an applied, small, domed disc. Hanging from each hoop is a gold wire with its upper part covered by spiral coiling, supporting a small baroque pearl. The construction and

embellishment of the hoop is very close to Stefanelli 1992, figs 176 and 177, two pairs of earrings from a second-century grave group from Rome; these do not, however, have pendants.

C. J.

BIBLIOGRAPHY
Marshall 1911, nos 2540, 2541.

109 Gold diadem ornament

First to third century AD

D 3.4 cm

From Egypt

Acquired in 1895

British Museum EA 26328

The ornament has eight rays or petals, each made separately and consisting of a base-plate with an escape hole for air and curved upper part. The petals are soldered to a central base around a central circular boss. Between every two rays are two granules of gold alternating with a single granule. A ring for suspension is soldered in the centre at the back.

This ornament is strikingly similar to a seven-pointed gold star worn on the forehead of the bearded man shown in portrait no. 21.

C. J.

BIBLIOGRAPHY
Tait 94, fig. 207; Parlasca and Seeman 1999, 138 no. 40.

109

110 Gold, amethyst and emerald necklace

Late second century AD

L 40.6 cm, WT 42 g

Provenance unknown

British Museum GRA 1917.6–1.2749
(Jewellery 2749)

The necklace features eleven egg-shaped amethysts between 1.3 and 1.7 cm long, open-set in plain gold collets with a ring at each end. The colour and translucency of the stones is thus fully displayed, since there is no gold backing. Between the amethysts are complex elements formed of a central rectangular box-setting about 3 mm deep with slightly oblique walls between two gold *peltae*. Flat loops beneath the *peltae* attach the elements to the rings soldered to the amethyst collets. The box-settings contain small emeralds, about 5 x 4 mm and cut perfectly flat. The terminals of the necklace are of *pelta* and triangle shape attached to a small hook at one end and a ring at the other. The last emerald at the ring end is set diagonally. Another (third from ring end) is missing, revealing sulphur in the box-setting.

Several of the necklaces in the early third-century hoard found in Lyon in 1841 have design elements in common with this piece (e.g. Comarmond 1844, nos 10, 11, 12, 14; Stefanelli 1992, fig. 229). Necklaces with amethysts and emeralds appear in mummy portraits of women of second-century date from various sites (e.g. no. 16).

C.J.

BIBLIOGRAPHY

Marshall 1911, no. 2749; Higgins pl. 61 B; Stefanelli no. 177, fig. 227.

111 Gold and emerald necklace

Second century AD

L 41.2 cm, WT 15.4 g

Provenance unknown

Townley Collection

British Museum GRA 1814.7–4.1203
(Jewellery 2731)

The necklace is composed of twenty-one emerald beads of varying size, though all in their natural hexagonal crystalline form, alternating with gold links. These links are flat quatre-foils made up of two figure-eight shapes soldered together. The form is probably intended to evoke a stylised knot of Hercules. The gold links are about 6.5 mm long. The clasp is of simple hook-and-eye form: the 'eye' is of twisted wire. At the hook end two gold links are placed together without an emerald between.

Emerald necklaces are worn by several women appearing in portraits of second-century date from Hawara and other Fayum sites. Often they are worn as part of an ensemble of necklaces, the others perhaps plain gold bands or chains to maximise the impact of the emeralds (e.g. no. 12). Gold and emerald necklaces remained in fashion throughout the Empire from the first to the fourth centuries AD. Many combine emerald beads with very simple gold links, but examples from the third-century Gaulish hoards from Vaise (Lyon, Rhône) (Lascoux et al. 1994, 20) and Eauze (Gers, Midi-Pyrénées) (Schaad 1992, 17, no. 1, pl. 1a) feature elaborate three-dimensional Hercules-knot links between the emeralds, while emerald beads alternating with lengths of standard loop-in-loop gold chain occur in the third-century treasure of Beaurains (Arras, Pas-de-Calais) (Bastien and Metzger 1977, B.1) and in the late fourth-century Romano-British treasure from Thetford (Norfolk) (Johns and Potter 1983, no. 31).

C.J.

BIBLIOGRAPHY

Marshall 1911, no. 2731.

112 Bead ornament with pendant discs

(illustrated p. 156)

First to third century AD

L 26.4 cm, WT 14 g

Provenance unknown

Franks Collection

British Museum GRA 1917.6–1.2709
(Jewellery 2709)

The beads are threaded on modern brass wire. The two principal types of bead are small orange-red hardstones described by Marshall as garnet, but looking more like carnelian, and spacer beads formed of a short spiral of fine gold wire. In addition, there are two small, blue-green faience beads and seven dark blue beads, probably of glass. Hanging from the string of beads are twenty-nine gold-and-pearl pendants. These consist of a pearl capped with gold at each end and a wire loop from which hangs a small gold disc with a cut-out (making a crescent shape) occupied by another small pearl on a wire. The disc element of one pendant is lost, and next to this defective pendant are two additional ornaments, an oval dark green glass bead and a small faience, *uraeus* pendant. The twisted gold wire which attaches the *uraeus* to the necklace looks modern.

Some elements of the necklace may well be alien, though no doubt ancient, in particular the green bead and the *uraeus*. In the absence of any history, there must be some doubt about the overall integrity of the piece, though its appearance is akin to the hair ornament worn by the subjects of some Neronian portraits (e.g. Walker and Bierbrier 1997, no. 16).

C.J.

BIBLIOGRAPHY

Marshall 1911, no. 2709.

110, 111

112, 113

113 Decorated cylindrical amulet case

Second to third century AD

L 2.1 cm, D 8 mm, WT 3.3 g

Provenance unknown

British Museum GRA 1917.6–1.2983 (Jewellery 2983)

A gold cylinder on which no join can be seen, closed at each end with a disc held in place by the rubbed-over edge of the tube. There is a single, central, ribbed suspension ring with granulated decoration at its edge, both front and back, in the form of a triangle of ten grains. The front triangle is at the centre of the first of

three rows of granulated decoration. Beneath it, in the centre of the second row, is a rosette of seven grains. The rest of the granulation consists of alternating single grains and triangles of three grains.

A very small, single-looped amulet case with simple granulated decoration now in Mainz is dated by Deppert-Lippitz to the late Hellenistic period (second to first century BC; Deppert-Lippitz 1985, no. 35, Taf. 14). However, close dating of tubular amulet cases is difficult, and there is no established typology.

An amulet case is worn by the boy portrayed on the panel excavated by

Grenfell and Hunt at er-Rubayat (no. 46). The portrait may be dated to the Severan period by association with the portrait of the woman found in the same tomb.

C.J.

BIBLIOGRAPHY
Marshall 1911, no. 2983.

Papyri

114 Papyrus written in black ink, licensing two painters of mummy masks

First century BC

H 20.5, W 20 cm

Provenance unknown

Vienna, private collection,
Inv. P. Vindob. Barbara 58

The Greek text may be translated:

> Maron and Marres, who have had written permission to paint and work with gold in the nome of Arsinoe for twenty-three years, send greetings to Phratres and Psenobastis. We have granted you the right to work in your profession as painters and gilders for the temple and on mummy portraits of this nome, and at the same time you are permitted to travel [...] throughout the nome as long as you make your monthly payments to your nearest bank from the month Thot to the month Mesore. [...] bronze drachmas a month, which comes to 1006 drachmas for 12 months and the five extra days at the end of the year [...].

The painters Phratres and Psenobastis are thus licensed by the painting workshop of Maron and Marres to travel through the Fayum as painters of mummy masks in exchange for a monthly fee. The mummy masks here referred to consisted of papyrus or linen board, that is a kind of papier-mâché made of old papyrus sheets or linen fabric pasted together in layers, formed on a model and subsequently coated with plaster. The face was then generally covered with thin gold leaf and the rest of the mask was painted. Gold, associated with eternal life because it was so durable, played an important part in Egyptian religious thinking.

That painting was subject to state control is hardly surprising, for Egypt's bureaucracy was extremely well organised. It is interesting that a painter's activity was restricted to a single nome – possibly the two mentioned here had an exclusive monopoly in the painting of masks. The artists worked for temples and also apparently for private clients.

The light brown papyrus is of medium quality, nearly complete on the right and at the bottom, trimmed in a curve at the top and pieced together from two sections; in places the vertical strips of papyrus have been detached, and the verso side has no writing. The sheet was removed from mummy wrappings, in fact from a pectoral, which explains the trimming at the top. The papyrus is unpublished, though an article on it is being prepared by Prof. W. Clarysse, Louvain.

U.H.

BIBLIOGRAPHY
Doxiadis 1995, 237 illus. 32; Parlasca and Seeman 1999, 200 no. 107; Seipel 1998, 188f no. 65.

114

115 Letter from Senpamonthes to her half-brother Pamonthes, written in black ink on papyrus

Second or third century AD

H 21, W 11 cm

From Thebes

Former Salt Collection

Paris, Musée du Louvre, Département des Antiquités Égyptiennes N2341

The Greek text may be translated:

> Senpamonthes to her brother Pamonthes: Greetings! I have sent you the embalmed body of my mother Senyris, with a label around her neck, via Gales, son of Hierax, in his own boat, having taken care of the entire cost of transport myself. The mummy can be recognized from: a shroud with a pink coating on the outside; her name inscribed on the belly. I wish you good health, brother. Year 3, eleventh day of Thoth [8 September]. [On the reverse side:]

To Pamonthes, son of Moros, from his sister Senpamonthes.

This letter, an altogether extraordinary document on funerary practices, was written by Senpamonthes to her 'brother' Pamonthes, regarding the transport of her mother's mummy. The word 'brother' should not mislead us: it was used in private letters in a sense that was not strictly familial. In this case, the expression used by Senpamonthes, 'my mother Senyris', shows that Pamonthes did not have the same mother. Their two names, though common in the Theban area, might also mean they belonged to the same family. It is therefore likely that Senpamonthes's correspondent was her half-brother. And it is in that capacity that she requested his help.

Required as much by religious tradition as by the law to see that her mother received the proper funerary rites (*kedeuein*), Senpamonthes found herself obliged to send the mummy (*taphe*) away, which indicates she did not live near the family necropolis, where it was customary to bury one's dead. After the embalment she therefore had the body transported by a certain Gales (a unique name, which must be an orthographic variant of 'Kales'), probably on the occasion of his undertaking a journey. The formulation does not

115

115 (reverse)

suggest that he was a professional in the transport of mummies, as was the case in the *Hamburg Papyrus* 174.3, which speaks of a boatman who specialized in the delivery of mummies (*ploion nekregon*).

The transport of a mummy, which had to remain intact if it was to survive in the hereafter, was a risky matter: the body could be damaged, stolen or confused with another. Precautions had to be taken. Senpamonthes took several: she equipped the mummy with a label (*tabla*), which, attached to its neck, contained the necessary information (name of the deceased and destination). But such a label could be lost or stolen; she therefore inscribed the name of the deceased on its shroud (*sindon*), a procedure well attested elsewhere. A mummy from Hawara serves to confirm the double precaution set out in this letter: the name of the dead man, Diogenes, is written on the shroud as well as on the label found attached to the mummy (Boswinkel and Pestman 1978, 229–30). Finally, Senpamonthes sent the letter ahead to alert her brother of the body's arrival, to signal that the transportation costs had already been taken care of (and therefore that Pamonthes did not have to pay for anything), and to give a description of the mummy to prevent possible confusion. The Greek expression (*sindon estin ektos ekhon chrema*

rhodinon) was not always properly understood: the incomprehensible *chrema* was corrected to *chroma*, 'colour'; however, it is in fact a (spelling) error for *chrima*, 'coating' (the word had this meaning especially in its later variant *chrisma*). It was common for the shroud to be covered with a fine coating of stucco, which was in turn painted. The pink colour in question was often used during the Roman period.

J.-L.F.

BIBLIOGRAPHY
A. J. Letronne and W. Brunet de Presle, *Notices et extraits des manuscrits de la bibliothèque impériale* (Paris 1865), 234 (no. 18 bis); K. Sudhoff, *Ärztliches aus den griechischen Papyrusurkunden* (Leipzig 1909), 194–5; U. Wilcken, *Grundzüge und Chrestomathie des Papyruskunde* (Leipzig and Berlin 1912), vol. 2, 577–8 (no. 499); H. Boswinkel and P. W. Pestman, eds, *Textes grecs, démotiques et bilingues*, Papyrologica Lugduno-Batava (Leiden 1978), 230–31; J. Hengstl, *Griechische Papyri aus Ägypten* (Munich 1978), 152–3 (no. 59); K. Parlasca, J. E. Berger, R. Pimaudi, *Al-Fayoum*, ed. Franco Maria Ricci (1995), 195 (French edition); B. Boyaval, 'Le transport des momies et ses problèmes', in F. Hinard, ed., *La mort au quotidien dans le monde romain* (Paris 1995), 109–15 (esp. 111); Walker and Bierbrier 1997, 187 no. 250; Aubert and Cortopassi 1998, 159 no. 106.

116 Papyrus written in black ink, listing the expenses of a burial

Second or third century AD

H 13 cm, W 42 cm

From Soknopaiou Nesos (Dime); purchased by Theodor Graf 1892/3

Vienna, Österreichische Nationalbibliothek, Papyrussammlung, Inv. P. Vindob. G 24.913

The Greek text may be translated:

List [of expenses] of a burial: ears of grain 12 drachmas 2 obols, earthenware jar 2 obols, minium pigment 4 drachmas 19 obols, wax 12 drachmas, myrrh 4 drachmas 4 obols, honey 4 obols, tallow 8 obols, linen 136 drachmas 16 obols, death mask 64 drachmas, cedar resin 40 drachmas, essence for the linen 4 drachmas, good oil 4 drachmas, wages for Turbon 4 drachmas, lamps 24 drachmas, cost of an old cloak 24 obols, sweets 20 obols, wheat 16 drachmas, ferment 4 drachmas, dog [statuette] 8 drachmas, small mask [= child's mummy mask?] 14 drachmas, 2 *artabae* bread 21 drachmas, pine nuts 8 obols, wreath 16 obols, women mourners 32 drachmas, transportation by donkey 8 drachmas, side dish [wheat gruel] 12 obols, which comes to drachmas 440 chalkoi 16.

The list includes embalming substances such as cedar resin,

116

essence for the linen, and good oil. The largest expenditure was for linen, for many metres of linen bandages were required for wrapping a mummy. Yet the death mask, at 64 drachmas, comes to nearly half as much as the cost of the linen. Other purchases, such as the ears of wheat (sheaves are depicted as funerary gifts on tomb steles from Terenuthis) and loaves of bread (which frequently appear on the offering tables in mummy painting), served as funerary gifts. The minium pigment was possibly used for colouring the outer shroud, which is often a strong red. The entry for a small mummy mask (= child's mummy mask) could indicate that this was the burial of a woman together with her child, but this is pure speculation. The 'dog' listed at 8 drachmas may have been a dog statuette (= Anubis) meant to protect the deceased. Another possible interpretation is that there was a mummified dog. Then the small mask could possibly be thought of as a papier-mâché case for it.

The wreath of leaves and flowers was placed around the mummy's neck. Tallow and lamps were employed in the burial service. Note especially the outlay for women mourners, whom one could apparently hire for burials, and for Turbon, possibly a gravedigger. The costs of transportation by donkey probably have to do with carrying the mummy to the grave.

A third column on the papyrus, which shows no connection to the previous text, reads: 'List of receipts: Cost of a young camel drachmas [...], cost of a donkey 124 drachmas.'

It becomes apparent how high the costs of a burial might be if one considers that in the second century an annual income probably amounted to between 200 and 300 drachmas. The expenses listed thus amounted to nearly two years' income, a sum surely only affordable by the upper middle class.

The original edge of this light brown papyrus is partially preserved on all four sides. The piece provides a good example of how papyrus rolls were constructed and cut into individual sheets for customers. The first seam, where two sheets of papyrus were pasted together into a roll, is 1.5 cm from the left edge, the next one is 21 cm from the right edge, and the remnants of a third seam can be seen 3 mm from the right edge. The individual sheets were roughly 20 cm wide.

U. H.

BIBLIOGRAPHY

K. Wessely, *Papyri N. 24858–25024 aliique in Socnopaei insula scripti (Studien zur Palaeographie und Papyruskunde XX)* (Leipzig 1922), no. 56; H. Drexhage, 'Einige Bemerkungen zum Mumientransport und den Bestattungskosten im römischen Ägypten', in *Laverna* 5 (1994), 167–75, esp. 167ff; H. Harrauer, 'Bestattungskosten', in *Die Wüste spricht. Papyri der Österreichischen Nationalbibliothek*, exh. cat. (Salzburg 1996), 78f no. 67; D. Montserrat, 'Death and Funerals in the Roman Fayum', in Bierbrier, *Portraits and Masks*, 33ff, esp. p. 40 (English translation of papyrus text with many misinterpretations); Seipel 1998, 190f no. 66; Parlasca and Seeman 1999, 201 no. 108.

Portrait

117 Chalcedony cameo portrait bust of the younger Agrippina, wife of the Emperor Claudius and mother of the Emperor Nero

About AD 49–59

H 9 cm, W 5.5 cm, TH 5.2 cm

Provenance unknown

British Museum GRA 1907.4–15.1 (Gem 3946)

The cameo is broken off at the base of the neck and at the lower nose.

Part of the empress's tunic survives at the right lower edge. The hair is parted centrally and brushed to either side of the head in

117

a series of increasingly tight waves. Around the face is a row of tight snail-shaped curls; above the ears these are arranged in two tiers.

The face is full, with a prominent squarish jawbone. The eyes are set wide apart beneath a low brow; the eyebrows are not indicated. The mouth is small and the expression sullen.

The bust is carved in the round with the remarkable skill typical of imperial cameos of the Julio-Claudian era. The flesh is highly polished to contrast with the matt surface of the hair with its mass of engraved detail.

The empress's hairstyle was copied by many subjects of mummy portraits and gilded masks (e.g. nos 1, 27).

P. R.

BIBLIOGRAPHY

S. Walker and A. Burnett, *Augustus. Handlist of the Exhibition* (BM Occasional Paper 16, 1981), 21, no. 228 (bibl.); W. Megow, *Kameen von Augustus bis Alexander Severus* (1987), 40, 301, pls 19–20, no. D33.

Select Bibliography

Full titles of works cited in abbreviated form in the catalogue and in the essay, 'A Note on the Dating of Mummy Portraits', are given below. Further reading recommended by Kurt Gschwantler is listed by author and title only. For a full bibliography, the reader is referred to the corpora of mummy portraits published by Klaus Parlasca, and of painted plaster masks by Günther Grimm. In this catalogue, references are given to these corpora, and to publications by Petrie, including Journals and Notes made at the time of excavation. Reference is also made to A. F. Shore's guide as the major preceding British Museum publication. Some literature published in more recent years is also included.

AJA
American Journal of Archaeology

Aubert and Cortopassi 1998
M.-F. Aubert and R. Cortopassi, *Portraits de l'Égypte Romaine* (Paris 1998)

Bastien and Metsger
P. Bastien and C. Metzger, *Le Trésor de Beaurains* (Wetteren 1977)

Berger and Creux 1977
J. E. Berger with René Creux, *L'Oeil et l'éternité: Portraits romains d'Égypte* (Paudex 1977)

Bierbrier, *Portraits and Masks*
M. L. Bierbrier (ed.), *Portraits and Masks. Burial Customs in Roman Egypt* (London 1997)

Borg 1996
B. Borg, *Mumienporträts. Chronologie und kulturelle Kontext* (Mainz 1996)

Borg 1998
B. Borg, *'Der zierlichste Anblick der Welt...' Ägyptische Porträtmumien* (Mainz 1998)

BMQ
British Museum Quarterly (London 1926–73)

Buberl 1922
P. Buberl, *Die griechisch-ägyptischen Mumienbildnisse der Sammlung Theodor Graf* (Vienna 1922)

Comarmond
A. Comarond, *Description de l'écrin d'une dame romaine trouvé à Lyon en 1841* (Lyon 1844)

Corcoran
L. Corcoran, *Portrait Mummies from Roman Egypt (I–IV Centuries A.D.) With a Catalog of Portrait Mummies in Egyptian Museums*. The Oriental Institute of the University of Chicago Studies in Ancient Oriental Civilisation No. 56 (Chicago 1995)

Dawson and Gray
W. R. Dawson and P. H. K. Gray, *A Catalogue of Egyptian Antiquities in the British Museum. 1. Mummies and Human Remains* (London 1968)

Deppert-Lippitz
Barbara Deppert-Lippitz, *Goldschmuck der Römerzeit im Römisch-Germanischen Zentralmuseum* (Bonn 1985)

Doxiadis 1995
Euphrosyne Doxiadis, *The Mysterious Fayum Portraits. Faces from Ancient Egypt* (London 1995)

Doxiadis 1998
E. Doxiadis, Ἀπὸ τὰ Πορτραῖτα τοῦ Φαγιοὺμ στὶς Ἀπαρχὲς τῆς Τέχνης τῶν Βυζαντινῶν Εἰκονων (Herakleion 1998)

Drerup 1933
H. Drerup, *Die Datierung des Mumienporträts. Studien zur Geschichte und Kultur des Altertums XIX I* (Paderborn 1933)

Ebers 1889
G. Ebers, *Eine Gallerie antiker Porträts. Erster Bericht über eine jüngst entdeckte Denkmälergruppe* (Berlin 1889)

Ebers 1893
G. Ebers, *Die hellenistischen Porträts aus dem Fayum, an der Hand der Sammlung des Herrn Graf untersucht und gewürdigt von Georg Ebers* (Leipzig 1893; English translation: New York 1893)

Edgar, *Coffins*
C. C. Edgar, *Catalogue général des antiquités égyptiennes du Musée du Caire: Graeco-Egyptian Coffins, Masks and Portraits* (Cairo 1905)

Edgar 1905
C. C. Edgar, 'On the dating of the Fayum portraits', *Journal of Hellenic Studies* 25 (1905), 225ff

Graul 1888
R. Graul, *Die antiken Porträtgemälde aus dem Grabstätten des Faijum* (Munich 1888)

Graul 1889
Zeitschrift für Bildende Kunst (1889), 9ff, 39ff

Grenfell and Hunt
B. P. Grenfell and A. S. Hunt, *The Oxyrynchus Papyri Volume III* (London 1903)

Grimm, *Mumienmasken*
G. Grimm, *Die römische Mumienmasken aus Ägypten* (Wiesbaden 1974)

Grimm, G., *Alexandria. Die erste Königstadt der hellenistischen Welt* (Mainz 1998)

Heurgon
Jacques Heurgon, *Le Trésor de Ténès* (Paris 1958)

Higgins
Reynold Higgins, *Greek and Roman Jewellery* (London 1961, 2nd edn 1980)

JEA
Journal of Egyptian Archaeology (London 1914–)

Johns 1996
Catherine Johns, *The Jewellery of Roman Britain* (London 1996)

Johns 1997
Catherine Johns, *The Snettisham Roman Jeweller's Hoard* (London 1997)

Johns and Potter
Catherine Johns and Timothy Potter, *The Thetford Treasure, Roman Jewellery and Silver* (London 1983)

Jucker 1984
H. Jucker, Rez. Parlasca I, II, III, *Gnomon* 56 (1984), 542–7

Kent and Painter
J. P. C. Kent and K. S. Painter, *Wealth of the Roman World* (London 1977)

(**Select Bibliography** *continued*)

Laffineur et al. 1988
R. Laffineur, A. Forgeau and
A. Hermary, *Amathonte III. Testimonia
3. L'Orfèvrerie. Ecole Française
d'Athènes, Etudes Chypriotes VII*
(Paris 1988)

Lascoux et al.
Jean-Paul Lascoux, François Baratte,
Catherine Metzger, Gérard Aubin,
Marie-Claude Depassiot, *Le Trésor de
Vaise* (Lyon 1994)

Ling, R., *Roman Painting* (Cambridge
1991)

Mack, *Masks*
J. Mack (ed.), *Masks. The Art of
Expression* (London 1994)

Marshall 1907
F. H. Marshall, *Catalogue of the Finger
Rings, Greek, Etruscan and Roman,
in the Departments of Antiquities,
British Museum* (London 1907; repr.
1968)

Marshall 1911
F. H. Marshall, *Catalogue of the
Jewellery, Greek, Etruscan and Roman,
in the Departments of Antiquities,
British Museum* (London 1911; repr.
1969)

*MDAIK
Mitteilungen des Deutschen
Archäologischen Instituts Abteilung
Kairo* (Berlin, 1931–)

*MEFRA
Mélanges de l'École Française de Rome*
(Paris 1931–)

Murray, Smith and Walters
A. S. Murray, A. H. Smith and
H. B. Walters, *Excavations in Cyprus*
(London 1900)

Nowicka, M., *Le portrait dans la
peinture antique*, Bibliotheca antiqua
22 (Warsaw 1993)

Parlasca I, II, III
K. Parlasca, *Ritratti di Mummie.*
In A. Adriani (ed.), *Repertorio d'arte
dell'Egitto greco-romano.* 2.ser. I
(Palermo 1969), II, III (Rome 1977,
1980)

Parlasca, *Mumienporträts*
K. Parlasca, *Mumienporträts und
verwandte Denkmäler* (Wiesbaden
1966)

Parlasca and Seeman 1999
K. Parlasca and H. Seeman (eds),
*Augenblicke. Mumienporträts und
ägyptische Grabkunst aus römischer
Zeit* (Frankfurt 1999)

Petrie, *Hawara*
W. M. Flinders Petrie, *Hawara, Biahmu
and Arsinoe* (London 1889)

Petrie, *Objects*
W. M. Flinders Petrie, *Objects of Daily
Use* (London 1927)

Petrie, *Portfolio*
W. M. Flinders Petrie, *The Hawara
Portfolio: Paintings of the Roman Age*
(London 1913)

Petrie, *Portraits*
W. M. Flinders Petrie, *Roman Portraits
and Memphis (IV)* (London 1911)

Pfeiler
Bärbel Pfeiler (= Barbara Deppert-
Lippitz), *Römischer Goldschmuck des
ersten und zweiten Jahrhunderts n.
Chr. nach datierten Funden* (Mainz
1970)

Pfrommer, M., *Göttliche Fürsten in
Boscoreale. Der Festsaal in der Villa
des P. Fannius Synistor*, 12. Trierer
Winckelmannsprogramm 1992 (Mainz
1993)

Popović
Ivana Popović, *Les bijoux romains du
Musée National de Belgrade* (Belgrade
1996)

Preisigke, *Sammelbuch*
F. Preisigke, *Sammelbuch griechischer
Urkunden aus Ägypten* (Strasburg
1915)

Reinach 1914
A. Reinach, 'Les portraits Gréco-
Égyptiens', *Revue Archéologique* 4,
sér. 24 (1914) 2, 32–53; 5 (1915) 2,
1–36

Rose, C.B., *Dynastic Commemoration
and Imperial Portraiture in the Julio-
Claudian Period* (Cambridge 1997),
esp. cat. nos 74, 116

Schaad et al.
Daniel Schaad (ed.), *Le Trésor d'Eauze*
(Toulouse 1992)

Scheibler, I., *Griechische Malerei der
Antike* (Munich 1994)

Seipel 1998
W. Seipel (ed.), *Bilder aus dem
Wüstensand. Mumienporträts aus dem
Ägyptischen Museum Kairo* (Vienna
1998)

Shore
A. F. Shore, *Portrait Painting from
Roman Egypt* (2nd edn, London 1972)

Smith, R. R. R., *Hellenistic Royal
Portraits* (Oxford 1988)

Stefanelli
Lucia Pirzio Biroli Stefanelli, *L'Oro dei
Romani, gioielli di età imperiale* (Rome
1992)

Tait
Hugh Tait (ed.), *Seven Thousand Years
of Jewellery* (London 1986)

Thompson
D. L. Thompson, *Mummy Portraits in
the J. Paul Getty Museum* (Malibu,
California 1982)

Walker and Bierbrier 1997
S. Walker and M. Bierbrier, *Ancient
Faces: Mummy Portraits from Roman
Egypt* (London 1997)

Williams 1924
C. R. Williams, *The New York
Historical Society Catalogue of
Egyptian Antiquities Numbers 1–160:
Gold and Silver Jewelry and Related
Objects* (New York 1924)

Winkes, R., *Clipeata Imago. Studien zu
einer römischen Bildnisform* (Bonn
1969)

Glossary

acroterium
Ornament on the corner of an architectural pediment (*Lat.*).

akh
The form in which the blessed dead were believed to exist in the netherworld.

ankh
Hieroglyphic sign for 'life'.

ansa
Handle, loop or clamp (*Lat.*). See also *tabula ansata*.

archon
Chief magistrate (*Gr.*).

atef-crown
Headdress worn by Egyptian gods, comprising a tall crown flanked by ostrich feathers and surmounted by a solar disc.

ba and *ba-bird*
Spirit-form of the individual, approximately corresponding to the personality; represented as a bird with a human head.

balteus
Sword-strap worn over the shoulder, often richly ornamented (*Lat.*).

bole
Fine compact clay, used as a ground for painting.

C.A.T. scans
Computerised Axial Tomography scans.

canopic jars
The four vessels which contained the preserved viscera of the dead.

cartonnage
Lightweight material consisting of layers of linen and plaster, used in the manufacture of mummiform coffins and funerary masks.

cestrum
Small pointed graver (*Lat.*).

chignon
Coil of hair pinned up at the back of the head.

clavus (pl. *clavi*)
Vertical purple stripe on a Roman tunic (*Lat.*), at Rome a sign of rank but in Roman Egypt of general affiliation to Rome.

contabulatio
Mantle worn across the chest in a thick band of folds (*Lat.*).

dalmatic
Full tunic with wide sleeves and broad *clavi*, worn in late antiquity.

entasis
The convex shaping of a column shaft for optical effect.

ephebate
Group of youths selected at the age of fourteen for education in the gymnasium, forming the elite of the Greek communities of Roman Egypt.

epistyle
Block set over column capitals, often comprising a moulded architrave and frieze.

fibula
Ornate brooch resembling a modern safety-pin, used to fasten a mantle.

fillet
Narrow band or strip.

gall (iron gall) ink
Ink made of a suspension of iron salts in gallic acid obtained from oak or nut-galls.

guilloche
Ornate pattern resembling braided ribbons.

himation
Mantle (*Gr.*).

Horus lock
Lock of plaited hair worn at the side of the head; a distinguishing feature of Horus the child, hence symbolic of youth.

impost
Rectangular block above a column capital, used to support an arch.

ka
The creative life-force of an individual, which comes into being at birth and continues to exist after death.

kalathos
Basket (*Gr.*).

kantharos
Chalice (*Gr.*).

knot of Hercules
The reef-knot associated with the hero Hercules, used in classical antiquity as a symbol of fertility.

lappet
Part of a wig or headcloth, hanging at the side of the face or on the shoulder.

lucky knot/tie
Garland bound with ribbons, carried by the deceased.

lunula
Crescent (esp. pendant jewel).

melonenfrisur
Plaits of hair tied back from the face to give the appearance of segments of melon (*Ger.*).

modius
Corn measure (*Lat.*).

murex/'real' purple
Costly purple dye produced from shellfish (*murex*), notably at Tyre.

nome
Administrative district of Egypt.

orans
Gesture of prayer with arms outstretched (*Lat.*).

pallium
Mantle (*Lat.*).

patera
Shallow bowl used to pour libations in pagan religious ceremonies (*Lat.*).

pelta (pl. *peltae*)
Voluted crescent-shaped shield carried by the Amazons and much used as a decorative motif in Greek and Roman art (*Lat.*).

Pentelic
White fine-grained marble quarried from Mount Pentelikon, near Athens.

protome
Ornamental figure projecting from surface of object.

Rishi coffin
Type of anthropoid coffin popular in the 17th and early 18th Dynasties, distinguished by feathered decoration on the lid (Arab. 'feathered').

sagum
Short dark cloak worn by soldiers (*Lat.*).

shen ring
A bound loop of papyrus rope signifying the universe encircled by the sun and, by extension, protection.

stola
Tubular garment worn over the tunic by Roman women of exceptionally high social status (*Lat.*).

strophium
Woman's garment, similar to the modern brassière, consisting of a band of cloth which covered and supported the breasts (*Lat.*).

tabula ansata
A tablet with triangular projections at the sides (*Lat.*).

taenia
Cloth band or tie (*Lat.*).

tang
Long narrow projection from an object.

tondo
Circular painting or relief.

torus
Rounded convex architectural moulding, esp. of a column base (*Lat.*).

udjat-eyes
Eye of the god Horus, widely used as a protective amulet.

unguentarium
Small narrow flask for perfume (*Lat.*).

uraeus (pl. *uraei*)
Cobra identified with the goddess Wadjit (patroness of lower Egypt); worn on the brow of the king's headdress.

Venus ring
Crease on the neck indicating fleshiness, often a sign of youth.

wadj-sceptre
Amulet resembling a domed papyrus stalk, where green colour denoted the new growth of plants and, by extension, resurrection.

was-sceptre
An animal-headed staff held by Egyptian deities, signifying dominion or control.

Egyptian Deities

Anubis
Embalmer-god, responsible for the mummification of corpses and protection of tombs. Represented as a black jackal or a jackal-headed man.

Isis
Sister-wife of Osiris, and mother of Horus. With Nephthys, mourned the dead Osiris and assisted in his resurrection.

Maat
Egyptian word for 'right' incorporating the concepts of 'truth' and 'justice'. Represented as a woman wearing a single feather on her head-dress.

Nephthys
Sister of Osiris; with Isis, mourned the dead Osiris and assisted in his resurrection.

Nut
Sky-goddess and mother of Osiris.

Osiris
Major deity associated with fertility, death and resurrection. Probably originally a chthonic fertility god, he came to be regarded as the ruler of the netherworld.

Ptah-Sokar-Osiris
A composite deity incorporating the principal gods of creation, death and after-life.

Ra-Horakhty
Solar deity compounded of the sun-god Ra, creator of the universe, and Horus of the Horizon. Represented as a falcon-headed man.

Sarapis
God introduced into Egypt in the Ptolemaic period having the characteristics of Egyptian and Greek gods. He is represented as a bearded man.

Chronology

Here dates are given for dynasties of rulers, Egyptian, Greek and Roman, to clarify references in the text.

Pharaonic 3000–343 BC

Persian 343–332 BC

Macedonian 332–310 BC

Ptolemaic 310–30 BC

Julio-Claudian 30 BC–AD 68

Augustan 27 BC–AD 14

Tiberian AD 14–37

Claudian AD 41–54

Neronian AD 54–68

Flavian AD 69–96

Trajanic AD 98–117

Hadrianic AD 117–38

Antonine AD 138–93

Severan AD 193–235

Lenders to the Exhibition and Photographic Acknowledgements

ANN ARBOR
Kelsey Museum of Archaeology, University of Michigan, Ann Arbor (81–2); photograph by Paul Jaronski

BALTIMORE
Goucher College, Towson, Maryland, on loan to the Walters Art Gallery, Baltimore (64); courtesy of Goucher College, on loan to the Walters Art Gallery, Baltimore, Maryland

BERKELEY
Phoebe Apperson Hearst Museum of Anthropology, University of California, Berkeley

BERLIN
Ägyptisches Museum und Papyrussammlung, Staatliche Museen zu Berlin (4, 7, 51, 56, 79); photography © BPK, Berlin, by Christa Begall (7), Margaret Büsing (4), Jürgen Liepe (56) and G. Murza (51)

Antikensammlung, Staatliche Museen zu Berlin (30–34, 39); photography © BPK, Berlin, by Johannes Laurentius except (34) by Christa Begall

BROOKLYN
Brooklyn Museum of Art (10, 44, 45); photography by Oi-Cheong Lee

CAMBRIDGE
Fitzwilliam Museum, University of Cambridge (53); by permission of the Syndics of the Fitzwilliam Museum

DUBLIN
National Museum of Ireland, Dublin (46)

EDINBURGH
Royal Museum, National Museums of Scotland, Edinburgh (13); courtesy of the Trustees of the National Museums of Scotland

HEIDELBERG
Sammlung des Ägyptologischen Institut der Universität Heidelberg (87)

LIVERPOOL
School of Archaeology, Classics and Oriental Studies, University of Liverpool (96–7)

LONDON
The British Museum, London: Department of Egyptian Antiquities (1–3, 6, 8, 11–12, 17, 19, 21–2, 24–6, 28, 40–42, 55, 57, 75, 88, 93–5, 109); Department of Greek and Roman Antiquities (35, 58, 100–102, 104–8, 110–13, 117). By courtesy of the Trustees of the British Museum; photography by the Photographic Service, J. Rossiter, I. Kerslake, P. Nicholls and S. Dodd

Freud Museum, London (36, 48)

The National Gallery, London (29, 38)

Petrie Museum of Egyptian Archaeology, University College London (5, 20, 27, 59, 83); by courtesy of the Petrie Museum

MALIBU
The Collection of the J. Paul Getty Museum, Malibu, California (37, 43, 47, 60, 61)

MANCHESTER
The Manchester Museum, University of Manchester (15, 23)

OXFORD
Ashmolean Museum, Oxford (14); by permission of the Visitors of the Ashmolean Museum

PARIS
Musée du Louvre, Département des Antiquités Égyptiennes, Paris (50, 54, 62–3, 65A, 74, 86, 89–90, 92, 99, 115); photography © Gérard Blot/RMN (62, 63), © Hervé Lewandowski/RMN (50, 54), © Georges Poncet/Musée du Louvre (74, 89, 115) and Christian Larrieu/Musée du Louvre (99)

Département des Antiquités Grecques, Étrusques et Romaines (49); photography © Gérard Blot/RMN

PROVIDENCE
Museum of Art, Rhode Island School of Design, Providence (80); photography by Del Bogart

SWARTHMORE
Swarthmore College (78); photography by Oi-Cheong Lee

TORONTO
Royal Ontario Museum, Toronto (18)

VIENNA
Österreichische Nationalbibliothek, Papyrussammlung, Vienna (116)

Private collection (114)

All other objects are in the collection of the Metropolitan Museum of Art, New York; photography by Oi-Cheong Lee.

Photographs used in the essay by Kurt Gschwantler are courtesy of the Kunsthistorisches Museum, Vienna (fig. 1); Soprintendenza Archeologica per le Province di Napoli e Caserta (figs 3, 5, 6); the Metropolitan Museum of Art, New York (fig. 8); the British Museum, London (fig. 9); the J. Paul Getty Museum, Los Angeles (fig. 9); and BPK, Berlin, © BPK (fig. 10).

Concordance of Catalogue and Museum Numbers

Catalogue Number	Walker & Bierbrier Number	Museum Number
1	15	British Museum EA 74709
2	17	British Museum EA 74716
3	18	British Museum EA 74713
4		Berlin, Ägyptisches Museum 10974
5	20	Petrie Museum UC 19608
6	21	British Museum EA 74707
7		Berlin, Ägyptisches Museum 19722
8	23	British Museum EA 74718
9		Metropolitan Museum of Art 11.139
10		Brooklyn Museum of Art 11.600–B
11	26	British Museum EA 74708
12	34	British Museum EA 74712
13	33	Edinburgh, Royal Museum of Scotland 1951.160
14	35	Oxford, Ashmolean Museum 1911.354
15	36	Manchester Museum 5378
16	37	British Museum EA 74706
17		Toronto, Royal Ontario Museum 918.20.1
18	40	British Museum EA 74705
19		Munich, Antikensammlung 15013
20	45	Petrie Museum UC 19610
21	46	British Museum EA 74714
22	47	British Museum EA 74704
23	49	Manchester Museum 2266
24	51	British Museum EA 74710
25	52	British Museum EA 74703
26	53	British Museum EA 74717
27	58	Petrie Museum UC 28084
28	59	British Museum EA 69020
29	76	London, National Gallery 3931
30		Berlin Antikensammlung 31161/15
31		Berlin Antikensammlung 31161/2
32		Berlin Antikensammlung 31161/6
33		Berlin Antikensammlung 31161/49
34		Berlin Antikensammlung 31161/9
35	79	British Museum GR 1890.9-21.1
36	83	London, Freud Museum 4947
37	84	Malibu, J. Paul Getty Museum 74.AP.11
38	85	London, National Gallery 3932
39		Berlin Antikensammlung 31161/8
40	88	British Museum EA 65345

Catalogue Number	Walker & Bierbrier Number	Museum Number
41	89	British Museum EA 63394
42	92	British Museum EA 65343
43	96	Malibu, J. Paul Getty Museum 81.AP.29
44		Brooklyn Museum of Art 54.197
45		Brooklyn Museum of Art 41.848
46	94	Dublin, National Museum of Ireland 1902.4
47	95	Malibu, J Paul Getty Museum 79.AP 142
48	97	London, Freud Museum 4946
49		Musée du Louvre MND 2047 (P217)
50	100	Musée du Louvre AF 6884
51		Berlin, Ägyptisches Museum 11651 09.181.8
52	101	Metropolitan Museum of Art 09.181.8
53	102	Cambridge, Fitzwilliam Museum E5.1981
54	98	Musée du Louvre AF 6883
55	104	British Museum EA 5619
56		Berlin, Ägyptisches Museum 11651
57	13	British Museum EA 74719
58	106	British Museum GRA 1890. 8-1.2
59	107	Petrie Museum UC 14768
60	108	Malibu, J. Paul Getty Museum 81.AP.42
61	109	Malibu, J. Paul Getty Museum 78.AP.262
62		Musée du Louvre N 2733 P212
63		Musée du Louvre N 2733 P211
64		Baltimore, Walters Art Gallery (Loan from Goucher College) TL 1990.26.1
65	112	Metropolitan Museum of Art 18.9.2
65A		Musée du Louvre AF 12541
66		Metropolitan Museum of Art 09.181.6
67		Metropolitan Museum of Art 09.181.5
68		Metropolitan Museum of Art 09.181.7
69		Metropolitan Museum of Art 09.181.3
70		Metropolitan Museum of Art 09.181.2
71		Metropolitan Museum of Art 01.181.1
72		Metropolitan Museum of Art 08.202.8
73		Metropolitan Museum of Art 09.181.4
74		Musée du Louvre N 3408
75	116	British Museum EA 6715
76		Metropolitan Museum of Art 44.2.2
77	118	Berkeley, Phoebe Apperson Hearst Museum 6/21378b

Catalogue Number	Walker & Bierbrier Number	Museum Number
78		Swarthmore College, Dennison 375
79		Berlin, Ägyptisches Museum 15979
80		Providence, R.I. School of Design 59.030
81		Ann Arbor, Kelsey Museum 88723
82		Ann Arbor, Kelsey Museum 88617a-m
83	134	Petrie Museum UC 19615
84		Metropolitan Museum of Art 19.2.6
85		Metropolitan Museum of Art 11.155.5
86		Musée du Louvre E 27152
87		Heidelberg, Ägyptologisches Institut der Universität 7
88	141	British Museum EA 29477
89		Musée du Louvre AF 2128
90		Musée du Louvre AF 6705
91		Metropolitan Museum of Art 12.182.46
92	164	Musée du Louvre E 21360
93	167	British Museum EA 189
94	168	British Museum EA 57358
95	170	British Museum EA 65337
96	171	Liverpool, School of Archaeology E.89
97	172	Liverpool, School of Archaeology E.3
98		Metropolitan Museum of Art 25.3.219
99	180	Musée du Louvre AF 6440
100	184	British Museum GR 1872.6-4.1109-10
101	185	British Museum GR 1899.12-1.4,5
102	189	British Museum GR 1917.6-1.2719
103		Metropolitan Museum of Art 10.130.1509-11; 24.2.9-10; 18.2.19-20; 20.2.26
104	195	British Museum GR 1872.6-4.602
105	196	British Museum GR 1917.6-1.2680
106	201	British Museum GR 1917.6-1.2672-3
107	206	British Museum GR 1872.6-4.583
108	207	British Museum GR 1872.6-4.1493, 1494
109	208	British Museum EA 26328
110	209	British Museum GR 1917.6-1.2749
111	210	British Museum GR 1814.7-4.1203
112	213	British Museum GR 1917.6-1.2709
113	216	British Museum GR 1917.6-1.2983
114		Vienna Private Collection P. Vindob. Barbara 58
115	250	Musée du Louvre N2341
116		Vienna, Nationalbibliothek P. Vindob. G 24.913
117	252	British Museum GR 1907.4-15.1